Extra Cash for Women

By Susan Gillenwater and Virginia Dennis

Writer's
Digest
Books

Cincinnati, Ohio

Library of Congress Cataloging in Publication Data
Gillenwater, Susan, 1947-
   Extra cash for women.

   Bibliography: p.
   Includes index.
   1. Women—Employment. 2. Self-employed. 3. Part-time employment. I. Dennis, Virginia, 1930-
II. Title.
HD6072.5.G53   650.1'024042   82-2679
ISBN 0-89879-061-1   AACR2

Illustrations by Tom Dusterberg.
Book design by Charleen Catt.

Dedication

We dedicate this book to our families, who have been patient, helpful, and understanding throughout, and to all the women who may benefit from its contents.

Acknowledgments

We would like to acknowledge the confidence, faith, and guidance given us by Bernadine Clark, and the staff of Writer's Digest Books.

Contents

Introduction

How can you hope to pay for new tires on the family RV or your daughter's med school tuition? How can you afford the Gucci handbag you've been dreaming about or save enough to take that trip to the Galapagos Islands?
The answer is *extra cash*.

This book will help you get it. It'll give you ideas on how you, the woman at home, can get the extra cash you need to make life in the eighties a little easier and a lot more fun. We'll show you countless ways to indulge your creativity, boost your self-esteem, enhance your lifestyle—and make a profit. Whether you're young or old, rich or not so rich, a high school dropout or a college graduate, a shut-in or a health buff, there's something here for you. And you're not alone. Every day more students, homemakers, wives, mothers, and grandmothers begin to tote business cards and brochures promoting their home businesses. Women all over the country are discovering the real significance of the extra cash they've earned by working from their homes. As mad money, spare change, or savings, extra funds represent a new freedom for women at home.

What do two women from central Ohio know about women working from home? Plenty. We've done many of the jobs we describe in this book; between the two of us, we have thirty years of home work experience. We've wrapped gifts, made cheese balls, typed manuscripts, painted apartments and milked goats, among other enterprises to make ends meet. We've chosen to be headquartered at home because, as wives and mothers, we already have one full-time profession although our need for extra cash has prompted us to put our talents to more financially rewarding work. We've enjoyed the excitement that every would-be entrepreneur knows. And we've faced the uncertainties: Is my product good enough to charge money for? How long will my family put up with TV dinners? Will I be able to get a loan? How do I keep from hugging the first customer who raves about my nut bread? The questions are here, along with answers we've lived with—or learned from.

In addition to our own experiences, we've met, interviewed, heard about, read about, corresponded with, and listened to hundreds of other women engaged in businesses of every kind, at every level of operation from full time to spare time. Many of their stories are told in these pages, with the hope that their successes will encourage you and their mistakes will keep you from finding out the hard way. You'll find ideas to spark your imagination and tips to help you push ahead with your plans. We'll teach you the importance of planning your money-making venture and give you hints on getting your business off the ground.

Once you've read this book, the only one who can hold you back is you. If you're willing to work hard, plan carefully, and commit yourself to your enterprise, chances are you'll reap both joy and profit. (Luck can't hurt, but don't rely on it.)

We know the snags, the snares, and the delights of working from home, and we'd like you to write us with questions and comments about your home business. We may not be able to answer every question or ease every circumstance for you, but we'll try to steer you to someone or some group who can.

Send a self-addressed, stamped envelope to:

Extra Cash for Women
Box 227
New Albany, OH 43054

We look forward to hearing from you. Share your questions and your stories. Ask us about writing a book or promoting a product, tell us how you spent your first profits. We're interested in you.

Home-Based Doesn't Mean Homebound

(What's involved in being headquartered at home and at work)

The 1980s champion a time-honored tradition: the home-based woman. You, in fact, may be one, and you choose not to seek employment outside the home for one or more reasons. You may not want to leave young children with sitters or day-care centers. You may not be able to work nine-to-five because you are caring for elderly parents, acting as a teacher's aid at your son's school, or helping with your church's fund-raising campaign. Maybe you're home-based because you got tired of punching a time clock and feeling unfulfilled as a tiny cog in a large corporate machine. You may think you lack skills or that your qualifications are outdated for today's job market. Or you may be staying home because you can't find the job you trained for in a glutted work force and a down-spiraling economy.

Making up a big chunk of that labor force are women who work outside the home—51.6 percent of American women between the ages of sixteen and sixty-five. Some have freely chosen the outside working world because they enjoy the bustle it demands. Others don't see how running a vacuum, washing windows, and scrubbing down the back porch are going to help ease the family money crunch. To earn extra cash, they feel compelled to join the masses who contend with rush-hour traffic, packed parking lots, crowded lunch lines, booked-up babysitters, and standing-room-only buses.

Whether you have a full-time job outside the home or full-time responsibilities in the home, chances are that you could use extra cash, because paying bills and eking out a so-so existence aren't enough. You want real butter for special occasions. Just once you'd like to buy a Bill Blass dress instead of a J.C. Penney. The following is a good example of how working from your home can make a difference in both your financial and personal outlook.

Kit P. is a young, single woman in Ohio who has been on both sides of the job fence. She was an eight-hour-a-day executive secretary for an oil company lobbyist and is now a self-made businesswoman with a successful home typing service. Her secretarial job paid a decent salary ($15,000 annually), but it just wasn't enough for Kit to get ahead. She had hoped to buy a condominium, but on her secretary's salary the best she could do was share an apartment. After she met her monthly expenses (rent, food, utilities, gas, insurance, etc.), she wasn't left with much for unexpected or irregular charges, like hairdresser appointments, cosmetics, new clothes, entertainment, auto repairs, office-related contributions, and an occasional pizza. Kit knew she was spinning her wheels. She had no money left for savings, vacations, or emergencies, and at this rate she would never save enough money for the down payment on a condominium.

She began moonlighting as a typist in the evenings and on weekends. She put posters and ads on the bulletin board in the student center of the state university, offering to type term papers and theses. Though at first she only had a few jobs, as time passed, her work load and income increased. But her late typing hours began to make her cranky, tired, and less efficient at her daytime job. She tried to explain her strained finances to her boss, but he gave her an ultimatum: Give up the typing service or the job. Kit cleaned out her desk and left.

She pondered her situation for awhile and decided to start a full-time home typing business. She borrowed $500 from her parents, agreeing to pay it back with interest as soon as possible. Kit then began a full-fledged advertising campaign. She had business cards and advertising flyers printed and sent them to commercial businesses and typing agencies. She made personal calls to companies in her city and left them her card. She advertised in local newspapers. Within two months, Kit was overwhelmed with work and had to hire help.

Being home-based has cut her expenses by $100 a month. She doesn't *need* a closetful of expensive dresses anymore; she can wear blue jeans if she wants. She doesn't need a weekly hair appointment, either. After only five years of business, her annual income is now better than $20,000, and she has recently moved into her new condominium. As a business person, she shoulders many more responsibilities than she did as an employee, but she reaps plenty of new rewards. Kit knew what she wanted and needed, and she took advantage of her skills to build a successful home-based business that could get it for her.

Being home-based doesn't mean being homebound. In fact, it may be the situation that *frees* you—to pursue interests, improve skills, *and* add to the family's discretionary income. A home-based job uses your home as the anchor for your money-making operation. It might be the place where you do the actual work (sewing drapes, touching up photographs, baking tarts), or it could be your headquarters for meeting customers, taking orders, scheduling appointments—whatever running your business demands. Every resourceful venture, from operating a telephone answering service to being a professional clown at children's parties, can be conducted (at least in part) from a home base. But at-home businesses don't happen on their own. That's where your ingenuity comes in. Dictionaries define "ingenious" as being something akin to . . . clever, original, inventive. To earn extra cash today, that's exactly what a home-based woman needs to be. She must be able to recognize and take advantage of her situation, knowledge, talents, and skills.

Ingenuity can turn ideas into cash. Isn't that what this country is founded on—people with creative ideas and the intelligence and stick-to-itiveness to make them work? Henry Ford had the foresight to recognize the potential of the automobile and the gumption to get assembly lines rolling. Mary Kay Ash (founder of Mary Kay Cosmetics) and Jean Nidetch (founder of Weight Watchers) used the realization that people want to look their very best to build multimillion-dollar businesses. The American public is accustomed to rubbing elbows with ingenious people in industry, education, entertainment—even in their own neighborhoods. You could be one of them.

Whether you are eighteen or eighty, your opportunities for home-based employment are practically endless. Think of all the jobs you do around the house (both the ones you enjoy *and* those you put off as long as possible)—everything from cleaning the crystal to walking the dog. Some of the things you do well may be the very jobs other people (maybe even people you know) would love to have someone do for them. Make an honest appraisal of your skills and talents, what you can do and what you might enjoy doing for others. Begin by looking at yourself and your lifestyle. If you love animals and happen to have a barn and corral in your backyard, why not consider boarding horses for extra money? If your singing voice calms your unruliest daughter, maybe the town's day-care center could use you one afternoon a week. Anything that you (and others) think you do well, or for which you have the personality, a knack, or a good location, is worth considering as a money-making idea.

Home-based employment has many advantages over traditional eight-hour days spent in offices, factories, or stores. It can allow you to set your own hours (three or four hours a day or the same eight-hour shift as your husband), be your own boss (no supervisor to work for or dress code to follow), spend time with your family (they'll appreciate it, and you won't give up the joy of seeing your kids grow up day in and day out), and still contribute to the family till. "Homework" can be economical, too, as was illustrated by Kit's story earlier in the chapter. You can custom-tailor your work at home to fit your particular situation, your wants and needs. One woman we know of operates a home-based mail-order selling business that allows her to stay with her handicapped teenage son while earning the extra money she needs.

A big part of finding the home-based job that best fits your situation is deciding whether you will work full-time, part-time, or in your spare time. How do these options differ and which one suits you best? Your choice will depend on the amount of time you want to invest and the amount of income you need to earn. If you plan to be the main financial support of the family, you should choose an occupation that can support full-time work: A typing or cleaning service or a sewing and alterations business. But even these jobs may vary in marketability from one place to another; what provides full-time work in a college community may be a better part-time effort in a resort town. Typing term papers will keep you busy during winter quarter if you live near the state university, but there aren't many students looking for typists in Fort Lauderdale in April.

Part-time works great if you only need a supplemental income. Maybe you want to continue volunteering at the hospital and taking gourmet cooking classes and still be wife, mother, and businesswoman. Writing, babysitting, and operating a shopping service are all workable part-time jobs.

Consider spare-time employment if you have only a small amount of time to invest and only need occasional extra cash. Holding a children's story hour, doing craftwork for holidays, and offering an envelope-stuffing service can all be fashioned into good spare-time money-makers. It's impossible to pigeonhole jobs because any job can be full-, part-, or spare-time, depending on you, your situation and location, and what you want to do.

Regardless of what you select as a home-based occupation, you may feel the need to brush up before offering your skills to the public. Whether you're cooking gourmet meals, upholstering furniture, or selling greeting cards by mail, you must be good enough to charge for your product or service. If your skills or your business qualifications need a boost, your confidence probably will, too. There are several ways to beef up your background: (1) by taking classes through colleges, universities, adult and continuing education programs, YWCAs and YMCAs, and correspondence programs; (2)

by attending movies and lectures in your field of interest, using libraries regularly, and visiting businesses related to your work; (3) by reading newspaper and magazine articles and talking with people knowledgeable in the area to keep abreast of trends and innovations in your field; and (4) by working with experts (mentors) in your chosen field and getting hands-on experience under their guidance. All of these contribute to your gaining necessary expertise.

Getting Serious

Have you ever had a "can't miss" moneymaking idea that your spouse, friends, or relatives shot down with criticism and doubts? Have you ever verbalized a potentially profitable scheme, and found that no one takes you seriously? When you get little or no encouragement for your ideas, they sometimes begin to sound absurd even to you. Granted, you can't expect cheers for some half-baked idea like making airbags for typewriters or starting a shoelace boutique for tennis shoes in the neighborhood shopping mall, but if your idea makes sense, hang in there.

The truth is you can't take a whimsical notion or a casual intention and hope to make it work. Feedback from others *is* important. Many nightmarish problems in would-be home businesses can be traced to a lack of planning and foresight. Your moneymaking idea must be sound, carefully prepared, and capable of bringing in extra cash.

You can't escape some initial homework to learn the basics of starting a business. A thorough investigation of what you're getting into will help you decide if your idea is workable and whether you have the knowledge and starting capital to activate it and the time, space, and operating money to keep it going. Too much can't be said about paying attention to business basics. (More on this throughout the book.)

Don't let verbal punches from well-meaning friends knock the wind out of your sails. Use those remarks in a positive way: Let them help you try harder and be more determined to succeed. By using friends, neighbors, and relatives as a sounding board, you can learn to anticipate future problems, learn a lot about what Joe Public is and isn't responsive to, and learn over and over again that running a business is a multidimensional challenge. There will be many who are eager for your success, and many who expect you to fail. And there are those who frankly get satisfaction from saying, "I told you so." You'll have to prove yourself to the skeptics who can't imagine your being able to balance the family budget by cranking out homemade linguine. You are not the only person in these cruel shoes, however; so don't let family roadblocks and less-than-enthusiastic onlookers stop you. There are enough women brimming with ideas, talent, and capabilities to start a separate political party of self-made business people. The ones who stand apart are those who have taken the time and trouble necessary to turn an idea into reality.

Trust your instincts and abilities. You know yourself best. And there are some people, the famous Phil Donahue for one, who truly believe you can succeed. Donahue has done more for women than panty hose. Since its inception, his daily program has been a showcase for female ingenuity and accomplishment. He and other less vocal supporters are your cheering section. (Maybe your husband does have faith in your newest brainstorm; chances are your sixteen-year-old brags to his friends about his creative mom.) Put as much time, planning, and self-encouragement as you can into your idea because you believe in it—and yourself. Sooner or later, it's going to pay off.

What Category Are You In?

Home-based women are as diverse as their business ventures. They represent every marital status, educational level, and socio-economic group. They live in New York City; Macon, Georgia; and Casper, Wyoming. Perhaps their only unifying feature is a desire to feel psychologically or financially resourceful.

If you are a wife and mother, you have an important job and, we might add, a very fulfilling occupation. Running a home is not an easy task, and the woman who does it well should feel proud. Sometimes, though, being a home manager isn't enough, especially if your husband's salary doesn't quite cover the expenses. Even if you do have enough to go around, you may need to do something besides household tasks for your emotional well-being. Maybe, after years of caring for the family, you have an "empty nest" and time on your hands. Maybe you're feeling a little bored, and playing bridge every afternoon or getting a full-time job downtown just doesn't appeal to you.

If you are single by choice, you are the master of your financial existence. You have chosen to remain single to be near ailing parents, to fulfill career ambitions, to remain free to travel and relocate, or for any of a number of reasons. You may enjoy independence and the challenges of self-sufficiency. There are also many newly single women around the country, who have hard facts to face; and finances are usually the most pressing issue. If you are divorced and have children still in school, you may want to stay home to give them security. You may feel apprehensive about entering or reentering the job market in your middle years. But earning extra cash suddenly has priority in your life. If you are widowed, you probably feel similar tensions. You may not have much confidence in your skills as a breadwinner, because you've been a full-time homemaker until now; yet you need something to take your mind off your loss and to help pay the bills.

If you are alone and sick or disabled, whether confined to bed or a wheelchair or just confined to your home, you may need or want to work. Having a "job" can enrich your mental health as well as your pocketbook.

If you are past traditional retirement age, you may want to find some kind of work or activity to keep your life interesting. If you're not in good health, maybe you'd like to avoid making a pastime of complaining about aches and pains. A meaningful work-at-home project will change your outlook and make your conversations with friends and relatives more enjoyable.

If you are a young woman living alone, a college student in a dormitory or a recent high school graduate trying to make it on your own, you probably welcome opportunities to earn extra cash. Perhaps you are in poor health, have no transportation or an impossible time schedule, or simply don't enjoy working in the public eye. Home-based work could be the perfect arrangement for you.

Whether you are young or old, healthy or disabled, married, single, divorced, or widowed, you can benefit from reading further and thinking about the opportunities you have for turning spare time at home into extra cash.

Budgeting Your Time

You'd better face the fact, here at the beginning, that a home-based business of any size will drain your spare time. For a single woman without a full-time job it may be easy to find time to get a business off the ground. For a woman who happens to be a wife and mother, it will require more effort and creativity, because she has to juggle time and energy among many responsibilities. In either case, you'll have to practice good time management and learn the art of flexibility, if you aren't practicing it already.

You can start by becoming more organized and efficient: Do the laundry, cleaning, and shopping once a week instead of every day. Learn to schedule family times (trips to the zoo, building a campfire) when you can snatch spare minutes. Don't get ruffled if your Christmas cards aren't out by December 10th. Don't waste time on luxuries like soap operas and bowling leagues. Make more time for your business by giving up extra activities like bridge clubs and luncheons with friends. (If they're really your friends, they'll understand your commitment.)

Once you've started a business, energy management is essential, too. Don't keep late hours unless absolutely necessary; forget about late movies or all-night political discussions with friends. Don't plan dinner parties and gatherings when you have to be up at the crack of dawn the next morning. Save these activities for days when you're less busy. Never plan more work than you can realistically do: Don't accept a big last-minute wallpapering job to be completed tomorrow. Don't use all your energy washing windows if you're scheduled to teach a disco dance class that evening. Don't retype your grandmother's recipe file if you've promised to write a speech for a city council member by five that afternoon.

Besides managing time and energy, you're going to want to corral the support of your family. Especially if your spare-time job turns into a full-time business, you'll need all the bolstering you can get. If you serve as the family maid, cook, and chauffeur, you may have to solicit some help from the other people who live in your house. Your family's reaction is unpredictable: It could be good, bad, or changeable. Regardless of how they react, you should always be straightforward with them. Talk things over and try to get them involved in your endeavors. Point out that the whole family will benefit from the extra income. Your venture could mean the new car your son is craving, the swimming pool your husband dreams of, or the prom dress your daughter can't live without.

You, your family, your business—which gets top priority? That's a question only you can answer. Your business may require as much attention as a newborn baby. But you can't neglect your family or yourself.

Pilar W. is a New York wife and mother and the owner of the Velvet Unicorn, a unique gift shop that sells things like matchbook holder frames and crystal wind chimes. She had always wanted to be her own boss, and this was a way to have a job and still be able to spend time with her family. She opened the shop three months before Christmas and launched a massive advertising campaign. The ads paid off, and Pilar found herself spending up to eighteen hours a day in the shop. The store was open six days a week from nine to nine. When she wasn't selling, she was unpacking, rearranging, or gift wrapping the merchandise, cleaning up, or keeping the books. Initially, her husband and daughters were enthusiastic, but after weeks of disrupted life, their interest waned. Their home was in shambles, and the preteen girls were getting a crash course in the art of homemaking. Pilar was too absorbed in the business to notice. Nothing else mattered, not even herself. She rarely slept more than four hours a night; she was cranky and exhausted, but determined to succeed. Sales were high; morale was low.

On New Year's Eve, Pilar's husband said he wanted them to live "as a family" again and that he would get a divorce if things didn't change soon. The shock of his statement caused Pilar to reflect on how important her family was to her and how much she missed their supper-time discussions. She realized they hadn't even gone Christmas shopping together (an annual tradition). But she loved the shop, too, and the independence it gave her. She didn't want to lose either of them. After a long and emotional session with her family, Pilar decided to hire two dependable women to help her run the store and a qualified bookkeeper to work behind the scenes. She realized that much of the work of running the shop could be done from her home: directing employees, ordering stock, planning displays, and writing and placing ads, for example. Pilar is home most evenings now, and on nights when she must be in the shop, she and her family share a basket dinner in the backroom. It was rough going for awhile, but the marriage-family-business mix worked, and Pilar learned the advantages of working from a home base.

You are an individual, not an extension of your family. You've spent years loving and nurturing them; you shouldn't feel guilty about recruiting their help. They stand to benefit, as you do, both monetarily and psychologically. Many women are emotionally stronger when they feel they are contributing toward their families' welfare; and a family profits from interacting with a confident, self-assured woman.

What Goes In and What Comes Out

As a would-be entrepreneur, you're probably filled with enthusiasm and impatience, along with a thousand questions and uncertainties. You're eager to become an honest-to-God businesswoman. You want to be calling the shots in your life. You're looking forward excitedly to the day when you hang out your shingle and welcome in droves of customers. Right now you're not worrying about getting enough work, paying taxes, keeping the books, or any of the other details of operating a business. You're intent on having your business dreams come true. Though it's hard to see clearly through a blur of expectations, you'll have to answer some hard questions and clear up real doubts before you begin. There aren't ready answers or guaranteed assurances for the concerns that follow.

"Do I have a product or service that people will buy?" Look around and see what's for sale, what's being offered to the public. What isn't available that people want or need or could benefit from having? What product line could use a little competition in your town? If your idea's rooted in good sense and sound judgment, feel confident that there's probably a market for it. But be willing to admit it when you know a pet idea will never float.

"Will my motivation hold up under long hours and the barrage of paperwork and expenses? Will I still enjoy my work when it's more than a hobby, not something to do only when I get the urge?" For your business to grow and flourish, you have to love it. If you don't tend it the way you would a child, you can't expect glowing results. Your motivation to forge on will spring from many sources: your financial need, your determination not to let others down, your own fear of failure. But mostly it will come from your drive to be successful. You'll generate enough energy to make it work.

"What am I willing to sacrifice?" Be prepared to lose most of your spare time and spare energy, and much of your family time. It isn't uncommon for a self-employed person to spend fifty to ninety hours a week making her business work. Of course, the time you invest depends on your intended result. You may have to sacrifice some privacy, too. And you'll probably have to deal with people who don't approve of your spending so much time devoted to something besides your family. If your business flounders, you may also sacrifice good credit, depending on your financial state and whether you borrowed money to get started.

"How do I keep from bungling my finances? I don't know much about tax laws and I can't read legalese. What should I do about planning for retirement?" Unless you're very familiar with tax breaks, deductions, and bureaucratic language, it's probably wise to enlist the services of a professional accountant. He or she will be qualified to answer your questions and keep you on the right track. As for a pension, it's true you won't have "the company" taking care of your retirement, because suddenly *you* are the company. Consult with your financial advisor about an IRA or Keough plan to suit your needs. (More on this in Chapter 2.)

"What if I fail? How will that affect me—and my family?" It's natural to be concerned about this very real risk, but there are also ways to minimize it. Always have an alternative to keep you going, a "Plan B."

You can further minimize your risk by having someone who can handle emergencies when you're not available. Never back yourself into a corner by being the only person who can do your job.

Along with your questions come doubts. Is this the *best* way to boost your self-esteem? Are you really bored? Is it natural to *love* to work, and is it selfish to work only for your emotional health? How much can you really alleviate the family's financial pinch with your business? These feelings about yourself and your home-based situation are important considerations in determining whether an at-home business could work for you.

Once you've recognized your anxieties, answered your questions, and confronted your doubts, you should allow yourself the luxury of anticipating the joys of a home business: the feeling of being self-reliant; the exhilaration of a sale; your pride when a customer says, "That's perfect," on seeing your work; the flexibility of being your own boss; the delight of treating your family to dinner out when you finally turn a profit; the heady experience of being *needed* for your financial contributions to the family; the fun of meeting new people; the frivolity of spending your own money. When you opt for a home business, you get the whole package: the risks and sacrifices, the elations and rewards.

In the following chapters, we'll take a look at hundreds of opportunities for a home-based woman in search of employment. Your ingenuity will help you add to our list of moneymaking ideas. Whether you elect to work only a few hours each week or to expand your newfound occupation into a full-time business, we're willing to bet that the financial rewards will be matched by your feelings of self-worth and achievement. Some of the jobs we have listed were once thought to be "men's work." These days, women are employed as petroleum geologists and telephone installers, as house painters and auto repair workers. Being home-based doesn't mean you're homebound, with skills and talents limited to the three Cs: cooking, cleaning, and child care. The only real limitations you face are those you impose on yourself.

Suggested Reading

Behr, Marion, and Wendy Lazar. *Women Working Home: The Homebased Business Guide and Directory.* Norwood, New Jersey: WWH Press, 1981.

Feingold, Norman, and Leonard Perlman. *Making It on Your Own: Small Business Opportunities for Women, Retirees, Young People, Handicapped.* Washington: Acropolis, 1980.

Ferner, Jack D. *Successful Time Management.* New York: John Wiley & Sons, 1980.

Ilich, John, and Barbara Schindler Jones. *Successful Negotiating Skills for Women.* New York: Playboy Paperbacks, 1981.

Levinson, Jay C. *Earning Money without a Job.* New York: Holt, Rinehart & Winston, 1979.

McQuown, Judith H. *Inc., Yourself.* New York: Warner Books, 1981.

Seltz, David, and Mary Leslie. *New Businesses That Women Can Start and Successfully Operate.* New York: Farnsworth Publishing, 1977.

Simon, Arthur C. *How to Start a Business and Make It Grow.* Ventura, California: Future Shop, 1978.

Sommer, Elyse and Mike. *The Two Boss Business.* New York: Butterick Publishing, 1980.

Winston, Sandra. *The Entrepreneurial Woman.* New York: Bantam Books, 1979.

Winston, Stephanie. *Getting Organized.* New York: Warner Books, 1979.

Getting Down to Business 2

(The unavoidable legal/financial aspects of going into business for yourself)

Dreams and luck don't bring home the bacon. Every prosperous businesswoman spends a major part of her time, attention, and effort in pursuit of her main objective: showing a profit. For *your* business to prosper, you must understand the marketplace, but first you must "know thyself." Starting a business is a time for determining whether you've got what it takes.

It's a time for realizing that the only certainty in running your own business is that there will always be risks. Taking those gambles in stride calls for effective planning, perhaps the most important ingredient of your fledgling business. You wouldn't take a husband, three noisy kids, and a dog on a week's camping trip without planning what clothes to take, how much money to allow for gasoline, camping fees, and unforeseen expenses, and whether to buy a new first aid kit. Neither should you think of investing time, money, and energy in any kind of moneymaking venture without plotting its takeoff and flight. According to the Small Business Administration, about 80 percent of new businesses fail each year, and lack of planning is a major reason why.

We've divided this chapter into several sections, each highlighting a broad area of the facts you must face before you start mentally spending your profits. The place to begin is where you are: Determine what you have financially and what you want or need; then plan the steps that will bridge the gap between the two.

Though you may want to have a home business for any of the personal reasons discussed in Chapter 1, you're certainly hoping to earn extra cash in the process. How often do you run short of money, paying half the electric bill and letting your credit card payment slide so that you can finance your husband's root canal? Do you postpone home improvement projects like retiling the bathroom or replacing the family-room carpet? Are you going out less and resenting it more, giving up your weekly French lessons, and grudgingly wearing last year's clothes? Are you driving your clunker of a car into the ground and trying to do your own plumbing repairs with only a vague idea of what to do with wrenches and snakes? You're not alone: All over the country people are finding themselves in similar predicaments, in need of extra cash to make ends meet.

Finding Your Financial Self

To know what direction you should take or how big a money-making operation you should tackle, take stock of your current situation. Seeing your financial picture will help you decide how much you'd like to earn and what you can afford to invest. It could mean the difference between running a profitable venture and just scrimping along. Compiling a picture of your financial situation at the outset is also a good way to get some insight into what's involved financially in planning a home business.

The following method of tallying up your present income and outflow might seem like complicated busywork, but in the long run, it will save you time, money, and disappointment. There seems to be shock value in actually seeing the figures in black and white. You suddenly know why last year's $.50 raise never seemed to make a difference at the end of the month and why you had to cancel your vacation trip to the Rockies.

Getting a financial picture of yourself doesn't take much time, and most of the needed information can be found among your canceled checks. The exercise which follows is important for several reasons: It will help you to budget your income better, and it will help you to determine where you might economize, whether you can afford any major investments (such as a home business), and how much more you need to earn to make life a little smoother.

All you need to complete the exercise is a pencil and a clean sheet of 8½x11-inch paper. An inexpensive calculator would be helpful and can be a great investment; it can save you time, frustration, and paper and prevent costly mistakes in figuring monthly bills, annual income taxes, and overhead and supply costs.

The financial picture in Table 2-1 is based on information we gathered during 1979 and 1980 in an informal telephone survey of more than one hundred single-income families living in the Midwest. Each survey participant was a family of four living in a city or a suburb, with one automobile and an annual income of $13,000-$15,000.

Table 2-1

Monthly Cash Flow Chart

(1) Monthly Net Income	(2) Fixed Monthly Expenses (outflow)	(3) Annual Bills
$1,000	$ 135 Auto loan	$400 Real estate taxes
	130 Utilities	200 Auto insurance
	300 Food	300 Home insurance
	250 Rent or mortage	360 Medical insurance
	75 Gasoline & auto expenses	180 Life insurance
	50 Clothing & charge accounts	
	120 Monthly costs of items from column 3 (1,440-12)	
	50 Miscellaneous expenses (5 percent of monthly income)	
	100 Savings (10 percent of monthly income)	
$1,000	$1,210	$1,440

Monthly cash flow—$1,000 - $1,210 =$-210

To do your own monthly cash flow chart, write the total amount of your monthly net income in column 1. Itemize all of your fixed monthly expenses, including bank loan payments, house mortgage or rent payments, and estimated utility and food costs, in column 2. List any annual bills, such as: taxes (real estate and personal) and insurance (life, auto, medical, and home), in column 3. Break the total amount from column 3 into monthly installments by dividing it by 12. Then add this monthly average to column 2.

Because maintaining a savings account is a good idea anyway and essential when starting a business, figure 10 percent of your monthly income as savings. Add this amount to column 2. Calculate 5 percent of your monthly income as an allowance for miscellaneous, not-planned-for expenses such as dinner out, a magazine, furnace repairs; add this amount to column 2.

This mathematical exercise should give you a pretty clear picture of where all your money goes. Now you have to face the bottom line. Total all the expenses in column 2 (including the 10 percent for savings and 5 percent for miscellaneous items), and subtract this from your monthly income in column 1. If you're lucky, column 1 is larger than column 2 and you have enough for a new lawn mower or a down payment on a couch. If, however, you're like so many other Americans trying to cope with inflation, which can put today's hamburger at the price of yesterday's steak, the difference between column 1 and column 2 will suggest that your spare time could well b⌐ used in earning some extra cash.

Down to Brass Tacks

If you've concluded that a home business could be just the thing to make your monthly cash flow picture healthier, read on. We've made several important discoveries about being in business, from our experiences and from the many interviews we've conducted with women who've hurdled all the obstacles en route to success.

Remember the old adage about needing to have money to make money? It's true for all businesses, large and small, part-time and full-time. In most cases you'll need start-up money for materials, supplies, and advertising and money to cover operating costs for an undetermined amount of time. Most new businesses don't show an immediate profit, so you've got to have enough funds to operate for at least six months. And there are several ways you can get your starting capital.

Joan B. of Massachusetts had a garage sale to raise money for baking supplies for her first three wedding cake orders. Today, she employs three other bakers and a delivery person, and *she* works mainly with customers, planning their wedding desserts. You might be able to take in ironing, babysit, pawn your jewels, or sell the bicycles that have been collecting dust in the garage to raise some funds to kick off your particular business venture.

Maybe you can trim your initial costs by renting (instead of buying) equipment you need for your business (e.g., an industrial sewing machine, a rug shampooer, extension ladders). Out of your earnings, you can stockpile some money to buy your own.

If you have no way to raise the money yourself, you may have to apply for a loan. Whether you get it will depend on your credit rating, the amount you want to borrow, and the way you plan to use the money.

Bank Talk

If you're a single woman, you've probably already established a credit rating. It's often nearly impossible to have a job outside your own home without having a car; that could be where you first came in contact with the value of good credit. Without it you couldn't have bought that endearing gas guzzler or the shiny compact with the squeaky brakes. Maybe one of your parents or a friend cosigned on a bank loan for your car, or you worked out an arrangement through the credit union where you work. Now you're making the regular monthly payments that establish a good credit rating for you. You're on record with the credit bureau in your area.

Establishing good credit before marriage can be quite an asset to any woman needing financial assistance. The Equal Credit Opportunity Act, signed by President Ford in October 1974, makes it unlawful for any creditor to discriminate against an applicant on the basis of sex or marital status. But if you married before establishing credit in your name, you may not have any. "Well," you say, "didn't I pay off that TV set last summer, and haven't I written a check for the car payment for the last thousand years?" Maybe you have, but unless at least one of those items was bought and financed in *your* name, or in both your name and your husband's, then *you* don't have a good credit rating; in fact, you don't have a rating at all.

If you don't have a personal credit rating, the next step is to get one. The first thing to do is to open a checking or savings account in your name only. Open charge accounts in your name at local stores and keep payments up to date. Make sure that your next major purchase is financed in your name only or in the names of both you and your spouse. Make regular installment payments. Your conscientiousness will reflect stability and mark you as a good credit risk.

If none of these ways of establishing credit are available to you, ask the bank to lend you some money. If you want a loan of $500 and the bank wants collateral worth $500, open a savings account in the bank, deposit the $500, and use the account as collateral. Naturally, you'll lose a little money because the interest you'll be paying on the loan will be greater than the interest you'll be earning from the savings account, but it'll be worth every penny to establish your credit rating.

Good personal credit could take some time to build, so put your plan into action several months before you hope to start your business. Besides local banks, other places to look for a loan are finance companies and credit unions. Be sure to compare interest rates. (Finance companies may charge a slightly higher rate than most other lending firms.)

When your business is firmly on its own feet, you may want to establish credit on a commercial level. That means being listed with Dun & Bradstreet. For a yearly fee, your business will be listed in the annual publication of this commercial credit bureau. If you need a business loan later on, the lending firm will likely check your business credit rating in Dun & Bradstreet before lending you the money.

Getting a Loan

Some businesses don't need a large initial outlay. But chances are you'll have to borrow some funds for "start-up." Begin small, and if possible, use your savings rather than borrowing. It's always nice to start with a clean slate—in this case, a loan-free business. As mentioned earlier, figure how much it'll take to keep your business afloat for six months, including costs of all supplies, equipment, salaries, transportation, and postage, plus rent, utilities, maintenance, and other expenses. Many new entrepreneurs have failed because they didn't have enough capital to hold out until the profits began flowing.

Darcy M. of Alabama started a diet clinic in her basement, offering weigh-ins, exercise equipment, and discussions with experts about diet foods. After three months she was in trouble because she didn't have enough customers to make the payments on the exercise equipment. To buy the equipment in the first place, Darcy had to get her husband to sign a note guaranteeing payment, and he was angry when he learned he would have to pay back the loan. In desperation, Darcy put on an extensive word-of-mouth advertising campaign to bring in more customers. In three more months she was back on her feet and making the loan payments herself. She realized she'd gone into business on a shoestring, and she vowed never to get herself into that bind again.

If you see yourself as a budding entrepreneur, but the figures in your checkbook show that you need to borrow some money, begin preparation for a loan application by putting together another kind of financial picture of yourself and your chosen business venture. (Your accountant or financial adviser could help with this.) List your assets (cash on hand, inventory, stocks and bonds, and business furniture and equipment) and your liabilities (outstanding debts). Define your intended business arrangement (sole proprietorship, partnership, corporation). Project your business future on paper: Show how much you expect to earn, where you plan to sell your product or service, how much your inventory and supplies will cost, and how you intend to meet your expenses.

Most banks will expect the following information from you when you apply for a new business loan:

- a brief description of your business: type, market, operation, start-up date;

- a description of your business location and the terms of occupancy, with a copy of the lease, if applicable;

- a résumé of your education, experience, and present duties (and the same for your partners, if any);

- a breakdown of the sources of funds (including other loans as well as the money you and others plan to invest in the business);

- a list of equipment to be purchased, with respective costs; be prepared to pay 20 percent in cash or show investments (in office equipment, materials, supplies, cars, truck) already made;

- monthly profit and loss projections for three years (a breakdown of the anticipated cost of goods sold, the net sales, gross profit margins, expenses, and net and accumulated profits);

- personal financial statement (a complete picture of what you own and what you owe; your tax return is a good statement addition).

Prove to the bank loan officers that there is a need for your business venture and that you are a good credit risk. Have requests for your service or orders for your product in writing; document the market research findings (see Chapter 3) that show your area would support a sandwich concession at the park or an industrial cleaning service. Be professional in your presentation and in your plans for conducting your business. Be confident and enthusiastic, but be realistic about your chances of getting the money you need. A cosigner may help secure your bank loan. Don't feel insulted if you're asked to come up with a reputable person who believes enough in you and your idea to agree to pay back the loan should you default.

All of this may sound a little scary, but remember that the worst possible thing that can happen is that your loan request will be turned down. If that happens, rethink your business plan and head for another lending institution.

In your eagerness to be resourceful, don't overlook the Small Business Adminstration (SBA); it exists to serve people like you. It distributes loans to small businesses according to carefully outlined standards. Current SBA guidelines define a small business as one that's independently owned and run and that doesn't have a major impact in its field. The SBA specifies how many employees and how much income a business can have and still be "small." Not every kind of loan request is filled. You can't get a loan to start a publishing business, for example. And you can't borrow money to pay off other debts. (More on the activities of the SBA later in the chapter.)

Turning Your Idea into a Company

When your loan is approved and you have money to work with, give your company a name and register it at city hall (more on this in Chapter 3). Obtain a permit or license to do business in your city and county. Once you're properly registered and licensed, go back to the bank and open a company account.

As a business, your operation will fall into one of three ownership categories. It may be a sole proprietorship, a partnership, or a corporation. A **sole proprietorship** is the least complicated and least expensive method of setting up a business. It works for one person or a married couple. In a sole proprietorship, you file your business tax statement as part of your personal tax return; the company is your personal asset.

A **partnership** arrangement is for a business with more than one owner. A limited partnership is one where one or more partners do none of the operating or decision making and contribute only a specific amount of funds to the business, with no responsibility beyond that amount. A general partnership exists when two people share authority and responsibility (personal and legal) for running the operation. Each partner files a financial statement for the business, showing her share of profit or loss, with her own tax return. The death of one of the partners legally dissolves the partnership.

A **corporation** is a legal arrangement in which people who own stock control the company. Its greatest advantage is that it holds no personal liability for its owners (in contrast with the sole proprietorship and the partnership). Corporations are complex, with their own regulations and paperwork. You can incorporate your business for several hundred dollars; there are books on the market that will tell you how. Nevertheless, unless you are well versed in legalese, it's best to hire a good accountant and a good lawyer to go through the process for you.

Whichever of the three business arrangements you elect to use, seek the advice of a qualified consultant. He or she will also be able to advise you about a **retirement plan.** There are two pension savings plans you may want to consider. The current Keogh law not only allows you to set up an ordinary pension plan with a savings account, but also gives you tax advantages for a nonmonetary savings plan, such as investment in antiques, land, diamonds, and other valuables. The Individual Retirement Account (IRA), created by Congress in 1974, provides millions of Americans with a tax incentive to save money for their retirement. The plan was originally designed to allow the self-employed and those wage earners not covered by qualified retirement plans to establish tax-sheltered retirement funds. Provisions for today's IRAs are even more attractive, although a Keogh plan still permits a larger yearly contribution. Get all the details, from financial institutions or the IRS, on how to prepare for your later years. No one is going to take care of this essential planning for you.

Insurance Concerns

Liability insurance is something every business should have. Regardless of how careful you are, accidents happen. Suppose you make and sell a liver pâté that gives your customers food poisoning (you thought the liver was fresh). Or your customer's cat is injured while in your care (you had no idea the kennel door was ajar so that the neighbor's boxer could get in). To protect yourself and your customers, check with your insurance company for complete details about the specific coverage you need. You may have to abandon your business idea if the insurance is too expensive. If you're determined to make a go of it in spite of high insurance costs, you may decide to incorporate your business, eliminating personal liability for your business operation.

Maggie M. of Ohio had all the space, equipment, and expertise to run a horseback riding school. She taught about twenty-five students. Everything was great until she discovered that, for her protection, she needed to get liability insurance costing over $100 a month. Maggie knew she would have to raise her fees to collect enough money to pay for the insurance. She also knew that many of her students (whose parents had to sacrifice some extras to finance their youngsters' lessons) would have to drop out. Disappointed, Maggie was forced to go out of business.

For some kinds of work you may need to be bonded. Bonding is a form of insurance you buy for your customer's protection and peace of mind. Transporting and guarding valuables and providing surveillance of houses and business property are services that may require bonding. A bonding company assures your customer that he or she won't suffer any loss. If you default, or if something happens to property in your care, your customer will be compensated by the bonding company. Look in the Yellow Pages for a reputable bonding company that can give you more details about bonding procedures and pricing.

Copyrights, Patents, and Trademarks

If you plan to sell an original product that you've created, you should consider protecting your rights to it. Copyright, which traditionally refers to protection of written materials, in fact can also protect music, patterns, and designs. Infringements of copyright are instances of people dramatizing, performing, reciting, publishing, filming, or otherwise using your original work (music, wedding dress patterns, or trivet designs) without your permission. The latest copyright laws give more legal protection than in the past. Anything created after January 1, 1978, is protected by copyright for the owner's lifetime plus fifty years.

Your application for copyright registration must be filed according to the latest laws, and you must follow exact procedures when giving others permission to use your property. As a copyright holder, you can't ignore some infringements and enforce others. You are responsible for protecting your interests. Write to the Copyright Office for a "Copyright Information Kit." To register a copyright, send $10 with the completed "Application for Registration of a Claim to Copyright" to the Copyright Office. Obtain the form free from: Copyright Office, Library of Congress, Washington DC 20559. (See Chapter 14 for more information on copyright.)

Perhaps your product would be better protected by a patent. You can patent a process, a machine, a manufactured item, or an improvement of any of these. You may want to secure a patent if your product can be described and manufactured and if it has unique qualities when compared with others used in a similar way. For example, a tool for opening paint cans might be patented if its design is new and unusual. Although securing a patent is time-consuming and expensive (sometimes taking up to two years and costing between $1,000 and $2,000 in legal fees), it protects your idea from being copied. To make sure you are the first to patent your item, you'll have to conduct a patent search or more likely hire a patent attorney or agent in your area to do it. Contact the Commissioner of Patents and Trademarks, Department of Commerce, Washington DC 20231, for procedures to follow.

Besides protecting your product, you may want to claim a product name or logo as your own. Though trademarks are most often secured by big businesses, there's no reason you can't get one. A trademark will protect your ownership of the product's name. The fee for registering a trademark is $35. Write for information to: Commissioner of Patents and Trademarks, Washington DC 20231.

Government Regulations and Tax Tips
Regulations and licensing deserve careful attention.

● First check with the local zoning board to make sure you're allowed to conduct business from your home.

● Secure a home business permit from the county licensing department. It will probably cost around $10 and be good for one year.

● Find out what kinds of advertising signs you can put up in your yard. Some communities have strict definitions of what's acceptable.

● You may be required to pay business rates on your telephone. Such rates vary from place to place but are generally higher than residential rates. For rules and prices in your area, check with your local telephone company or the agency that regulates public utilities in your state.

● In most places any kind of food-handling service requires a permit. To get and keep the permit, the business must meet various standards of operation and must pass regular inspections. Check with your board of health for details.

● For some businesses you may need a chauffeur's license, issued by the department of motor vehicles in your state. Plan to get one if you intend to transport people, pets, or cargo.

● If you're selling at retail, it's mandatory that you get a state sales tax license, more commonly known as a vendor's license. It authorizes you to collect sales tax for the state. With the vendor's license you will be issued a resale number enabling you to buy the materials/supplies for making your product without paying sales tax. Call your state licensing department for information on the collection of sales tax.

● Be sure to check the parking regulations on your street, so you can instruct your customers where to park.

● Contact the fire department and your local branch of the Environmental Protection Agency if you'll be burning anything that discharges any solid, liquid, or gas into the air.

● Special licenses may be required for practicing certain occupations. These vary from state to state but include such jobs as auto mechanic, electrician, and cosmetologist.

Many state offices offer valuable advice on setting up shop—from which agencies or governing boards to check with and what procedures to follow, to how to go into business with the fewest growing pains. If you can't find out which office can help you, write to the governor's office. Ask that your request be forwarded to the department that can give you the information you need.

Running a business is a complicated venture for the unseasoned amateur, especially when your business grows to the point where you hire people to work for you. Once you hire someone, decide to incorporate, or start a Keogh plan, you need a federal employer identification number. (Your own social security number is enough to identify a small operation.) When you hire employees, you are subject to regulations of the Occupational Safety and Health Administration and are obliged to pay whatever employment taxes are currently required.

Federal Tax. The IRS publishes *Tax Guide for Small Business,* which you should study and discuss with your financial adviser. This publication identifies the tax forms for which you are responsible and specifies what business deductions (such as travel, insurance, fees you pay to belong to professional organizations, and business phone calls) you can legally take.

For the first time since 1976, the IRS is permitting the home business person to write off expenses on a work place in the home even if the principal place of work is somewhere else. Suppose you operate a cleaning service or conduct nature hikes; even though the actual job is performed on your customer's property or in a public park, your home is where you run the business—where you negotiate and plan jobs, order supplies, keep the books. You don't have to perform the service or sell the product in your home to qualify for the deduction, but you must have a portion of your home set aside exclusively and used on a regular basis for conducting your business. If one-seventh of your home (measured by percentage of floor area or by number of rooms) is specifically designated as your work area, this is the portion of your home expenses (rent, depreciation, taxes, insurance, repairs, and utilities) that you can claim as a deduction.

Have your accountant or a competent tax return preparer give you expert advice on giving the government what you owe it and keeping for yourself what's rightfully yours.

Recordkeeping

But all the expert advice in the world won't do you much good if you don't keep careful, accurate records. The following summary represents the bare minimum of what you should account for in your home business.

Purchases. Business purchases (expenses) are whatever you have to buy or pay for in order to run your business: your equipment, supplies, clothing, and advertising. The scope of your expenses depends on your type of business. If you are a photographer, your expenses would include such purchases as cameras, film, developing materials, enlarging equipment, and paper. These must be recorded with proof: canceled checks, receipts, or bills of sale. (Your financial adviser will request these in order to complete your annual tax return.)

Betty J. did occasional typing at home for students and small businesses. Her business grew into a nearly full-time venture. At tax return time she went to an accountant for help. He asked for papers showing expenses, payments from customers, and so on. Betty knew some of the papers had been stuffed into drawers, crammed into notebooks, or lost. She had to pay the bank to look up canceled checks she hadn't saved, but she still couldn't take many of the deductions to which she was entitled, because she hadn't saved receipts. Betty learned an expensive lesson about conducting her business in a professional manner.

Deductions. Schedule C of your tax return has something called "Cost of goods and/or Operations" where you can account for materials and supplies you've bought for your business. The IRS defines deductions as the expenses of doing business. As mentioned earlier, the IRS allows you deductions for using a specific area in your home for operation of your business, as long as that space isn't used for anything else. You can deduct the depreciation of equipment you use to run your operation. And don't forget to deduct mileage on your family car while it's being used for business. (The current deduction is $.20 per mile.) Keep a notebook in your car and record your exact business mileage. You may be eligible for other business deductions; check with the IRS office in your area.

Income. Income means every penny your business takes in. Naturally, not every cent of your business income is profit, *but it must all be accurately recorded anyway.* After you've entered in a ledger all your purchases, deductions, and earnings, your accountant will have a fairly good picture of the financial shape your business is in. Your actual taxable profit will be what is left over at the end of the year, after the expenses and deductions have been subtracted from your income.

Financial Friends

If you aren't qualified to do your own books, don't hesitate to solicit the services of a reputable bookkeeper or accountant. Ask your business friends to recommend the people they use. It's important to find someone with whom you can communicate easily. Besides helping to set up your books and showing you how to keep your records, he or she will be qualified to answer many questions you have concerning your business, such as how to get an E.I. (employer identification) number or where to pay your monthly federal tax deposits. You'll find that much of the work and worry can be lifted from your shoulders for a monthly fee that generally runs between $35 and $50. Accountants are seldom paid a retainer by a small business person; they are usually paid monthly or quarterly.

Choosing other financial friends (like lawyers and bankers) carefully is an excellent practice for the beginning business person. These experts work as consultants for your business or negotiators in times of trouble—when you need an extension on your loan payment, for example. Keeping any budding business afloat financially is tough enough, and some lawyers' fees may seem exorbitant. (Many lawyers even charge clients for their telephone time.) But having a good contact in the legal field is invaluable. To locate a reputable lawyer, call the local bar association, or ask your business acquaintances for their lawyers' names. Bankers are also good people to know. They can give you good advice on how to effectively conduct your banking. Loans are often more easily secured from bankers who have come to trust your judgment and recognize your commitment to your business.

Use the Small Business Administration

Speaking of consulting experts, the Small Business Administration is perhaps your greatest champion. This government agency is dedicated to the birth and development of independent small businesses in America. As mentioned earlier, the administration grants loans (of up to $150,000) to qualified applicants. It can give you advice on buying and selling (wholesale and retail) and pricing, and it publishes charts and workbooks on keeping business records. One of the SBA's specialties is counseling. It also sponsors workshops that provide information on starting and operating a small business. The SBA offers nearly two hundred pamphlets covering every aspect of business management, including a "Tax and License Checklist" for your state and city. Call a district office of the SBA or request a list of publications and their prices from the Small Business Administration, Box 15434, Fort Worth TX 76119.

Another valuable contact for your home business is the Service Corps of Retired Executives Association (SCOREA), an agency of the SBA made up of retired men and women who make their managerial skills and advice available free of charge to owners and managers of businesses. The group has eight thousand members, organized into ten regional divisions, sixty-five districts, and 375 local chapters.

Getting any new business on its feet is a monumental undertaking; it can't be achieved overnight. Regardless of how many get-rich ideas you read about, or how many "I made a million" stories you hear, reality is more humdrum. You'll get back just what you put in. You'll need plenty of common sense, some hard planning sessions, a sound approach to making money, enough up-front funds to get things rolling, and the ability to hang in there until they do. Add a twist of luck to all your efforts, and you may just find extra cash in your pocket.

Suggested Reading

The Complete Encyclopedia of Legal Knowledge for Small Business Survival. Leesburg, Virginia: Citizens Law Library, 1980.

Kamoroff, Bernard. *Small-Time Operator: How to Start Your Own Small Business, Keep Your Books, Pay Your Taxes and Stay Out of Trouble.* Rev. ed. Laytonville, California: Bell Springs Publishing, 1981.

Lane, Marc J. *Taxation for Small Business.* New York: John Wiley & Sons, 1980.

Lerner, Joel J. *Bookkeeping and Accounting.* New York: McGraw-Hill, 1978.

Loffel, E. W. *Financing Your Business.* New York: John Wiley & Sons, 1978.

Mackevich, Gene. *The Woman's Money Book.* New York: Bantam Books, 1979.

Nelson, Paula. *Joy of Money: A Contemporary Women's Guide to Financial Freedom.* New York: Stein & Day, 1975.

Pomroy, Martha. *What Every Woman Needs to Know about the Law.* New York: Playboy Paperbacks, 1981.

Porter, Sylvia. *Sylvia Porter's New Money Book for the Eighties.* New York: Avon, 1980.

Rice, Jerome S., and Keith Libbey. *Making the Law Work for You: A Guide for Small Businesses.* Chicago: Contemporary Books, 1980.

Strassels, Paul N., and Robert Wool. *All You Need to Know about the IRS.* New York: Random House, 1979.

Weinrauch, John G., ed. *How to Get Credit.* St. Paul: Research Advisory Services, 1978.

Contact: Internal Revenue Service (the address and telephone number of the nearest office are listed in your telephone directory) for a copy of *Tax Guide for Small Business.*

Small Business Administration, Box 15434, Fort Worth TX 76119, for a list of available pamphlets on small business management.

Marketing your Product, your Service, Yourself

3

(The importance of advertising)

The IRS estimates that there are currently seven million Americans operating part-time businesses out of their homes. That's a lot of enterprising people, and the ones who are making it don't rely on luck to bring in customers. The bottom line is sales, and if you hope to entice the public to your weekly flea market or get them to buy your velvet initial pillows, you, too, will have to become "business wise." That means learning how to sell your product or service and, in a sense, yourself. In business jargon it's called marketing—the sum total of activities designed and coordinated to sell a product or service.

Marketing principles are usually grounded in common sense. They suggest, for example, that the jewelry you make from seashells would be more salable in Iowa than in Florida, since only a few stores (if any) would feature such items in the Midwest. The marketing-minded Miami businesswoman might consider selling her jewelry nationally through the mail instead of trying to compete with the other Florida beachfront gift shops.

This chapter identifies some marketing techniques you should know about in launching your business. Do you recognize the importance of identifying your target customers, pricing your product fairly, and promoting it to your best advantage? You can't afford *not* to recognize it if you intend to operate in the black.

Marketing Yourself

Before you try selling your doll clothes or offering to scrub walls in townhouses, you must first present yourself as a serious entrepreneur and adopt the kind of **professional manner** that leads customers to comment, ''That's the kind of person I enjoy doing business with.'' Don't underestimate your abilities and strengths. If you're not confident, how can you expect your customers to have confidence in you and your business? Conducting yourself and your operation according to sound, ethical, fair business practices is an important first step in establishing yourself as a professional.

Louise M. of Idaho learned the importance of professionalism early in her bakery operation. To get rid of all the breads, cakes, pies, and cookies she made every day, she used to sell everything that was left by late afternoon at ridiculously low prices. It wasn't long before most customers waited until late in the day to shop at her home bakery. Louise was losing money. After much thought she realized she wasn't being fair to herself. She decided to mark down her prices the day *after* the goods were baked, and she set aside a rack for day-old goodies. Louise's profits increased. She still sells almost everything she bakes, but now she makes a profit. Louise's professional attitude about selling top-quality goods at reasonable prices saved her business.

Assertiveness is another attribute that contributes to a successful venture. You must have the conviction that what you are offering to the public is the *best, most* helpful, *least* expensive, or some other appropriate superlative. And you must be ready to assert your opinion and back it up with facts. Don't let anyone undermine you, your product, or your service. (By the same token, it isn't good business practice to run down the competition. Competition is healthy; it can spur you to make your product or service so desirable that people won't be able to resist the coconut hearts or flannel doll pajamas you make.)

Alice R.'s assertiveness led her to a solution that kept her community service alive. This Illinois homemaker put together a newsletter listing homes for sale ''by owner.'' She distributed the newsletter herself to grocery stores and drugstores in her city. After several weeks she was ready to give up the idea because distribution kept her on the road practically day and night. Sales were good, and feedback was positive; but she was worn out, and her husband and children complained that they never saw her. There had to be a better, more efficient way to distribute the newsletters. Alice took the initiative to call the news agency that distributed magazines and newspapers all over town and asked if they would distribute her product. The contract she now has with the news agency puts her newsletter in more stores than she'd ever hoped. Newsletter sales are up so much that Alice doesn't worry about distribution costs anymore, and she has more time to compile and edit her product, as well as more time to spend with her family. All because she was assertive enough to convince someone else to take a chance on her business.

Whether you're babysitting, tending lawns, delivering prescriptions, or taking photographs, being committed to success and rallying to find solutions to the problems that will inevitably surface could mean the difference between profit and loss.

Professionalism and assertiveness in a home business must be matched by **thorough preparation and hard work.** Don't leave anything to chance. Make sure from the start that you have a quality product and that you have learned everything there is to know about the services you will perform for others.

Susan B. and Edith W. of Rhode Island worked for years as secretaries to various physicians and dentists. Using that experience, they started a new service in their area: setting up offices for doctors who were establishing new practices, local physicians who were moving to new offices, and out-of-towners who were relocating to the city. Susan and Edith found offices and negotiated leases for the professionals. They decorated the offices and chose carpeting, draperies, and furniture. They had phones installed and ordered stationery, business cards, and office supplies. They secured the services of an accountant and a billing agency. When they finished their jobs, all the doctors had to do was walk in and start working. The hard work paid off. Their clients enthusiastically recommended them to associates because of their thoroughness and competence.

Professionalism, assertiveness, hard work—they're some of the basics of marketing yourself. When you believe in your *own* marketability, you can begin the marketing process for your product or service.

Research

Before you advertise and promote your "can't miss" idea, you'd better do some research to make sure you have a clear shot at success. If your budget is bulging, you can leave this to the marketing experts. Let them survey attitudes and send questionnaires. But if you're like most home business hopefuls, your budget is already strained; so plan to do some market research on your own.

Analyze the area in which you live. Who lives there? What are their interests, hobbies, and jobs? What are their backgrounds? Their concerns? What's the average income level? How big is the student population? How many professional people and business owners are there? Assembling a profile of your market will help you to determine if there's a need for a breakfast-in-bed service or a do-it-yourself furniture refinishing shop. You should also determine whether your community's need for your product is long-term, short-term, or seasonal. How will such fluctuations (if any) affect your profits? Are you likely to have repeat customers, or are one-time sales more probable? The answers to these questions will enable you to plan accordingly. Talk to people and—more important—listen.

Market research isn't just for products. You should conduct similar research on services you plan to offer. By surveying your community you may find that young singles would support a wake-up service; families with children, a babysitting service; students in college, a boarding house; professional people, an office design service; businesses, a typing service.

As part of your research, **check out your competition.** How many others are offering similar services? What special bonuses or incentives do they give their customers? Can your area support another stationery shop or another alterations service? If similar businesses are booming—if their owners are turning customers away or working more hours than they'd like— chances are good that demand is strong enough to welcome a new enterprise.

Nancy C. of New Jersey wanted to start a day-care center in her home. She learned that there were already several centers in the community but that they had long waiting lists. This reassured her that there was a need; so after checking with the zoning board and complying with all the regulations of the board of health, she secured a license and opened her day-care center— to an eager and grateful public.

Frannie L. of Arizona was not as lucky. She lives in a community made up mostly of retired people. Frannie has always loved to knit, crochet, macrame, and embroider. A store manager agreed to place her handmade items in his store on consignment. But sales were sluggish. Frannie had to take back her fine sweaters, plant hangers, and embroidery. She realized later that many of the elderly people in her community were also craft workers, making gift items in the spare time they had so much of.

Whether you're selling macrame plant hangers or purple-martin birdhouses, **test your market** before expending a lot of time, energy, and money. Offer your product or service on a small scale to a carefully selected audience, noting all their reactions. If you want to offer a quilt-making class, start teaching on a one-to-one basis. The grapevine will undoubtedly give you some feedback. If other people show an interest in your class, then you can plan for the extra work space you'll need. Trying out your service might postpone your official entry into the business world, but it'll keep you from making a big investment in a hopeless venture. When you do open your doors to the public, you'll have a better idea of what people are looking for.

Laura Z. of Nevada was allowed to hang and sell her framed paintings—mostly large landscapes—in the lobby of the local library. She spent a lot of time there, listening to library patrons comment on her work and mention other types of paintings they would like to buy. Many people said they would buy small paintings of birds, butterflies, and geometric designs to use in wall groupings in their homes. Six months later Laura displayed her work again, but this time she showed both large and small paintings. The smaller works sold quickly, and she took orders for specific paintings. Laura's informal market test paid off in increased sales.

Market research can't guarantee your business's success, but it'll help you design, package, and promote your service or product in a way that minimizes your risks and maximizes your potential to turn a profit.

Product and Service Design

Armed with valuable feedback and carefully analyzed market research, design, redesign, and rethink your product or service so that it fits the needs of your potential customers. If you want to start a typing service, for instance, examine all the possible variations: being on call, specializing in statistical typing, offering a delivery service. And consider the consequences for you: getting called late at night to finish something by early morning, having to buy a new typewriter, needing reliable transportation. Then develop your product or service to make it attractive for your customers and easy-to-live-with for you and your family.

A part of designing your product or service is deciding how to **package** it to make it more attractive to customers and to make it stand out from the competition. If you're making cookies, package them in attractive reusable containers. If you're babysitting for children, have "educational" games and toys for them to play with, suitable for their age groups. Make your product or service pleasantly unforgettable. The way you present your business to the public could well determine whether someone gives your garage sale ad a second look or samples your newest ice cream flavor.

The market research you've done will translate into valuable foresight. Once you're in business, keep watching for people's reactions and asking for feedback; consider their spoken and implied suggestions. You may need to change your service or product slightly to better suit your customers.

Arlene E. of Washington was a master cook; she decided to use her skills to cater dinner parties. She advertised in newspapers and on community bulletin boards, but only a few of the responses she got were about her dinner parties. Most of her calls were from people asking if she made up party trays of meats, cheeses, and relishes. It didn't take her long to realize that she could be more successful designing and delivering party trays for informal gatherings and receptions. She changed her ads accordingly and was pleasantly surprised at the influx of calls. In no time, she was getting repeat customers: People who had called her to supply food for wedding receptions began calling her to cater their small parties, too.

Pricing

One of the hardest things to decide when running a home-based business is how much to charge. There's often a fine line between selling yourself short and not selling at all because your price is too high. When setting a price for your product or service, consider your time, effort, skill and training, materials, and overhead (that includes all your expenses except labor and materials). Also make note of what the competition is charging.

Sally M. of Connecticut was making Christmas wreaths from wire, pine cones, and artificial fruit and selling them at craft bazaars and flea markets for $25 each. Although they were well made and attractive, they didn't sell, because others like them were going for $15. Better to price slightly lower than you'd like initially. Build up a following for your product. Once people are hooked on your chocolate covered pretzels or the rug shampooing job you do, they won't balk at a moderate price increase.

But if you start selling at unrealistically low prices, it's not easy to raise them drastically because customers will feel betrayed. Underpricing in the beginning may even cause your customers to think that your product or service is inferior to others on the market. They don't expect you to produce a good product and sell it at a loss.

Try to set an honest price, both for you and the customer. Don't reduce your prices for friends and relatives; fairness should underlie all your transactions. Your customers should know they're getting some of the following: reasonable prices; lower prices than a larger outfit would charge; top-quality merchandise; fast, dependable service; personal attention; and convenience.

No matter what you charge, sooner or later you must evaluate the cash-flow balance sheet. After considering your time and expenses, you may find that to make money you'd have to charge more than anyone would be willing to pay. That's the time to reconsider your needs and desires. If you're keen on providing this *particular* service or product, evaluate what you are gaining or saving by having a home-based business. Your expenses are clearly not what they'd be if you were working at a nine-to-five job in a sky-scraper downtown. You probably save on clothing, gasoline, auto maintenance, parking, lunch, and babysitter fees. Working from home gives you other advantages: having flexible working hours, being your own boss—all the things you can't quantify. By rethinking your pricing in this way, you might find you can live with a lower return. Maybe you can't get $15 for every plant box you paint, but when you consider all the nonmonetary benefits you reap from your venture, getting $10 may not be at all disappointing.

Advertising

When you've researched your potential market and designed, packaged, and priced your product or service, you're ready to tackle perhaps the most crucial part of your marketing campaign. If people never hear about your exquisite wooden coasters, how will they ever buy them? Decide how much advertising you need and what funds you have available to do it.

In October one year Anne M. of Minnesota, a ceramics buff, decided to earn the money she needed by selling mugs personalized with names and initials. Reaching customers was her biggest problem since she had only $100 to spend on both advertising and materials. Her planning efforts indicated she could spend $15 (15 percent of her capital) to advertise in two newspapers in her area. To supplement those ads, she posted notices on bulletin boards in office buildings, laundromats, grocery stores, and libraries, advertising "My Mugs" for $2.50 each. Her November newspaper ads yielded responses from Christmas shoppers, who spread the word for her after they got their mugs. Her posters in office buildings gave many bosses the idea of giving mugs to their employees as holiday gifts.

How much you sell and to whom may depend on how well you advertise. But first you have to give your business a name—one you've carefully chosen. Be sure you've secured your home business license or permit and registered at city hall. Your license is good for one year and should be displayed in your work area. (You should have already decided on the legal arrangements of your business: Is it a corporation, a partnership, or a sole proprietorship? See Chapter 2.) Since you're registered at city hall, a person who calls and inquires about someone doing your type of work may be directed to you. Another place to announce the establishment of your business is in the legal notices section of your local newspaper.

Dream up or have someone design an appropriate **business logo**—a distinctive combination of words, letters, and symbols to identify your product or service. Your logo (short for logotype) is like a name tag—an identifying label; very often it's the way people remember your business. Your yard or plant care business might be identified by a circle with a green thumb inside; a sewing service could be advertised, with or without words, with a sign showing two needles stuck in a spool of thread. Use your logo on business cards that you distribute to potential customers. Put your logo on stationery you've designed yourself or ordered from a printer.

You may want to consult a clip art book filled with designs, pictures, and emblems in the public domain (which means they are not copyrighted and can be used by anyone for any reason, including advertising). Clip art books can usually be found in the fine arts department of a public library. Hart Picture Archives is a series of clip art books with pictures related to weather, food, furniture, and the trades and professions. If you find a picture you want to use in your business's advertising campaign, make a photocopy of the page. Then clip whatever you want out of the copy and paste it onto the original from which your business cards, stationery, postcards, envelopes, signs, or billing statements will be printed. If you're a good sketch artist, you may want to draw the design yourself. Print and pictures can be enlarged or reduced at most printing shops, so don't worry too much about precise dimensions for your sketches.

Business cards can help you sell your product or service; they're a reflection of the quality of your work. The most expensive place to buy business cards is usually an office supply store. You can save some money by buying them from a copying service; you'll save even more by making them yourself. You can design them or consult an artistic friend for ideas.

There are several ways to make your own business cards. The least expensive is to divide a standard sheet of typing paper ($8^{1}/_2$x11 inches) into sections the size of business cards. Then type or use press-type lettering to spell out your message in each section. A typical business card might look like this:

```
[LOGO SPACE]
   DROP-IT-OFF-AT-MY-HOUSE
Anything & Everything Cleaning Service
  941 Main Street • Anytown, USA
                     JANE DOE
                  555-341-8976
```

Take your sheet of paper to a printing company, and select paper for your cards. Naturally, paper prices may influence your choice: so ask to see all the styles, colors, and textures, and ask about prices. Index paper has a rough texture, but it comes in several colors and makes an attractive business card. (It's also cheap.) Index paper for 250 cards will cost you around $5—including printing and cutting fees. If the printer won't cut the paper into business card size, you can do it yourself with a good paper cutter at a public library or school.

If the cost of printing the cards is still too high for your budget, try hand lettering the cards yourself on bright-colored paper or poster board. Done with precision and care, a little originality can do a lot for promoting your business. Another thought is to trade your product or service to a printer in exchange for having your cards printed.

Consult a printer who can give you advice on creating the kind of business image you hope to project. The colors, paper stock, and style of your business cards and stationery should be appropriate for your business. Rugged-looking cards made of heavy-duty paper might be appropriate for a firewood delivery service. Pastel-colored stationery and a smiling baby logo would reflect an artist who does oil paintings of infants.

Put your advertising money where it'll do the most good. A shotgun advertising approach scatters a lot of information, but it doesn't always hit the most responsive customers. Tailor your ads to appeal to your intended customers—the people you identified in your market research. If you're a photographer, decide what you want to photograph: children, animals, valuables, landscapes. If you plan to specialize, you'll advertise to a smaller group of people. As with every other facet of running your own business, planning is the key. If you're like most home-based entrepreneurs, you want to stretch your advertising dollar as far as it will go.

While you're allocating your advertising budget, don't overlook the advertising and promotion possibilities that don't cost a penny. **Word-of-mouth** goes a long way; satisfied customers are often your most effective promoters. Their raves about your homemade chicken soup or the piano music you provided for the supper club may hold more clout than the half-page ad you take out in the local newspaper. This "free advertising" is gratifying to you and gives your business a shot in the arm.

And what about **publicity?** That's the free advertising you get from newspapers or magazines or from radio or television interviews. If your product or service is unusual or new to your area, or particularly significant at a certain time of year (e.g., dandelion removal in the heat of summer), call the managing editors of local newspapers or magazines. Tell them about your business and explain how their readers would benefit from knowing about it. You may or may not get an interview out of it, but at least you've told one more person about your operation. Call area radio or TV show hosts who often feature people with stories to tell. Tell them why you would make an excellent guest on their shows. Your home business might fit into the "success story" or "where-there's-a-will-there's-a-way" category, always popular with viewers and listeners.

Send **news releases** to local publications. These, also called press releases, are short publicity statements disguised as news. Most editors run a certain number of them in every issue. Prepare your news release by typing a short paragraph (double- or triple-spaced with wide margins) giving all the important facts about your home-based operation. The following example should give you an idea of what kind of information to include.

For immediate release

Tiny Tours for Tots is a new service for children aged three to six years. Mary Smith, director of the operation, which is headquartered on the east side of town, is a former kindergarten teacher. In her new business she takes youngsters to the zoo, the circus, movies, amusement parks, and playgrounds on Saturday afternoons. The philosophy behind the business is that there's plenty of learning and fun out there for youngsters to enjoy. For $5 each, children, in groups of four to eight, are picked up in a red minibus at the city shopping mall at designated times. The duration of each activity tour is three hours, with snacks of cookies and juice served on the bus. The children are returned to the mall for pickup by their parents at a specified hour.

To make reservations for an afternoon of fun for your children, or to learn more about Tiny Tours for Tots, call Mary Smith at 964-9880 during regular business hours.

Consider sending along a glossy photograph of yourself or your business site, or an on-the-job candid. Include your name, address, and phone number, plus postage if you want the photograph returned.

Publicity and word-of-mouth advertising don't completely fill the marketing needs of most businesses. Though you may not have the capital for expensive ad campaigns, a few well-placed ads can give you a good return. Post attractive notices and your business cards on appropriate **bulletin boards** located in grocery and specialty stores, laundromats, schools, churches, universities, libraries, offices, and hospitals. People who frequent these establishments check the boards for babysitters, sale items, lost and found items, swap and trade options, lawn care and typing services, gifts, and anthing else they're in the market for.

Newspapers. A continuous ad in the classified section of the newspaper will be one of the best investments you can make to advertise your business. Discounts are usually given for ads run regularly over an extended period of time. Seeing your name and telephone number every day lets people know that your business is not here today and gone tomorrow. If your name or logo becomes familiar to the community because of the regularity of your ad, newspaper readers will recognize your dependability.

Magazine advertising. If you have a service or product that would appeal to a particular group, advertise in trade journals, papers, or magazines that interested people would subscribe to. If you hope to type manuscripts for writers, advertise in *Writer's Digest* magazine and other writers' journals. If you make personalized golf club covers, sport and golfing publications would be appropriate for your carefully written ads.

Magazines need advertising material two to three months ahead of the publication date. If a magazine ad seems right for your business, be prepared to use a big chunk of your advertising budget. A three- to four-line classified ad generally runs between $40 and $50 an issue. Larger display ads run in the neighborhood of $350-$400 for one-twelfth page to nearly $3,000 for a full page. Of course, each magazine has different rates, so check prices carefully.

Circulars. Have circulars printed describing your service or product and listing prices. Distribute them door-to-door in the area you hope to reach. If possible, offer a special price or a bonus for the first week after the circulars are passed out. This will encourage customers to try your product or service while the price is low and the invitation to buy is personal.

Yellow Pages. Many people check the Yellow Pages when looking for a service they don't use regularly. If your business falls in this category, consider an ad with Ma Bell. Would it generate enough business to pay for the added cost of a business phone plus the cost of the ad?

Any business phone comes with a standard Yellow Pages listing, but a space ad is quite different. For an extra fee, the phone company will help you design and write your ad—or they'll do it for you. Their ads can be quite expensive, ranging from approximately $25 per month for one-half inch of column-width space to $1,000 per month for a half page. Again, prices vary around the country.

Signs. A sign on your door or in your yard is a good idea if there are no zoning laws against it. Check the regulations before erecting any signs. If word signs are not allowed in your area, consider a sign without words that explains your product or service—maybe a picture of rabbits if you want to sell rabbits you've bred or a picture of flowers if you're selling plants from your greenhouse. If yard signs are prohibited, you could have a sign painted on your car door and leave the car parked in your driveway.

Catalogs. Catalogs are expensive advertising tools, but they're the best way to advertise when you have a large assortment of goods to sell. A catalog is a particularly good idea for mail-order selling; you can include a self-addressed, postage-paid order form. Let your customers pay by check, money order, or credit card. Of course, you'd have to make advance arrangments with the credit card company, and you should be prepared for the extra bookkeeping and accounting created by catalog sales and credit customers.

Brochures. Brochures can be passed out locally or mailed to your prospective customers. Check on postal regulations, and consult your printer for advice on paper stock, weight, and cost, so you can advertise as economically as possible.

Portfolio. Make up a portfolio—a visual demonstration of your service or product. Show this when you contact potential customers. Sometimes pictures can explain more plainly than words the special qualities of your business.

Demonstration Tapes. If you're in the entertainment business and trying to sell your talents, make a demonstration tape of your act, voice, or music. If the person you want to see is busy, you can leave your tape so he or she can hear it at a more convenient time, and you can pick it up later. These tapes can also be mailed out of town to prospective clients. It's a good idea to have more than one copy of your tape.

Advertising Agencies. If you're fortunate enough to have a large advertising budget, and if you want to build a full-time operation, you might consider using the expert services of an ad agency. Ad writers often get a commission from the client equal to 15 percent of the cost of each ad they place; sometimes they also get payment from the magazine or newspaper where an ad appears. Ad agencies are often effective (though expensive) tools for advertising purposes; but their work by itself doesn't guarantee sales.

Only you can decide which is the most economical and most effective form of advertising for your home-based business. Do you want to attract enough customers to earn a few dollars a week, or do you want to attract a large number that will keep you busy all the time? How much money do you have for operating expenses? Encourage word-of-mouth advertising, take advantage of free publicity, and use well-placed, inexpensive ads. If you don't get the response you want, rethink your advertising plan; it could be the key to increasing your profits.

Try to determine which of your advertising methods (signs, newspaper or magazine ads, word-of-mouth, flyers, bulletin board notices) is getting you the most customers. When possible, ask your customers where they heard of your product or service. For mail order, code your ads so that when the order forms are returned, you'll know which magazine or newspaper they came from. Are you reaching the people you want? Are they responding as you'd hoped? If your newspaper ad for home-baked wedding cakes gets little response after a few weeks, stop the ad. Place notices in church bulletins. Leave your business card with stores who sell or rent wedding attire and with places that print wedding invitations and announcements. Contact caterers and florists who "do" weddings. Chances are your phone won't be silent for long. Carefully planned advertising campaigns more than pay for themselves.

Sales

The goal of the marketing process, and the reason you spend hours designing catalogs, posting signs, and distributing business cards, is to "make a sale." Whether you offer a product or a service, you are essentially "selling" something. (In your enthusiasm to get started, don't forget that if you're selling a *product* retail, you need a vendor's license. See Chapter 2 and Chapter 13 for details.) Whether you're offering a pet-sitting service or creating greeting card verse, being *in business* means having customers, and staying in business means keeping them coming back for more. Chapter 13 highlights a number of specific sales opportunities for home based entrepreneurs, but here we take a brief look at the variety of methods you can use to land a sale.

Direct Sales. Direct sales is a face-to-face experience with a customer. It can mean selling door-to-door, setting up a stand at the mall or on the street corner, or doing business from your front porch. The main advantages of direct sales are that you have low overhead, that you can recruit family members to help in an emergency, and that you can set your own business hours. The disadvantages of selling from home include potentially higher utility bills; customers traipsing through your home; paperwork, supplies, equipment, and worries you can't leave at the office; and customers who call you with minor complaints at any time of day. Being headquartered at home but selling door-to-door or in a public place eliminates some of the drawbacks of home selling, but increases some of your costs (gasoline and rent, for example) and raises new concerns, such as transporting goods and materials safely and having enough on hand when you need it. Weigh the pros and cons of the various direct sales options carefully; if you enjoy people contact, you'll be able to resolve the frustrations and realize the rewards direct sales holds.

Thelma V. of Virginia is a crochet expert and the wife of a career Navy man. Since she had a lot of spare time and needed extra money, she decided to give crochet lessons in her home. She advertised in the PX that for $25 per person she would give ten two-hour lessons. She got lots of responses, and everything went well until several of her students started knocking at her door at all hours, asking for guidance in finishing a project. They were all close neighbors, many of them friends, and Thelma felt obligated to drop everything and help them. After a while Thelma and her husband, Ralph, were sick of the annoying interruptions. Committed to the original offer, Thelma finished the ten weeks of lessons. Then she made arrangements to teach crochet at the YWCA near the base. She'd found that "direct selling" from her home was tying her down too much.

Selling on Consignment. Consignment selling is a kind of direct sales handled by someone else. In this method, shops agree to exhibit and sell your products (usually crafts and handmade items) and to pay you a percentage—usually between 75 and 85 percent—of the selling price. The advantages of selling on consignment are that you have a place to show your merchandise and that you don't have to use your own space or spend your time playing saleswoman. The disadvantages are that your items may not get the care in handling and display that you would give them yourself, that you make less money since you split the profits with the shop owner, and that there's usually a lag between the time an item sells and the time you get your share of the money.

Barbara D. of New Hampshire works at home, making ceramic flower pots, ashtrays, candy dishes, wall decorations, and lamps. Some of these items sell from her home; others are displayed in area gift shops. When Barbara began selling on consignment, she found that some shop owners were more professional than others in the way they handled her merchandise and forwarded her payments. Sometimes when she visited the shops to collect her money, she saw broken or chipped items on display. She heard the excuse that some items were sold at a lower price because they'd been damaged. She lost money, too, when shop owners reported one or two of her pieces stolen. She lost merchandise when a couple of shops closed without warning, and the owners disappeared. Barbara is now more particular about which stores she does business with. She checks them out several times to see how well they are run, how neat they are, how attractive the displays are, how carefully the merchandise is handled, and how often it is dusted. She asks the proprietors for both personal and business letters of reference.

Telephone Sales. Home businesswomen who enjoy using the phone might consider telephone sales. Both products and services can be sold by phone. If you clean carpets, call home owners about your service in the spring. The hint from you that their carpeting could use some freshening after a winter of having salt and grime tracked in could be just the nudge they need to give you the job.

If you plan to sell by phone and to use the phone only for business purposes, the full cost can be a tax deduction. The telephone can also save you time and gasoline. The biggest drawback to telephone selling is that people aren't always receptive to this kind of solicitation. They may respond to your call in a less than enthusiastic way. But once you build a good reputation, people wll recognize your name and your business. Chances are they'll be calling you.

Mail Sales. Selling by mail means advertising your product or service in newspapers, catalogs, periodicals, and magazines and then taking orders and delivering merchandise through the mail. Mail ads rely on snappy words, vivid illustrations, or photographs to entice readers to buy. They list either a home address or a post office box number for incoming orders. Single (usually nonperishable) products, such as cookbooks, herbs, spices, and quilts, are often advertised and sold this way. Enticing product descriptions, generally lower prices, and the convenience of shopping from your recliner in the living room appeal to busy professionals and dedicated bargain hunters. Magazine ads can be very expensive, however, so be sure to place yours where you'll get the most mileage out of them.

In addition to products you make, your mail-order business could feature products distributed by wholesalers listed in the *Thomas Register of American Manufacturers*. (More on this in Chapter 13.) The advantages of mail sales are that you won't have customers in your family room and that you don't have to dream up ways to decorate a showroom. Mail-order establishments are little more than warehouses for inventories. The disadvantages are the expenses of advertising and mailing and the need for extra space in your home for the products you'll be storing.

Rosy L. of Utah makes delicious candy. Six years ago, to make extra money for Christmas shopping, she placed an ad in the paper and put her business cards on bulletin boards around town, offering to make peanut clusters, chocolate drops, turtles, and chocolate and peanut butter fudge. As an added convenience, she offered to pack it in tins and mail it anywhere.

After the first year, she found that business was good but that the high price of the tins she used for shipping cut her profit too much. The next year she packed her candy in heavy cardboard boxes, but got complaints that the candy sometimes got mashed en route and was not as fresh as when it was in the tins. Finally she found plastic containers in the five-and-dime store, wrote to the manufacturer, and made a deal to buy them direct, which cut costs. The following year Rosy used these containers and got no complaints.

Business is better than ever. Rosy has a post office box where she picks up all her orders. During November and December, the busiest months, her husband helps her with packing, wrapping, and shipping. She has many repeat customers every year. She charges $10 a pound, plus shipping costs, and last year she cleared over $800.

A home business (be it carving the emblems of local high school sports teams into wooden bookends or telling stories to children at the YWCA) needs customers and sales to succeed. How you market yourself, design your product or service, and advertise your business will affect your sales. And the marketing process doesn't stop when you turn a profit or make your first million. Looking at new markets to tap and better ways to reach potential customers are ongoing activities for any home-based woman committed to keeping herself in business.

Suggested Reading

Anthony, Michael. *Handbook of Small Business Advertising*. Reading, Massachusetts: Addison-Wesley, 1981.

Biggles, Barry. *The Copy Catalog*. New York: Pantheon Books, 1981.

Brannen, William H. *Small Business Marketing: A Selected and Annotated Bibliography*. Chicago: American Marketing, 1978.

Breen, George E. *Do-it-yourself Marketing Research*. New York: McGraw-Hill, 1977.

Caples, John. *Tested Advertising Methods*. Englewood Cliffs, New Jersey: Prentice-Hall, 1974.

Girard, Joe. *How to Sell Yourself*. New York: Warner Books, 1981.

Hyatt, Carol. *The Woman's Selling Game*. New York: M. Evans & Co., 1979.

Roman, Murray. *Telephone Marketing: How to Build Business by Telephone*. Rev. ed. New York: McGraw-Hill, 1977.

Sarnoff, Dorothy. *Speech Can Change Your Life*. New York: Dell, 1970.

Shafiroff, Martin D., and Robert L. Shook. *Successful Telephone Selling in the Eighties*. New York: Harper & Row, 1982.

It All Starts with an Idea

4

(A smorgasbord of both taken-for-granted and unconventional money-making ideas)

The title says it all. Before you start planning to set up shop, you must have an idea. This chapter is a smattering of jobs and job ideas that we've discovered by mail, telephone, personal interview, the grapevine and smoke signal. The first half of the chapter includes those everyday jobs that we know exist (*somebody* has to stock vending machines) but that we might overlook because we're bent on finding unique spare-time work. The second section suggests creative, unconventional jobs that have worked for many different reasons: A woman's personality makes her a hit as a clown; students in a small college town welcome another boarding house; a home-based woman's ingenuity and determination make her the perfect contest participant. They are jobs whose success depends largely on a person, a place, a circumstance, or a specific need. They are jobs first realized in the imagination and then made workable by a gung-ho search for excitement—and extra cash.

Home-based women out there are doing anything and everything known to humanity. It would therefore be impossible to write about every potential job, but this chapter aims to whet your appetite and alert you to the possibilities. Some of the jobs require time spent away from home; some demand that you have your own transportation. But they all represent real ways to earn money while headquartered at your home address. Researching those ideas that appeal to you is the place to begin.

Tried and True

Tried and true jobs are like blue chip stocks—just waiting to be cashed in. They include everything from selling Christmas trees to sweeping chimneys. They evolve from our lifestyles, the technological improvements of our day, and the needs of human beings. They are jobs done to ensure safety, dispense information, and provide social services. They are jobs found in Olympia, Washington, and Orlando, Florida; they kept coming up in our conversations with home-based women around the country. Though they've been tried by many others and found profitable, they don't just happen. All the basics of business sense and sound planning still apply.

Sales

Christmas tree sales can earn you a nice holiday bundle of cash. If you have a farm or own acreage and want to go into the Christmas tree business, you will naturally raise your own trees. If you start them from seedlings, they can be purchased for $.75 to $1 each and will take five to seven years before they're ready for cutting. Staggering the planting times will keep all of them from being ripe for sale at the same time. If you don't have your own growing space, the most practical and easiest method is to buy the trees from a Christmas tree farm. The price ranges from $.50 to $3.00 a foot. Pine, spruce, and fir are the most common varieties. Rent a vacant lot on a busy street corner or near a shopping mall, and get a vendor's license. You'll be in business until very late Christmas Eve.

Vending machines can earn you a decent spare-time profit. Check with local vending machine companies listed in the Yellow Pages if you are interested in buying a vending business; they will tell you about any permits or licenses required. (A vendor's license will be one of these.) The cost of a machine depends on its size and type. There are several kinds to choose from: self-photo vendors, personal item vendors, and food, cigarette, and drink machines. A refrigerated sandwich or soft-drink machine will obviously cost more than one that sells bubble gum or small toys and trinkets. Food vendors are profitable in many locations: hospital corridors, service stations, department store lounge areas. Toy and gum vendors are great in grocery stores and beauty salons. Two of the hottest "vending machines" these days are pinball machines and video games. Small restaurants and bars would be great locations for these. The vending company usually helps the buyer of a machine locate a well-trafficked spot for it. After you set up the machine, all you have to do is keep it well stocked and maintained and remove the money regularly. The person from whom you rent the space for your machine may get a share of the profits, depending on the deal you make at the start.

Demonstrators are used for everything from food processors to word processors. Many stores, distributors, and manufacturers advertise this job and give short training sessions on the product and the way they plan to exhibit it to the public. If you're considering this kind of "highly visible" work (demonstrators are looked at almost as much as the products they show to the public), don't forget that you'll be most convincing if you demonstrate items you like, believe in, or own yourself. If you play the organ or piano, you may land a job demonstrating it in area music stores. If you have delicate, manicured hands, you might notify local jewelers that you are available to model rings, watches, and bracelets.

Make decorated T-shirts to sell to clubs and organizations, amateur sports teams, fraternities and sororities, schools, and company bowling leagues. There might be restaurants, theaters, and other establishments in your city that could use the shirts to promotional advantage. If you live in a resort town or vacation area, your T-shirts could be big sellers in local gift shops. Shirts, transfers, and a heat press can all be purchased through a wholesaler. Ask a T-shirt retailer in your area how to locate a supplier, or check the *Thomas Register of American Manufacturers*. A start-up kit usually includes five hundred transfers, four dozen shirts, and one heat press, totaling around $1,000. The kinds of transfers you offer will depend on current public taste (maybe characters from the latest outer-space thriller or members of the World Series-winning team) and on what you are willing to sell. Shirts retail for $5-$8 each. Kids, teenagers, and even adults will flock to your door if you have the in transfer for this month.

Service

Inventory takers are always in demand. The work requires little training, apart from the procedural instructions given by employers. Watch the classified ads of the newspaper for inventories being taken in your community, or call some department stores and apply to help with their upcoming inventories. You'll need ready transportation, and you may have to spend long hours on your feet when inventorying an entire store. You should enjoy methodical work that demands careful counting of merchandise and tabulating of appropriate order numbers and quantities. The work is available year round but is especially common at year's end. This job could help you pay off your Christmas bills.

Chimney sweeps are not figures of the past. Fireplaces continue to be popular and are used around the country on cool evenings in autumn and winter. And in many homes wood-burning stoves have recently become an alternative to conventional heating. Chimneys should be cleaned at least once a year to prevent fire, improper functioning of the flue, and other dangers. They are cleaned with large brushes that screw onto poles. The brush-and-pole combination can be bought at a hardware store for $15-$40, depending on the size. Chimney sweeps' rates average between $35 and $45 per visit. Though you don't need to be certified or licensed to sweep chimneys and stoves, you should get plenty of practice before you start, and you should feel comfortable on rooftops. (You'll probably need at least one extension ladder and one stepladder.) Work with a sweep for a while before you advertise your own services.

A clipping service might serve individual customers and community groups, as well as businesses too small to hire a full-time clipping service. Your clients will be interested in material that is important to them or their operations (political articles for a city councilman, entertainment reviews and stories for a freelance theater critic, fund-raising stories for the Jaycees). Your customers will bring the source material to your house; you'll clip notes, pictures, and articles from magazines and newspapers, label each with its source and date of appearance, and present them to your customers regularly in a scrapbook or folder. You'll probably charge a flat monthly or weekly retainer, but it's best to check with larger clipping services to see what the going rates are.

Advertise on wheels. Build or buy several portable lighted signs and offer to put other people's messages on them and deliver them to locations around town. A sign will cost $500-$1,000; it can be towed behind any standard vehicle with a trailer hitch. Your only maintenance will be keeping your vehicle's tires inflated and making sure that all the lights on the signs are in good working order. For $30-$35 a day your customer can let the world know that Mary is celebrating her eightieth birthday, that Bill and Jean are marking twenty-five years of marriage, or that Pete is coming home after four years in the Air Force.

Run a boarding house if you have plenty of space in your home and are there most of the time. Provide rooms plus meals to people who rent from you. Modify your insurance policy, and be sure your neighborhood is zoned for boarding houses. Calculate your expenses, including higher utility bills, food for the meals you plan to serve your tenants, and more expensive insurance coverage. Charge enough to make a profit. To bring in more money, offer phone privileges and services like cleaning and laundry.

Rentals are a great way to earn extra cash. Following is a potpourri of things you can rent to other people; there are countless others you might think of that could meet particular needs in your area. Knowing where and when to advertise is often the key to success.

bikes
camping gear
clothes for weddings
costumes for parties
dishes and silverware
furniture (folding chairs, tables, etc.)
horses and wagons for hay-rides

party supplies (hats, decorations, etc.)
recreational vehicles
rooms, garages, yards
sports equipment
tools
vacation homes
umbrellas, rain gear, tents (for outside events)

Consider renting storage space. If you can provide storage for anything, from tricycles to tripods, from books to scuba equipment, you have a good (and relatively easy) way to make extra money. People are savers; they'd usually rather pack something up ("I might need this someday") than pitch it. You may have to adjust your insurance coverage if you offer a storage service; and ask your lawyer to draw up a contract form outlining exactly the terms you want in your storage rental agreements.

Special Skills

Dog training usually doesn't require that you be a licensed teacher or instructor. Maybe you've trained your own golden retriever and the neighbor's German shepherd, and you've enjoyed the challenge. If you love dogs, have been blessed with a double dose of patience, and know how to make pets do what you want them to do, you can get paid for sharing your skills with animal owners. Be sure you're comfortable handling the friskiest spaniel and the most lethargic basset hound. You'll need ample space for animals *and* their masters, since the owners should actively participate in teaching their pets to obey. Basic animal training requires no special equipment, as pet owners will provide six-foot leather leads and choke chains for their animals. Advanced training sessions would make use of jumps.

Taxidermy is the process (some consider it an art) of preserving the skins of dead animals. Don't count it out as a possible home-based job for you. Some states (Pennsylvania, for example) have examining boards before which you must mount certain species according to established standards and obtain a license to practice. Other states have no governing or licensing bureaus; most taxidermists in those states learn the craft from books and from professionals in the field. There are also a few taxidermy schools around the country. Taxidermists skin the animals (birds, fish, mammals), preserve the skins by treating them with a chemical preparation, stuff them, and mount them. The procedure often takes ten hours or more (depending on the kind of specimen and its condition—e.g., thin skin, loose scales), spread over three to four weeks because much drying or sitting time is required. If you have a good deal of patience and time and if you appreciate the unique joy of preserving the beauty of a prize catch or a huge rack, why not consider the taxidermy trade? Check out the requirements in your state, and if possible ally yourself with a practicing taxidermist. Especially in an area where hunters and fishers find sport, your enterprise will be welcome.

Translators make the world a little smaller. If you speak a foreign language *fluently,* offer to translate letters, contracts, and other documents for companies and individuals that on occasion do business or correspond with those who don't speak English. Advertise in business magazines. Skilled translators are often difficult to locate; clients will pay $20-$50 an hour for your communication expertise. Interpreting could also be offered at a similar rate.

Teach a skill like shorthand or a craft like candle making or an avocation like bird-watching. Teaching as a means to extra cash deserves ample discussion because it's a rare person that doesn't excel at something. And whether you teach a class of twenty-five or tutor one student, you are sharing your expertise with others. You have something that others want. In any case, when you teach, yours is a noble undertaking; you are helping to build a society of lifelong learners.

You may be a "born teacher," or you may have to work hard at being an effective stimulus for growth and change. No matter what your subject matter, your communication skills are all-important: You speak, listen, and react to students in a way that reflects your enthusiasm for what you teach. You are patient and interested in your students' needs. To teach in accredited programs, highly technical areas or licensed fields, you will need specific degrees and certificates; to teach your dog tricks or your neighbors aerobic dancing, you need only the expertise and the personality for the job.

If you would like to teach from your home, you must think how much space you will need. You can't teach twenty people to square dance in your basement, but you could hold a speed-reading class there. You may be able to rent space in schools, churches, or city clubs. If your subject can be easily taught on a one-to-one basis, and if you have transportation, you might choose to travel to your students' homes.

Equipment is another consideration: If you're teaching someone to water-ski, you'd better have a boat and access to a lake. In some cases, you may be able to rent equipment or have students bring their own (knives and wood for whittling, violins for practicing, cakes for decorating, etc.).

Costs to you and your students depend on what you're teaching. Palm reading, for example, requires little equipment; horseback riding involves major expenses. Figure hidden costs before setting your prices. Some types of lessons (horseback riding, skiing) may require liability insurance. Check with your insurance agent for further details.

Individual tutoring actually costs the student more money per hour, but you can earn more by teaching groups. A tutor often earns $12-$15 an hour for working with one student; a teacher can make $25-$35 an hour for instructing five students. To earn more money, you might consider selling supplies, apparel, and equipment needed by your students. Karate students, for example, must have proper dress; art and ceramic enthusiasts are constantly buying more paint and glaze.

You must decide whether you would be most effective working with children, teens, young adults, or the elderly. Each age group has learning characteristics you must be tuned in to. Kids have short attention spans and like active, get-up-and-go learning situations; teens enjoy learning things they can use right now—things that are relevant to their lives; adults are usually very specific about what they want to learn and why they want to know it; elderly adults generally have sharp minds, but they often have slowed reflexes, failing eyesight, or hearing loss. A teacher of all age groups must know how to deal with these diverse learning profiles. The snappiest children's storyteller may get only yawns from a class of middle-aged adults. Choose an age group, and decide whether you're at your best in front of a large group or more at ease with only a few listening and participating. The most outgoing, liveliest teacher may be ill at ease with an "audience" of one.

Teaching requires a real commitment. Once you set a class time or arrange a tutoring schedule, the show must go on—even if you'd rather be shopping or doing a crossword puzzle. Teaching may well involve preclass preparations and after-class reviews. A good teacher may have to miss the season premiere of her favorite TV show and may not be able to finish her needlepoint design by Christmas.

If you decide to teach, be sure you feel confident in your understanding of your subject (how "good" are you?) and in your ability to communicate that understanding to others. And be ready to *learn* a few things about your subject, because invariably you'll have a student who asks the most probing questions or suggests the most novel approach to solving a problem.

Though teaching ideas are presented and discussed throughout the book, the following list suggests some possibilities you may not have thought of.

accounting, home budget-
ing
cake decorating
canning or freezing tech-
niques
canoeing
ceramics
chess
computer use in the home
driving
edible plants
English (to foreigners)
first aid
furniture making
gourmet cooking, wok
cooking, ethnic cooking
graphic design
gravestone rubbings
handwriting analysis

judo
kite making and flying
Lamaze birth classes
magic
palm reading
pinochle, euchre, bridge,
backgammon
rock polishing
sign language
speed-reading
sports (tennis, golf, bowling)
waterskiing and snow ski-
ing
weaving
will preparation
wine making, wine appre-
ciation
wood carving

Agriculture

Breeding and raising salable pets, such as dogs, cats, birds, fish, snakes, and spiders can be profitable. If you are an animal lover, check further into this moneymaking idea. The skills, training, space, and equipment needed for breeding and raising animals depend on the kind of animal you work with. Most birds, for example, require a tranquil atmosphere, but guppies will breed under almost any condition, as long as they are underwater. Talk to experts who are knowledgeable in your area of interest. Initial start-up costs for a business like this are variable. (Some exotic birds can cost as much as $3,000.) License and permit regulations also vary; pet shop owners will be able to give you an idea of what to expect if you plan to breed gerbils or raise canaries.

Beekeeping can be a fascinating and profitable spare-time job. A hive of swarming critters can produce twenty-five to seventy pounds of honey a year. To start yourself in the business, you'll need a hive with interior frames, a swarm of bees, beekeeper's attire, and a smoker. Start-up costs should be around $125, a small investment considering that honey sells for $1.00-$1.50 a pound. Check with your county agricultural extension service on procedures to follow and regulations surrounding bee tending. (For example, in most places the hives must be inspected twice yearly.)

Fruit and vegetable pickers are crucial for a successful harvest season. If you're camping or living in an area where farmers could use extra hands at harvest time, hire yourself out to pick cherries, blueberries, tomatoes, apples, oranges, and other crops. This is a good job for the person who wants to work occasionally to supplement her income. It's hard, often tedious work that usually requires an early start in the day. The benefits, aside from monetary, are being able to work outside in the fresh air, being a part of the country's food industry, and having good temporary employment that doesn't tie you down for extended periods. Wages vary according to the region and the crop.

Try It—You Might Like It

Nontraditional money-making ideas are born out of your imagination, talents, and experience. You can invent a job, no matter who you are or where you live. The secret is in recognizing the opportunities around you. You don't have to be a Rhodes scholar or a prodigy to make available a product or service people want or need. But you do have to have insight into people's tastes, habits, and lifestyles.

Unconventional jobs may not thrive everywhere. A swimming pool maintenance business would find few customers in northern Alaska; but a sled runner sharpening service might be more welcome than the spring thaw. Some of these self-created jobs work because they're done in a particular region; others because they're geared to a specific market; still others because home-based entrepreneurs are determined to prove the worth of their ideas.

We talked to a young woman who throws cream pies in people's faces as a sideline. (She must have insight into her community's sense of humor.) But you shouldn't forge ahead with her idea without careful investigation of your own. She told us there's a major personal drawback to her part-time job: She's gained ten pounds working around such deliciously gooey things. (We wonder if she's ever had any threats of lawsuit or assault and battery charges.) Such are the unanticipated consequences of trying out little-known, untested, or high-risk job ideas.

As far as pricing goes, you created the job, so you'll have to determine the price, based on what you feel the public will pay for your talent, services, or product. There are usually fewer models for the following job ideas, and should you choose to take a similar route to extra cash, be prepared to blaze a few trails. Planning and risk taking are important in these jobs—as much a part of them as the novelty and excitement. Let your imagination run free, but keep your money in the bank until you do some research and careful planning.

Taking Over the Drudgery

Swimming pool maintenance is a great way to fill up your spare time and put change in your pocket if you live in a high pools-per-capita community. The work is not taxing and usually consists of: testing the water for chemical balance (with a small testing kit available at pool supply stores), vacuuming the surface, and scrubbing the sides and bottom. Offer your service to hotels and motels, apartment and condominium managers, and private pool owners, especially during vacation months.

You could also prepare pools for winter. Some need to be totally drained and some drained to just below the filter opening. Installing a winter cover usually means inserting bolts into the pool deck so there's something to attach the cover to. Keeping a pool free of debris during the off-season can save time and money the next spring.

Transporting boats is a necessity since sailboats, powerboats, and pontoon boats don't stay in the water forever. They need to be moved at one time or another, usually to the lake or river in the spring and into storage in the fall. Though many boat owners have their own trailers, they might welcome the chance to let someone else do the moving. If you plan to be a boat mover, start with the small ones. If you own a pontoon trailer or would like to invest in one, moving boats for other people can help you pay it off. A brand new trailer will cost you between $2,000 and $3,000; a good used one can probably be found for under $1,000. Advertise your boat transport service to marinas, yachts, boating clubs, and boat dealers.

Blacktop sealing is a treatment that should be given to blacktopped surfaces about every other year. You need only two supplies to do the job: a squeegee (an implement much like a wide rubber brush or broom, but with a solid blade instead of bristles), used for spreading the sealer, and the sealer itself (which looks very much like thin tar and usually comes in a five-gallon bucket). Both of these can be found in hardware stores, and you don't have to be a genius to use them. The process consists of pouring on small amounts of the sealer and spreading it very thin. It's like painting a horizontal wall. Sealing a double-width, fifty-foot driveway takes about three hours. A reasonable price for the job would be between $75 and $90. You could keep busy right in your own neighborhood; most people don't have the time or know-how to do the job themselves.

Waterbed maintenance is a potential money-maker because waterbeds have grown in popularity in recent years. They require a certain amount of care to keep them in top condition. Once a month a waterbed should be examined for leaks; the water level should be checked and chemicals added. The mattress should be cleaned with a plastic cleaner to keep it soft and pliable and thus prevent cracking. The frame should be checked to be sure there are no splinters that could puncture the mattress. This is work you must teach yourself or learn from experience in a waterbed store. Directions accompany each mattress, and supplies can be purchased from any waterbed dealer. Ask hotels, motels, and waterbed sales companies for their maintenance business and their customers'. You could also install the beds for the store you affiliate yourself with.

Install "for sale" and "sold" signs for local real estate brokers. Offer to maintain signs and give them a fresh coat of paint when needed. If a broker doesn't already have a photographer to take pictures of homes for the multiple-listings book (and if you can shoot good pictures), offer this added service. You'll need a car big enough to transport signs around town. You should be available to take down a sign as soon as the broker calls to tell you that a sale has been made. This job won't make you rich, but the spare change you'll make will be complemented by the reputation of dependability you'll build among the real estate agents in your town.

Corporate gift buying is a convenient, time-saving service that business executives and professional people in your city may welcome. They might be too busy to do their own shopping, leaving you an opportunity for making extra cash. You could handpick unusual items from wholesale supply houses (many in New York) and offer each of your clients a shopping bag full of things like brass key rings, "crystal" paperweights, pens and pencils, exotic coffees and teas, and candy and nuts. Your clients would then present these charming gifts to their clients, employees, and potential customers as promotional gestures. This job may require one or two New York shopping trips a year for you to select gifts that are rare in your part of the country. Order colorful bags from a paper products dealer for $.25-$1.00 each, fill them with the goodies (include matching tissue paper and message cards), and deliver them to your customers. Consult the *Thomas Register of American Manufacturers,* available in most libraries, for wholesalers.

Special Talents
Telling stories in your home weekday afternoons will keep eager tykes coming to your door. Parents who have appointments to keep or who want to do some shopping can drop their little ones off at your house. Kids will enjoy this more than being jostled around a shopping center; moms and dads will have peaceful shopping trips. A supply of stories can come from the library and from your memory and imagination. You could also read or act out stories and might even get the children involved in a few stanzas of "Goin' on

a Lion Hunt.'' (Consider offering them snacks and beverages, too.) Consult the zoning board, and check with your insurance agent on whether your current policy is appropriate for your venture; contact the health board if you decide to serve food. Advertise at libraries, nursery schools, and day-care centers. Charge $2-$3 a child for an afternoon of storytelling in your home.

Public speaking is a skill that few people have. And fewer still are ever comfortable with the task. If you are knowledgeable in a special field or have experience in a business or hobby, register with a speaker's bureau or your chamber of commerce and advertise to lecture in your city. Many schools, churches, and political, charitable, and civic organizations are always looking for appropriate speakers to address their members. If you're known as a world traveler or a horticulture buff, others might enjoy hearing about your escapades in the Orient or the greenhouse. You could show slides, movies, or pictures, play music, or distribute literature as part of your presentation. Charge a flat fee for your public speaking engagements. How much you charge will depend on your renown and on the demand for your special brand of entertainment.

Magicians and puppeteers are popular at children's parties. If you are an amateur wizard or puppeteer, cash in by performing at kids' get-togethers, school events, hospitals, and holiday festivities. You can make costumes for your puppets and can use scripts you've written or ones composed by people in the community. The script may include your singing, telling stories, and creating sound effects. You might have to make a large investment in props, stage sets, and other performance equipment. Try out your talents on family, friends, and neighbors before booking engagements.

Contestants have fun and sometimes profit. Many Americans are very competitive and truly enjoy contests, games, and all kinds of challenges. This country shows a near mania for competitions, including cooking contests and bake-offs, word puzzles, brainteasers, and cow-chip-throwing fests. There are contests to stretch your brain power, your strength and dexterity—and your luck. *The Contest Book,* by Kenn Dollar, Ruth Reichl, and Susan Subtle, can give you tips on how to enter and prepare for contests and possibly *win* some extra cash. You may not earn a bundle, but chances are your investment will be small and your return, in terms of satisfaction, will be high.

A diet club might catch on in your neighborhood if your community is as weight-conscious as the rest of the country. Many people can't stick to a diet unless they have the company of others who are trying to practice the same discipline. If you're a born organizer, start a diet club that meets once a week in your home; at each session have a weigh-in and share conversation with your customers while you serve dietetic beverages and snacks. Offer them low-calorie recipes; whip up a diet salad dressing and sell it at each meeting. Charge a nominal weekly membership fee—$2 or $3. Invite speakers who have already won the "battle of the bulge," and advertise their visits in the local newspaper.

Unusual Sales

Build lawn furniture and picnic tables from patterns you design yourself. Dexterity with hammer and nails, the know-how to read blueprints, and the ability to visualize spatial relationships are prerequisites of this work. In the summer put a few samples in your front yard with "for sale" signs on them. If you prefer intricate carpentry work, consider **building dollhouses,** with or without furniture. These sell for $50-$500 and may take fifty or more hours to complete. You'll have to start hammering in the spring to be ready for all your Christmas orders months later.

Make bumper stickers and sell them for cars, trucks, and campers. Use a bumper sticker printing machine that sells for $100-$150. (The machines are frequently advertised in craft magazines.) You'll use a standard adhesive-backed, vinyl-coated paper. Your bumper stickers can tout political figures and attitudes, promote popular causes and religious beliefs, and provide comic relief. Sell them by mail through newspaper and magazine ads and on consignment in printing and novelty shops.

Make up baby baskets to be given instead of the usual planter or vase of flowers, and deliver them to local hospitals or to homes of new parents. Include baby items such as diaper pins, lotion, powder, oil, and Q-tips; top it off with wine and cheese for the proud mom and dad. You could call your service Angels from Heaven and make the delivery of the basket a memorable occasion by dressing up as an angel.

Deliver balloon bouquets instead of flowers. A helium tank with a nozzle for inflating the balloons should cost under $100. Start delivering the bouquets around town as colorful centerpieces for children's parties or as cheer-up surprises for youngsters in hospitals. Women can send balloons to men when they don't feel comfortable sending flowers. The airy bouquets can even be sent to people at work. Offer to decorate the bouquets with satin ribbons or yarn and to write special messages on the balloons with paint or magic marker. Balloons might make a big hit at adult parties, especially with just the right phrases on them.

Make magnetic signs and sell them to small businesses, such as pizza places and real estate offices, to place on doors of company cars and service trucks for advertising purposes. These can also be placed on boats or on metal doors of buildings for identification. Magnetic sheeting comes in several colors, usually in pieces twenty-four inches wide, which cost about $1 a foot. You can paint or silk-screen the letters on the sheets, according to your customer's wishes. Advertise in the Yellow Pages under "Signs."

Have we stimulated your imagination? As you read the ideas in the following chapters, make note of the ones that appeal to you and try to think of variations that would suit you even better. Consider your talents, your resources, the amount of time you have to spend, and the needs of your potential clientele. You can find a way to make the extra cash you need.

Suggested Reading

Abrams, Kathleen and Lawrence. *Successful Landlording*. Farmington, Michigan: Structures Publishing Co., 1980.

Ellis, Iris. *Save on Shopping Directory*. Ottawa, Illinois: Caroline House Publishers, 1979.

Faligati, Evelyn. *Bzzz—A Beekeeper's Primer*. Emmaus, Pennsylvania: Rodale Press, 1976.

Hopp, Henry. *About Earthworms*. Charlotte, Vermont: Garden Way Publishing Co., 1973.

McFall, Waddy F. *Taxidermy, Step by Step*. Tulsa, Oklahoma: Winchester Press, 1975.

Platt, Charles. *T-Shirting*. New York: Hawthorn Books, 1975.

Rubin, Ken. *Drop Coin Here*. New York: Crown, 1978.

Siposs, George G. *Cash In on Your Bright Ideas*. Costa Mesa, California: Universal Developments, 1980.

Smith, Demaris C. *Starting and Operating a Clipping Service*. New York: Pilot Books, 1980.

Stamberg, Peter. *Building Your Own Furniture*. New York: Ballantine Books, 1981.

Subtle, Susan, et al. *The Contest Book*. New York: Crown, 1978.

Write: International Publications, Box 29193, Indianapolis IN 46229, for a free catalog of books on money-making ideas.

Garage Sales and Flea Markets 5

(Making money with your own junk and other people's, too)

Nearly every family in America is good for at least one garage sale or flea market booth a year. That's enough junk to build a second Mt. Fuji. The sales are prompted by many things—a move, children leaving home, spring or fall cleaning, dwindling storage space, redecorating projects, a new addition to the family, a hobby that requires more room, or just that long-overdue attempt at organization. Maybe it's time to part with the baby clothes in the cedar chest and the set of porcelain figurines Aunt Mabel gave you for Christmas nine years ago.

During our research for this chapter, we heard from Nita K. of Indiana, a young widow with two children to support. She earns the family income by operating a garage sale business known as Trash and Treasures. Besides coordinating garage sales in her community for a commission, she operates a weekend flea market. Nita believes garage sales and flea markets could be the answer to overpopulation in this country—maybe even the world—because if we all had our basements, attics, and closets cleaned out, we wouldn't be so crowded.

Well, garage sales and flea markets can't solve all our problems, but they might be a way to add extra money to the family budget.

Garage sales and flea markets are similar in both purpose and reward. A garage sale is a single sale in someone's garage, patio, basement, or yard. Garage sale merchandise consists of things people would otherwise throw away. The old adage about one person's refuse being another's riches is a fitting theme for the business. A flea market, on the other hand, is a group of individual sales run by different people selling a variety of goods in a designated area where they rent space. Flea market fare has been specially collected from antique shops, fire sales, bankruptcy auctions, discount outlets, estate sales, and even garage sales. Flea market booths often feature particular kinds of items—for example, glass dishes, old magazines, or jewelry. Selling your merchandise at a flea market can often bring you higher prices because you're exposing your sale to a wider public. Not having strangers wandering through your home or your yard is another advantage.

There are people who love to snoop out garage sales and flea markets and delight in fingering their way through secondhand merchandise. Sale hopping is a hobby for them, and they come home with any number of things they'll never use. There are also people who take it seriously; they work at it. They seek and find highly usable bargains and actually save themselves a lot of money. Both of these types are your potential customers.

Garage Sales

Before joining the garage sale circuit, you may want to consider a few things. Are you the kind of person who enjoys meeting and dealing with the public? Can you cope with strangers who want to haggle, and people who paw through your merchandise and insult your prices, the items themselves, and even your housekeeping? There is also a lot of physical work involved in setting up each sale.

If you're still sold on the idea of a garage sale, the next thing to do is to make sure it's legal to have one in your city. Check with city officials to see if any local laws will affect you. In many cases, none will apply. However, some communities limit the number and duration of sales held each year and put restrictions on the placement of advertising signs. Some communities require a permit to hold a garage sale, and the sale of certain items, such as firearms, ammunition, and explosives, may require a special permit. Sale of bedding, certain types of clothing, and food may also be restricted. Check local ordinances and state laws before stocking your tables. A few communities ban garage sales altogether. This is usually the result of a few greedy people abusing this privilege by holding continuous garage sales.

With all the preliminaries out of the way, you can concentrate on enticing the public with your sale. In order to do that, take time to plan your venture carefully. Garage sale failures are the result of improper planning: failing to check local regulations, underpricing or overpricing merchandise, not anticipating inclement weather or complaints from neighbors, posting advertising signs haphazardly or improperly, or underpricing your services. Have alternative plans ready—just in case the electricity goes out or it rains on all your watercolored signs.

Grace B. of Arkansas is a weekend garage sales coordinator. After accidentally selling an antique hand tool for a fraction of its value, she realized that her lack of knowledge had nearly cost her the credibility she was working so hard for. She decided it was time she learned how to accurately price garage sale items. She observed pricing standards at other garage sales and began to consult collectors and hobbyists about the value of merchandise with which she was unfamiliar. Now she feels more comfortable and professional in her weekend job.

No matter how confident you feel, start on a small scale at first: Hold a sale for yourself and then one for a friend or relative in the neighborhood. After you hold a few financially successful and problem-free garage sales, advertise in local newspapers to hold sales for others in your area. These could be held either at your home or the customers' homes.

Every year after spring cleaning or garage organizing, people pack up their discards and give them away to Goodwill Industries, Volunteers of America, the Salvation Army, church organizations, and other charities. They may get tax deductions for these donations, but many of them would rather get some cash for all those things they spent their hard-earned dollars on, and they'd be thrilled to find someone who could get it for them. This is where you come in. With your expertise in garage sale planning, you can hold sales for them or sell their things in your flea market booth. Seek out people who have an ample supply of prospective sale items bulging from their closets, basements, and attics, but who don't have the time, space, or knowledge to get rid of it themselves.

They can bring their stuff to you, and for a commission you'll sell it for them. Considering that you'll do most of the work, 20 to 25 percent of the selling price is a fair commission. You can do the pricing for those who don't have any idea how much their goods are worth. By visiting other garage sales, you'll learn how much merchandise usually sells for. Remember that rounded amounts are less confusing and don't require as much change on hand. Naturally, the more work you have to do, the more money you should make. So if you are asked to do the pricing, go for a higher commission.

Ellie J. of New Mexico is a student who has found the key to earning money during the summer months. To help work her way through college, she holds garage sales for people in town. She recruits potential garage sale sponsors mostly by word of mouth. Her satisfied customers are her best source of advertising. Ellie is great at pricing, arranging merchandise, and writing newspaper ads for the sales. She has netted an average of $1,200 a summer for three years. Ellie is a marketing major at school, and her experience in the "retail business" has helped her gain a perspective on what's involved in dealing with customers and running a moneymaking operation.

How does a garage sale get off the ground once you've decided to have one? The following step-by-step procedure should help you make yours a success.

1. Find out what you have to sell. Explore every cranny of your home, basement, garage, attic, car, boat, and camper. You may be shocked to see how much you have that you're willing to part with. If you're holding the sale for someone else, help them decide what to sell. Distribute to your potential clients a sample list of bestselling items and places to look for them. If you're coordinating the sale for someone else, keep it at the client's home if numerous items or any very bulky ones are involved. If there's only a small amount of merchandise, combine it with other wares at your home for one big sale.

Some things are hard to sell at a garage sale, especially expensive jewelry, antiques, guns, rare books, and other collectibles. If you plan to sell this type of merchandise, investigate other methods of sale. You might consider advertising in newspapers and periodicals appealing to serious collectors. Most people—even antique dealers and collectors—come to garage sales and flea markets, not to find a dusty gold mine, but to find a good deal, and that means a cheap price. Save your valuables for private, individual sales.

2. Find out what the competition is selling. Study the classified section of the newspaper; see how the ads are written and what they have to offer. Decide how you can make yours better. Go to other garage sales. Even if you've always been a garage sale junkie, start going with an analytical eye. Study every aspect of the sale and decide if it's a success. Try to figure out why—or why not. Talk to the sale's sponsor and ask which items are moving and which are sluggish. Ask what they would do differently next time. Make mental notes of prices of various items.

3. Set your sale date and buy an ad in the local newspaper classified section. Friday, Saturday, and Sunday are always good days for any type of sale, as long as you don't try to compete with a local craft show or the county fair. That kind of attraction will beat you every time. (Check on this by looking in the entertainment section of the newspaper.)

The cost of an ad in most newspapers depends on the number of words in it and the number of times it appears. Run it on the day of the sale and on the day before. To make the ad jump out at readers, order a type size larger than normal newspaper print if you can. You may be charged extra for it, but the results will be worth it. List your address at the beginning or the end of the ad; itemize the merchandise in the middle of the ad. If it's a Saturday *and* Sunday sale, say so, and indicate the hours of the sale. Don't list your phone number, and you won't be bothered by calls on the day of the sale. You might consult a classified-ad person for tips on making your ad readable and attractive. Your ad could look like this:

> COLOSSAL GARAGE SALE—4178 Fairway Blvd., across from Ajax Car Wash.—Baby Clothes, Toys, Books & Records, Antiques, Dishes, Little Girls' Dresses—size 6X. Sat. & Sun.,—June 17 & 18, 9 a.m. to 3 p.m.

4. Plan your advertising signs carefully. Good signs will draw more customers. Make them well in advance of the sale date. Be sure the writing is legible and large enough to read from a distance. Place one sign in plain view in your yard; if you live on a quiet, not-well-traveled street, place a sign at its intersection with the nearest major road, giving directions to your home.

5. How the merchandise is displayed is vital to any sale. Put similar items together; toys, dishes, and tools should be assembled neatly in separate areas. Create a gallery for artwork and picture frames by hanging them together on a wall or room divider. When space is available, fashion a roomlike setting for large pieces of furniture. If not, at least make sure they can be seen from the street, as furniture always draws customers.

Tables or other sturdy substitutes are a must for displaying most of your goods. You can use standard interior doors from your house or sheets of plywood or plasterboard, with home-made legs, cement blocks, bricks, or sawhorses to hold them up. What you use for tables doesn't matter; how it looks does. Be sure to keep it attractively organized; don't pile tables high with cluttered merchandise. Be sure clothes are clean and ironed, and whenever possible, put them on hangers. People stroll right past a box of wrinkled clothing. Crystal and china sell much better when they are sparkling clean, but a sturdy piece of furniture will probably sell with a few years of dirt on it. An important garage sale tip: The better something looks, the more money it will bring.

If your garage is too small to accommodate your sale, consider using your yard. Yard sales provide more space to display merchandise. Be aware, though, that a sudden rainstorm can create havoc: Clothing and upholstered furniture may be drenched in a few minutes. Having a table on wheels or a tent over your head might be a good precaution.

6. Be sure everything is priced before the sale. This encourages impulse buying from your customers. Overprice the major items a little; this gives you and the customer some haggling room. You should not cut your prices if the sale has just started, but as the day and the sale wear on, consider lowering the prices of all your merchandise.

Prices are more conspicuous on colored stickers, available at most office supply stores. This is an especially good way of pricing if you are selling consigned merchandise for someone other than yourself. You can use a different color for each person's goods. When an item sells, simply peel off the sticker and save it. When the sale is over, it's easy to tally up how much merchandise was sold for each sale contributor.

7. There are a few things that every sale should be equipped with: an extension cord for testing electrical appliances, a yardstick or ruler for measuring furniture and carpet pieces, and paper bags, boxes, and old newspapers for wrapping and bagging sold items. If you are selling clothing, provide a spot for your customers to try on the jogging suit or evening gown.

If you're holding a yard sale, a canopy would protect clothes from sun and rain. Lights are necessary if your sale runs until after dark, and if bugs are attracted because of them, provide a mosquito repellant. Last, but not least, you'll need plenty of cash on hand: at least twenty-five one-dollar bills and one roll each of quarters, dimes, and nickels should be sufficient for making change. A sales tax isn't charged for most one-time garage sales. However, depending on your location and the number of sales you plan to conduct, you may be required to pay. Check with your state sales tax department for complete details. Should you accept only cash? To be on the safe side, accept checks only from people you know and trust. A "Cash Only" sign posted in a highly visible place states your policy simply and effectively.

8. Try to start your sale at least thirty minutes earlier than the other sales in your neighborhood. More than half of your customers will probably show up before ten in the morning. Late morning hours are generally your busiest times. By starting earlier than your competition, you'll attract customers who still have money to spend.

9. To be recognized as the hostess of the garage sale, wear a bright name tag identifying yourself. Make sure any helpers you enlist are also easy to spot.

10. Make your customers feel welcome and comfortable. If you own a dog, tie it up. People won't stop at your sale if they're intimidated by a barking, snapping dog. Don't follow your customers around as though you're afraid they'll steal you blind. Wait until they ask, and then give them any assistance you can. Let them browse in peace.

11. What happens after the sale? Take down all the signs to discourage late comers. The unsold merchandise should be neatly packed and returned to the owners. Agree beforehand with your clients whether a handling fee will be paid for unsold merchandise.

Garage Sale Bestsellers

baby clothes	bedsprings
baby furniture	bicycles

books and records	mirrors
camping equipment	outdoor furniture
canning jars	picture frames
Christmas ornaments	pots and pans
clothing	rugs
dishes	small appliances
fireplace accessories	sporting equipment
handicrafts	televisions, radios, and
household furniture	stereos
houseplants	tires
inexpensive jewelry	tools
lamps	toys and games
lawn mowers	

Eileen R. of Virginia is a seventy-year-old grandmother affectionately known by her friends and relatives as a pack rat. She has a spare bedroom in her rambling house that is stacked with everything from end tables to broken toasters to bedspreads. Eileen collects everyone's discards for her yearly garage sale. People give her a call when they are bogged down with junk, and Eileen jumps into her Volkswagen bus and goes to pick it up. No matter what it is or how tattered, she makes it salable. The day of her sale she's up early arranging and organizing merchandise in an enormous garage right behind her house. At nine the doors officially open, and the customers start filtering through, nibbling the cookies and sipping the coffee she provides. Eileen uses the $200 to $300 she earns on her annual garage sale to go Christmas shopping with her sister in New York every fall. But even more than the money, she enjoys the year-round planning and the feeling of accomplishment the annual sale gives her.

Flea Markets

Flea markets are group sales that come in all sizes. They are held both indoors and out. Each one is a carnival of sales where as few as twenty entrepreneurs or as many as a thousand congregate and peddle a great variety of merchandise at individual booths. Though flea markets resemble garage sales, they have their own distinct appeal.

Flea market mania is a disease that is likely to strike anyone who attends one of these sales festivals. The first symptom is a heavy sensation in the chest when a flea market is sighted. Next comes a severe trembling of the hands as you try to steer your car past it. Finally a layer of jubilant perspiration rises up the back of your neck as you spot the first booth of used dishes. What a feeling!

A homemaker in New York told us that she once had flea market mania so bad that her house was filled to the rafters with flea market finds. She never found a good use for many of the items, so she rented a booth at one of the local flea markets and resold most of them. She figures it was like putting money in the bank when she bought the things and like withdrawing it with interest when she sold them. Every weekend she can be seen at a flea market somewhere in the state either buying or selling.

If you are a person who loves flea markets, think about becoming the coordinator of one, or consider adding to your income by renting a booth and selling your own merchandise.

1. To rent a booth, locate the manager of the flea market you're interested in. He or she will give you a complete list of rules and prices. Booth rental rates range from $3 to $15 for an eight-by-nine-foot space for a weekend. For an additional fee, some managers also rent equipment such as tables, risers, and extension cords—or you can bring your own.

2. Once you have rented a flea market booth, shop around for interesting items that can be bought cheaply for resale. Fresh merchandise is a must if you want your booth to be successful. Bankruptcy auctions are a good place to go to find salable goods. Friends and neighbors will also give you a lot of "junk" if you will haul it away free of charge. Trading with relatives and coworkers may also bring in some good items. You may consider taking things on consignment, getting 30 to 50 percent of the selling price for your share. This is a higher commission than garage sale organizers get.

3. Nearly anything can be bought at flea markets, but a few of the most popular categories are listed below.

antique dolls	bric-a-brac
appliances	celebrity memorabilia
Avon bottles	ceramics
baby clothes	clocks and watches
baseball cards	comic books

crafts	oak furniture
glass (Cambridge, Heisey, etc.)	old-fashioned clothes
	produce
houseplants	records and tapes
jewelry	"skin" magazines
leather goods	wicker furniture

4. What is the range of profit that you can expect to make? Well, that depends on many things. We interviewed Shirley P., who sells at flea markets in Ohio and surrounding states. Her profits range from $100 to $175 on a good day. Some days are better than others, and some she would like to forget. Pinpointing an average percentage of profit is nearly impossible since your profit depends on your investment in each item.

5. Will you need to charge sales tax? All but five states require tax on flea market sales. The states that currently do not charge a tax are Alaska, Delaware, Montana, New Hampshire, and Oregon. Consult the manager of each individual flea market regarding sales tax depositing.

6. Will you need insurance? Yes. The flea market owner is required to carry liability insurance on the building or property an its occupants. But each individual dealer must carry insurance on her own merchandise.

Lettie M. of Minnesota lives on a farm with her husband Howard. They grow everything from tomatoes and string beans to squash and turnips in their garden. Every summer weekend they load up the family pickup with produce and head for the flea market. Soon after they started, Lettie and Howard's produce stand became so popular that other flea market organizers in their area invited them to set up a booth. Their teenage daughters decided to join in and expand the business, and now the entire family spends summer weekends making money at various flea markets. Every fall, Lettie counts the summer's profits and plans for a Florida vacation when the Minnesota ground is frozen solid.

If you enjoy flea markets, think about starting one of your own. You'll earn your profit from booth rental rather than sales. Having a concession stand at the flea market and offering booth operators and their customers beverages and snacks can reap you even more profit.

The first step is to find a good location. Flea markets are held in vacant buildings of all sizes, at drive-in theaters, and in vacant lots. A real estate agent may be able to suggest prime flea market locations—along well-traveled routes. These places are usually rented, and the prices vary according to size and location.

Once you have a good spot, the next step in becoming a flea market promoter is to contact the city zoning board. That office can answer your questions concerning health, fire and safety codes. If you plan to feature firearms at your flea market, contact the Bureau of Alcohol, Tobacco and Firearms for details on firearm codes. These regulations depend on many things: location, number of firearms you plan to sell, how often you plan to sell them, and so on.

Secure liability insurance on the property and its occupants only. As mentioned earlier, each booth operator must carry insurance on his or her own merchandise.

Buy tables, lights, cleaning supplies, ladders, and other equipment for your sellers to rent from you.

Advertising is of the utmost importance in promoting a flea market. Costs depend on the amount of exposure you want and the media you choose. Prime places to advertise are television, radio, and newspapers. Advertising on TV and radio can be very expensive, but if you live in a large city and can't rely on newspaper and word-of-mouth advertising to bring in customers, consider buying some cheap air time late at night or very early in the morning. News of your flea market will reach a lot of night owls. Check with local stations for prices on off-hour advertising time.

As for your own pricing and collection policies, you must decide whether to accept checks and credit cards along with cash. Most flea markets are operated on a cash-only basis. We think this is the best policy, since you may need cash on hand anyway to make change for booths that are "low on $5's" or to operate a hot dog concession stand for hungry browsers.

Janelle R. is a teacher in California who wanted to earn some weekend cash. She had always been a camping enthusiast, and she realized that early spring is the time when getting recreational vehicle buyers and sellers together could mean extra cash. She decided to coordinate a specialized flea market featuring RVs and camping equipment.

Her first step was to check with city and zoning officials about fire and health codes. She estimated everything on paper to see if she had enough money on hand to finance the venture. She obtained a vendor's license and a permit to operate the concession stand she had planned.

She set the date and rented a vacant field for the sale in a very busy area. Her next step was to locate the sellers. Her numerous newspaper advertisements read like this:

ATTENTION CAMPERS

On Sat. & Sun., May 5 & 6, at 7380 State Route 23, between 11 a.m. and 7 p.m., I am holdng a used recreational vehicle and camping equipment flea market. Anyone wishing to sell their used RVs and/ or equipment, please contact me at [phone number and address] by April 30.

The response was good, and she rented fifty-seven spaces for owners and seventy-seven equipment booths. Janelle realized that this many owners would need hundreds of buyers, so she started advertising in the local and nearby newspapers. She even bought some cheap television and radio advertising time.

She was able to meet city fire and health codes by posting "No Smoking" signs and by renting several fire extinguishers and four portable toilets. She also consulted her insurance agent and bought liability insurance for the grounds and the customers.

She engaged the help of her two teenage daughters to operate the concession stand. Her son took admissions at the gate. The price was set at $.50 for adults; children were admitted free. Her husband helped out by acting as ground manager (directing traffic and parking, helping with heavy items) and admitted to having fun, even though he missed his usual game of golf.

Janelle's flea market netted her a profit of nearly $2,400. Encouraged by her venture, she decided to hold it every year. She has considered holding similar flea markets for boats, motorcycles, and even used cars.

Janelle's story reflects the variety of flea market and garage sale options available to the enterprising woman. If you can come up with one that fits your interest, it will probably fill your antique piggy bank, too.

Suggested Reading

Copeland, Irene. *Flea Market and Garage Sale Handbook*. New York: Popular Library, 1977.

Harmon, Charlotte. *How to Make Money Selling at Flea Markets and Antique Fairs.* New York: Pilot Books, 1974.

Jenkins, Dorothy H. *A Fortune in the Junk Pile.* New York: Crown, 1963.

Miner, Robert G. *Flea Market Handbook.* Stockbridge, Massachusetts: Berkshire Traveller, 1981.

Quertermous, Steve, ed. *Flea Market Trader.* Paducah, Kentucky: Collector Books, 1980.

Ullman, James Michael. *How to Hold a Garage Sale.* Chicago: Rand McNally, 1981.

Wasserstein, Susan. *Collector's Guide to U.S. Auctions and Flea Markets.* New York: Penguin Books, 1981.

Sitting Pretty 6

(House, garden, people, pet and property sitting)

Sitting can be profitable. We don't mean just sitting in a chair. We're talking about that age-old Saturday-night job of the American teenager: babysitting—or some variation of it. It's a job often taken for granted—until you're stuck without a soul to water your plants during your two-week vacation. Back when grandmothers were gray-haired ladies who baked cookies and knit sweaters, sitting was a family affair. There was always someone around to mind your store, house, or gerbils while you were away. But since grandma has put a rinse on her hair and gone out to sell real estate, and the kids are tied up with after-school sports, there is a great demand for good sitters.

Even if you're long past the teenybopper stage, there are still plenty of sitting jobs you can do. You can sit with children, the elderly, the lonely, or the ill. You can take care of plants, houses, businesses, pets, farm animals, and anything else that can't be tended by its owner. We talked to Lorie D. of West Virginia, who fed and milked her neighbors' goats when they were called out of town because of an emergency. Not only was she paid for her services, but she also got to keep and use the goats' milk.

No matter who or what you're "sitting," friendliness, patience, and punctuality, along with a respect for other people's possessions, are necessary for you to do a good job. No matter what the sitting circumstances, you need common sense and confidence to react calmly in an emergency. As a sitter you are responsible for people or things that hold value for someone else.

People-Sitting

The benefits of people-sitting are numerous. In addition to being exposed to different people and places (and often free food), you gain experience that could be helpful if you plan a career in teaching or social services. You discover how much patience and stamina you have. You get to know a great deal about children and their needs: how they think and react in various situations and what you can expect from them at different ages. You are exposed to older people: their wisdom, memories, insecurities, and strengths. You can bring joy to children's lives by showing interest in them and can provide stimulation to the sick or elderly by sharing conversation and company.

Sitting for children or adults is a weighty responsibility. Sometimes it's an easy task—e.g., when your two-month-old charge sleeps the entire time his parents are out. But it doesn't always go smoothly. You must be prepared for possible problems. To avoid difficulties, find out if your charge has any special medical problems or allergies or takes any medication. Determine at the outset just how much attention you must give to ensure his or her safety and well-being. Taking precautions and being prepared can prevent a child's falling out of a high chair or a sick person's missing an injection. Your responsibilities as a sitter can't be overemphasized.

When Mr. and Mrs. P. of Idaho go to church on Sunday evenings, they hire Lena M. to sit with Mrs. P's mother, Ruth, who is bedridden. At first Ruth didn't like the idea of having a "babysitter," and she complained loudly; but when Lena brought out a deck of cards one Sunday and suggested a game of gin rummy, Ruth's complaints stopped. Now the two of them play rummy every Sunday night. Ruth delightedly tells everyone who visits her that Lena owes her over $75 for the games she's lost.

People-sitting sometimes involves other jobs; for example, some customers may ask that you cook, clean, or wash dishes while you sit. (You can charge more for extra duties.) Trisha M. of Missouri babysits every Friday for Mary, her neighbor, who has three preschool children. While Mary shops, has her hair done, and runs errands, Trisha watches the children and cleans the house. She even secures the kids' help with dusting, straightening pillows and rugs, and other light work. The children love the cleaning "play" because it's different from having to pick up toys when mom's home; Mary benefits because she gets a break from her everyday routine. Trisha always plans a part of each sitting day to do something special with the kids. And with everyone pitching in, there's always time for baking cookies, going to the park with a picnic lunch, or taking a walk. Trisha has a warm, loving personality and a knack for bringing smiles to children's faces. She charges $5 an hour and makes $40 every Friday.

Sitting with Children

Classes to train child-sitters are given by the Red Cross, scout councils, and YWCAs and in home economics courses at junior and senior high schools. A certificate issued upon completing these classes can be presented to your potential customers as evidence of your qualifications. If you have a child-sitting certificate or good references from former customers, your services will be welcomed by your potential employers, who include the 41.6 percent of American working women who have children under the age of seventeen. With two-career marriages becoming common, there is a great need for good daily child care, which could translate into money for you. Parents need sitters for many different reasons. They may have to leave town for family emergencies; they may want to take vacations without the children; they may be single parents who must often travel on business. That's where you come in. Babysitting pays as much as $2 an hour and up these days and it is not uncommon to charge $35-$50 a week for keeping one child during the workday.

If you love children and have the training to care for them, consider starting a **nursery for preschoolers** in your home. It won't be long before you have a waiting list. Having several children to care for is more difficult than having one or two, especially if one or more of them are in whining or squabbling moods. And there are other things to consider as you plan your venture. Call your local zoning board to see if your neighborhood is zoned for a nursery or day-care center; check with the county auditor's office for tax requirements; contact the state licensing bureau for licensing requirements. You should also check regulations set by the fire department, the board of health, and state and local agencies. Often there are rules pertaining to the number of bathrooms available, the area of space per child, and so on.

You'll need baby swings, playpens, cribs, and strollers on hand for babies, and outdoor swings, sandboxes, tricycles, and kiddie pools for toddlers. Small stuffed toys, rattles, dolls, and balls are popular toys for both age groups. You will have to comply with regulations concerning the kinds and amounts of food you serve your charges.

Begin a **babysitting agency**. Check out each sitter (through references) before listing him or her on your roster. Collect small yearly fees from the people you list and take a 10 percent commission on each job you get for them. Parents will like this service because with one phone call they can get a reliable sitter whose work is guaranteed. Any responsible woman who has good organization and communication skills and who's had sitting experience could operate such a service. To be successful you must be a good judge of character and be able to fill a customer's need with just the right sitter. Promote your service with ads in the Yellow Pages and in newspapers.

Rent a space in or near a shopping center to **babysit while parents shop**. This would be a popular service for frazzled mothers and harried fathers trying to beat the masses of shoppers on weekends and during holidays. Check with the board of health, the county auditor's office, the state licensing bureau, and other agencies to be sure you comply with all regulations for offering this service.

Lanie M. and Suzanne K., two sisters from Georgia (who were both teachers), got the idea of starting a day-care center. Since they are neighbors and live right across the street from a major shopping mall, they seemed to have the perfect spot. They advertised in the neighborhood newspaper and passed out leaflets in the shopping mall. They babysat some children by the hour for shopping parents and others by the day or week for working parents. Later Lanie and Suzanne rented a small space right in the shopping mall; now business is booming because the center is very convenient for parents who are tired of coping with tired, cranky children. The women have decorated a small area to look like a picnic ground, complete with artificial turf and a picnic table, so that parents can share a picnic lunch with their little persons before or after they shop or work. Now the moms, dads, and tots have a happier outlook on shopping, working, and malls in general.

Sitting with the Elderly

As our population grows older, the demand for sitting services for the elderly will grow. For any number of reasons, older people may want or need someone to stay with them: Perhaps they have physical limitations or lessening mental faculties; they may be afraid to be alone, or they may long for people to talk to; they might need care temporarily while recuperating from illness. The work could involve giving medication to sick people or waiting on convalescents. It could mean writing letters for people, reading to them, or playing games with them. Good conversation, sincere interest, and a listening ear are usually appreciated most. Sitting with the elderly demands patience and understanding: They may be in failing health, have no appetite, want to stay in bed when they should exercise, or appear short-tempered and hard to please.

You may want to get special training to prepare you for the job. Hospitals and nursing homes often offer classes, which are required for nurse's aides. The courses teach such things as how to pick up a bedridden patient, how to oversee an elderly person's diet, how to recognize symptoms of illness, and how to better understand and appreciate the needs of the elderly. If you sit with an elderly person on a regular basis it's a good idea to consult with the family or the doctor about what your duties should include.

Specialized People-Sitting

Besides the young and old there are others who may benefit from your services. Sitting with "special cases" is a line of work for people who are trained in an area of expertise; they are observant and knowledgeable, able to recognize changes or symptoms in the people they look after. Stroke victims and heart patients often need someone to stay with them and to help with their therapy. Cancer patients, paraplegics, or those suffering from crippling diseases such as muscular dystrophy or multiple sclerosis sometimes need people to care for them at home while their families work, play, vacation, or shop. Drug addicts, alcoholics, and those who suffer from psychological disorders are some of the many other people who may require special attention. This could be spare-time work for qualified people—nurses, physical therapists, and social work or psychology students. Lay people with proper training can also offer sitting services. The Red Cross offers courses in cardiopulmonary resuscitation, a valuable skill for those who sit with heart patients; Al-Anon and drug treatment centers often sponsor training sessions for those who deal with alcoholics and drug addicts.

Joanne L. of Pennsylvania cared for her alcoholic father for eight years after her mother died. She brought him into her house to keep an eye on him and his drinking and learned quickly about the needs and habits of an alcoholic. To buy alcohol her father would use money she gave him for needed clothes; he would take things from her home and pawn them; he would even lie to get money. In desperation she turned to Al-Anon, an organization dedicated to teaching family members how to live with alcoholics. When she began to understand that alcoholism is a sickness and that her father was its victim, she started learning how to cope with the problem. After her father's death she did volunteer work in halfway houses, where alcoholics learn to cope with their problem before reentering society. She gave talks at local hospitals and rehabilitation centers. She began sitting for alcoholics whose relatives felt they had nowhere else to turn. Today she sits with alcoholics who have brain damage caused by their drinking or who are withdrawing from the drug. Some of her charges suffer from malnutrition because when they drink, they don't eat. Joanne sees to it that they eat and take any medication they need; she listens to them and informally counsels them. Joanne charges by the hour, day, or week, as some cases call for short-term sitting and others for a week or more. In addition to getting paid for her sitting jobs, she knows the real satisfaction that comes from helping others.

Animal-Sitting

Pets, like people, are tended, nurtured, and loved. If you thrill at the exuberance of a new puppy or delight in the feel of a fluffy kitten curled in your lap, you're a pet lover, and you know what we're talking about. There are millions of us around the country, and any pet food manufacturer can tell you that pets are big business. Pet lovers want the best for their dogs, cats, horses, canaries, or whatever. Knowing this, you can use your sitting expertise to serve animal lovers when they are away from home and make a nice income for yourself at the same time.

A natural love for animals is a prerequisite of this line of work. Chances are that if this idea appeals to you, you already know plenty about the animal world. You know that animals usually respond to patient and affectionate human beings. Handling them with calm, steady hands assures them of your good intentions and concern. Having animals of your own will qualify you for many animal care jobs, but you can learn more from books or by working for someone who cares for animals (a veterinarian, a pet shop owner, an animal breeder or trainer).

Regardless of where you live, you can profit from animal-sitting. City dwellers can go to clients' houses or farms to care for animals; those living on farms or on big lots in the suburbs may have the space needed to board dogs, horses, and other large animals. Some of these jobs might require added insurance, so check with your insurance agent before you offer animal-sitting services. Zoning and licensing rules vary considerably, so check with the appropriate offices for the regulations in your area. If you plan to care for pets at their owners' homes, your expenses will be minimal. If you intend to board animals at your home during their owners' vacations, your initial outlay will be much greater.

To become established in the animal-sitting business, become acquainted with veterinarians and pet shop owners and ask them to refer their customers to you. Stress the fact that you provide personal attention to every animal left in your care. Advertise in pet and farm magazines as well as in local newspapers.

Pets

Many people prefer not to take their pets along when they have to be away from home, and substitute love is better than no love at all. This can be a full-time or part-time business. Dogs, cats, birds, fish, gerbils, hamsters, mice, snakes, and other domestic animals need care and attention. Since each requires a different level and kind of care, the price you charge will have to be determined by you and the pet owner. The paragraphs below suggest a few animal categories you might consider sitting for. The equipment and space required, the special needs of the animals, and your understanding of them will determine which pets you are best qualified to care for.

Small household pets—gerbils, hamsters, mice, and guinea pigs—are the delight of many youngsters. You can board them, providing food, bedding, water, proper cages, and a temperature-controlled environment. All these animals are kept in cages and are easy to care for, as they scurry through exercise trails, occupy themselves with exercise wheels, and sustain themselves by eating ready-mixed food.

You can keep **fish** healthy while their owners are gone. A small bowl of goldfish can be brought to your home, but you must go to your customer's home to tend aquariums that house tropical specimens. An extra tank, with filtering equipment and heater, and water-testing supplies should be kept handy in case of an emergency in which fish might need to be transferred because of a foreign organism in the water, improper pH, or some other harmful condition. Especially when sitting for expensive saltwater fish, you should be knowledgeable about their care and habits and should be able to recognize and react to signs of trouble in the tank.

Although **cats** are independent creatures, they still need food, water, affection, exercise, and possibly medical attention when their owners are gone. Indoor cats can be watched in your home; special carrying cases are available for transporting them. To help the cat feel at home, have your customer bring their pet's favorite bed, scratching post, and toys to your house. Cats are seldom sick, but if they are listless and refuse to eat, they should be taken to a veterinarian. If you are hired to sit for outdoor cats, we suggest that you feed and water them in their home environment.

Canaries, parakeets, and other caged **birds** need constant attention in the absence of their owners. They should be transported in their own cages and kept in a warm room. Birds are delicate; they require gentle treatment and respond to soft voices. Their cages should be cleaned daily and their water replenished regularly. Bird cages should be covered at night to keep out the cold air.

When **frogs, toads, snakes, and lizards** are kept as pets, they don't live in ponds, swamps, or deserts, but in man-made environments suited to their needs and habits. If you plan to sit for pet reptiles and amphibians, get specific care and feeding instructions from their owners. The eating habits of these unusual pets vary according to their species; some snakes, for example, are fed only once a week. Don't sit for any poisonous animal unless you are trained in its proper handling.

Vacation plans are too often halted by the question, "Who's going to take care of Fido?" You can relieve frustrated vacationers of their dilemma and earn some money doing it. **Dogs** are the favorite pets of most people, and you can provide many services for their care if you are patient and gentle and have a love for animals. Feeding, watering, brushing, and exercising them while their owners are out of town are only some of those services.

You can offer to go to your customer's home once or twice a day to run or **walk a dog** that is housebound most of the time. Such exercise is vital, and many owners are too busy to provide it regularly or would prefer to have someone else do it. A **visiting service** can be provided for dogs whose owners are away from home during the day. You can stop by once or twice daily to feed and play with the poodle or dachshund or to let the schnauzer romp in the yard for a few minutes.

It might be a good idea to have a trial run—a few getting-acquainted sessions with a bulldog or a Saint Bernard—before you're left on your own with the dog. You'll have more fun visiting or walking a dog if both of you feel comfortable with the arrangement. Owners, too, will feel better about leaving their dogs in the care of a compatible sitter.

Dog boarding is a service you can offer if you have the right facilities. You need outdoor exercise runs with resting platforms and overhead protection from sun and rain. The indoor area must have adequate ventilation for summer and heat for winter. Food, water and care are your most basic responsibilities. A place to isolate sick dogs will be necessary, and a veterinarian should be on call at all times. In some areas a kennel license may be required. Check with the city licensing department for further information. Also check with the zoning board; local regulations vary considerably. Boarding charges usually depend on the animal's size, but for most dogs $3-$5 a day would be a fair price.

Farm Animals

Farmers have to forgo many a vacation, because it's difficult for them to find caretakers for their animals. The animals seldom leave their homes; so "sitters" must go to them. Their care may include feeding, milking, or brushing. Cows, goats, horses, chickens, and hogs are the most common farm animals. The price varies depending on their type and number.

Be sure you are qualified to care for horses, cows, or other animals before you seriously consider the idea. The job may sound glamorous—

or even easy—but in fact it requires a lot of on-the-job experience not held by the average animal owner.

As a rule, **cows and goats** are even tempered and mild mannered and are probably two of the easiest farm animals to handle. But since they require milking twice daily, they keep many farmers tied down on their farms. The feeding and milking of cows and goats is done at dawn and dusk and takes thirty to forty-five minutes apiece. You can charge $3-$5 per day for each animal.

Chickens are raised for both eggs and meat and cannot go untended for even a day. Baby chicks must be fed and watered, and the brooder must be kept warm to substitute for the body heat of the mother hen. You must be careful that the chicks don't get wet or drown themselves in the waterer. Other chickens must be fed and watered twice a day. Their diet depends on whether they are layers, fryers, or broilers. Have the customer instruct you as to the feed for the different types of chickens. If you are tending laying chickens, you must gather the eggs and store them in a cool place, or follow any other instructions given by the owner.

Horses are among the most beautiful and graceful creatures on earth. In action they are one thousand pounds of power and agility. They are used for everything from pleasure riding to farm work. Their daily care consists of feeding, watering, and exercising. They also need regular grooming. The minimum amount of space needed to board a horse is a twelve-foot square stall and one-half acre of securely fenced pasture. If you're a country dweller and happen to have an empty stall available, think about renting it to a horse owner. Full boarding (which means that you supply everything, including a stall, fresh bedding, and feed) will cost the horse owner approximately $130 a month, depending of course on the quality of the facilities. Since most horses can be fed for $50 a month, your monthly earnings would be $80 per horse.

Midge R. and Sally M. are two animal husbandry students in Ohio who cared for twenty-one quarter horses while the owner attended the cutting-horse finals in Texas. Since they had taken care of the horses on weekends, the owner felt confident leaving his animals in their care for a longer period. The women lived at the farm for a week and traveled back and forth each day to school. Their principal duties were feeding, watering, and exercising the quarter horses, plus feeding three dalmatians and a big yellow house cat named Morris. Midge and Sally were paid $100 for their week on the farm. They've been given several other animal-sitting jobs because of recommendations from their satisfied customers.

Hogs may be the original mud wrestlers, but to maintain their well-rounded figures, they must be fed. As their sitter, your duties would be to give them slop or hog mash twice a day. Since they are kept in pens at all times, tending hogs can be a relatively easy way for you to earn spare-time cash.

Plant-Sitting

Plants can do for the eye what music does for the ear. What is more vibrant than an African violet with a flush of growth, or a rose in full bloom? Without proper care they will shrivel and die. Caring for plants can be an opportunity for you to earn extra money. People who must be out of town for extended periods of time need plant-sitters. You can make house calls to water, mist, and fertilize the plants to keep them in good health. You can choose your own working hours, and you won't need special clothes or a huge cash outlay to get started in the job. If people rave over the thriving plants in your house and yard, you're probably qualified to care for the plants of others.

Goldie W. of Kentucky lives in a town house with a small, fenced patio, where she plants every inch of open space with beautiful blooming flowers. Hanging baskets decorate her redwood fence, and climbing roses trail everywhere. Her town house association holds a contest each year, awarding a prize to the owner of the most attractively decorated patio. Goldie has won this prize two years in a row. You can guess who the neighbors leave in charge of their plants when they're away. They pay Goldie according to the number of plants cared for, with an extra amount for the ones that require more time.

Some customers may bring their plants to your home. But not all plants take kindly to being moved. *Ficus benjamina,* the weeping fig, is especially susceptible to leaf drop when its environment is changed. It would be better to care for sensitive plants in their usual surroundings.

Besides house plants, outdoor hanging baskets, window boxes, and flower beds may need tending when their owners are away. If the owners are gone for extended periods of time, bushes, trees and the lawn may need care, too, not to mention gardens, which, if not weeded regularly, may grow into virtual jungles in no time. In Chapter 11 we'll explore these more strenuous plant jobs further.

You must base the amount you charge your customer on several things: how many plants need care; how far you must travel to care for them (consider your time and gasoline costs); and how difficult each plant is to cultivate.

Never agree to care for any plants that you know nothing about. If you enjoy horticulture, you've probably researched the peculiarities of many plant varieties, taken classes on plant care, or talked wth experts. But if you're unfamiliar with an exotic tropical plant, say so. Your customers will appreciate your candidness.

If you manage to bring an ailing plant to life while its owner is away, your service could include offering tips on keeping plants healthy. To be qualified to give advice on the health of plants, you must be able to examine them, recognize different diseases and pests that afflict them, and treat them successfully.

Laura Z. is a Vermont woman who loves plants and has always had a green thumb. During the summer she works full-time for Ida and Lena, widowed sisters who own Shades of Green, a large **plant shop and greenhouse**. She grows and tends the plants and is paid a handsome salary for her expertise. At the first sign of winter, Ida and Lena close up the shop and head south, and Laura is hired to sit with the plants until spring. She spends an hour or so daily, surveying the plants in the greenhouse, making sure that proper levels of heat, moisture, and light are maintained, and attends to ailing plants. In February she starts seedlings for early spring sales. She is paid $75 a month for her off-season sitting.

House-Sitting

Even if vacationers have no pets or plants at home, they may still welcome a sitting service. Whether home's a log cabin in the backwoods or a mansion in Beverly Hills, travelers want to know it'll be there *intact* when they return. Having someone who can be trusted to stay there or to come in periodically and check on things allows them to breathe easier. The rewards of this job are, obviously, the money and the satisfaction of knowing that someone finds you trustworthy enough to act as caretaker of a valued possession.

A house-sitter must be an observant person who not only has spare time, but also is conscientious about checking the house and prompt in noticing any potential problems. She must also be an organized person who uses a checklist of details to give the house a complete look-over.

If you find house-sitting an appealing spare-time idea, check with your insurance agent to see if liability insurance or bonding is necessary. This may vary from one part of the country to another.

Once you have agreed to house-sit for a customer, find out who else has a key to the house and when or if they might be using it. Advise customers who plan to be absent for more than a few days to remove their valuables and place them in a safety-deposit box or make other arrangements for them. Get the name of your customer's repair services in the event of an emergency.

House-sitting usually involves daily visits to the site to gather mail and newspapers. Each time you enter the house, check for such things as gas leaks, power outages, dripping faucets, and disarranged furniture or other objects. Also make sure that the locks have not been tampered with. You may be asked to mow the lawn or water plants if your customers are gone long. You could charge more for these duties and others, like dusting furniture, forwarding mail, or moving cars around in the driveway.

Rhonda S. and Julie R. both attend a university on Michigan's northern peninsula. Since many residents of that area go to Florida for the winter, Rhonda and Julie advertised in the local newspaper, offering to check the vacant homes while their owners were away. Many people answered their ad; some hired them for only a week or two, some for the entire winter. The girls check the houses twice a week to make sure they haven't been broken into and that everything is in order. They have the homeowners' telephone numbers in case of emergency. The arrangement works well: The girls earn extra spending money, and the homeowners don't worry about their empty houses.

Business-Sitting

Business owners have much time and money invested in their livelihoods. But they can't be around every minute to ensure their businesses' safety. There may be a market for a business-sitting service in out-of-the-way locations, known high-crime areas, or recently vandalized sections of town. Your clients could be businesses whose merchandise is expensive or sensitive to temperature or light. You can earn extra cash by checking on businesses during evening hours or vacation periods or when the owners are called away unexpectedly. You may have to be bonded or carry liability insurance to perform this service, so check with your insurance agent for information.

As a business-sitter, your duties could vary from checking on the security of windows and doors to monitoring heat levels in the stockroom, depending on the type and location of the business and on the merchandise, if any, involved. Determining a price to charge for your service will depend on the operation's size, its location, and your particular reponsibilities.

Sara C. is a Canadian woman who lives on an island a few miles from the mainland. During the winter the population of the island is approximately 2,500, but it swells during the summer tourist season. The island has several small businesses: a grocery store, restaurants, a gift and candy shop, a clothing store, and an antique shop. When the tourist season ends and crisp fall weather approaches, many of the businesses close their doors, and the proprietors head back to the warmth of their mainland homes. Sara's husband, Dave, is a schoolteacher on the island, so they are year-round residents. A few winters ago two of the stores were destroyed by fire. That's when Sara got the idea of being a business-sitter. The business owners jumped at her offer. Each store owner pays Sara $50 a month to check the heat and water pipes in the store and to watch for fire hazards, weather damage, and burglaries. Her sitting business assures the proprietors that their shops are looked at regularly by a concerned eye.

No matter which of the above categories you choose, you can build sitting into a successful business if you are knowledgeable, reliable and willing to take responsibility for someone else's valuables.

Suggested Reading

The American Medical Association's Handbook of First Aid and Emergency Care. New York: Random House, 1980.

Barkin, Carol, and Elizabeth James. *Complete Babysitter's Handbook.* New York: Wanderer Books, 1980.

Hersey, Jean. *The Woman's Day Book of House Plants.* New York: Simon & Schuster, 1963.

Kirk, Robert W. *First Aid for Pets: The Pet Owner's Guide to Emergency Care of Dogs, Cats and Other Small Animals.* New York: Dutton, 1978.

Meyers, Carole T. *How to Organize a Babysitting Cooperative and Get Some Free Time Away from the Kids.* Albany, California: Carousel Press, 1976.

Pommery, Jean. *What to Do Till the Veterinarian Comes.* Radnor, Pennsylvania: Chilton Books, 1976.

Smith, Lindon H. *The Encyclopedia of Baby and Child Care.* New York: Warner Books, 1980.

Cash from the Kitchen

(Cooking, baking, catering, party planning)

Americans love to eat. They savor concoctions whipped up on worn-out dormitory hot plates and in modern microwave kitchens. They eat meals, snacks, desserts, and appetizers. These millions of munchers, chewers, sippers, and samplers support a greater number of food suppliers than any other people on earth. Go to any major American city; you'll find fast-food, gourmet, health food, ethnic, regional, and family-style restaurants. You'll find groceries that stock everything from mincemeat to molasses, and discriminating shops that sell nothing but one special brand of herbal seasoning from southern Ceylon. And you'll find people buying these ingredients, because where there are eaters and eateries and a plentiful supply of eatables, you can bet there's also an ample supply of good cooks.

Some of these seasoned chefs and bakers are home-based women who are or could be getting paid for keeping the rest of us nutritionally satisfied. These are the women who can transform a shopping-cartful of groceries into a delectable beef Wellington or a mouth-watering quiche. Quite often these wooden-spoon wizards are the mothers, sisters, aunts, and grandmothers who have been preparing Sunday pot roasts, Friday night spaghetti dinners, and Thanksgiving turkeys most of their lives.

You may well belong to this honored, though sometimes taken-for-granted, brigade. Maybe you have a specialty of your own: cheesecake, anchovy pizza, barbecued chicken, or raisin almond fudge. Or maybe you're the brand of good cook that never flubs a soufflé, burns a tuna casserole, or makes soupy lasagna. Or if you *have* bumbled a few dishes along the way, you more than make up for it in the creativity department, turning leftovers into delicious canapés and hamburger into the juiciest meatballs in town. Whichever kind of good cook you are, it's certain that you beam with pride at your finished products and that you find great joy in the words, "I'll have seconds."

Tarna J. of Kansas started her homemade doughnut business five years ago at the urging of guests at her Halloween party. Since she already owned the doughnut-making equipment, she had to borrow only a few hundred dollars for start-up supplies for a part-time operation in her basement. She sells doughnuts to local restaurants and to some "mom and pop" grocery stores in her town. After all her expenses are deducted, she makes about $325 a month. She enjoys her job, and she likes being home with her husband and children, who sometimes help by adding powdered sugar or chocolate glaze to her doughnut treats.

Tarna was coaxed into starting her business, but that's just one way to get motivated. For most home-based cooks and bakers, the motivation comes from a desire to make money from the kitchen, after answering some hard questions about what that really involves. If you're thinking about cooking or baking for extra cash, these are questions you can't afford to ignore.

• *Do you like to cook?* Do you like to experiment and improvise with the most basic dishes? Do you find yourself collecting new recipes and perfecting old ones, cheerfully tolerating the continual mess in the kitchen? Do you usually go overboard when asked to cook or bake? (Instead of bringing baked beans to a potluck, do you whip up some meatball paprikash?)

• *Are you a good enough cook to get paid for your efforts?* Janet O. of Arizona realized she was a good cook when she was asked by a local Italian restaurateur to cook for his customers. She and her husband were dining at Leonetti's, and she ordered the house specialty, lasagna. Disappointed in its flavor, she told the owner that he should taste *her* version of the dish. Later that week she prepared a huge serving of it, made with the best ingredients: beef and pork, pasta, ricotta cheese, fresh herbs, and melted mozzarella cheese. She took it to the restaurant, reheated it, and served it piping hot. Mr. Leonetti was so impressed that he offered to supply her with ingredients and cooking pans if she'd agree to make her lasagna for his customers. Her trial agreement has turned into a long-term contract. Once a week Janet gives Mr. Leonetti a shopping order, and he sends what she needs to her home. Each day a messenger picks up the lasagna, assembled but unbaked. Janet has recently added minestrone soup to the menu, at Mr. Leonetti's suggestion. The quality control she gives the two dishes has landed her a contract with another restaurant in town. She loves the arrangement because it lets her cook and stay at home and it adds $225 a week to her family's income.

● *Do you get satisfaction from cooking for others?* Many good cooks love giving dinner parties because they feel confident that guests won't be disappointed. They'd probably cook even if people didn't have to eat. Satisfaction might come from your ability to turn an inexpensive cut of meat into a tender feast or from your talent for stretching a menu to accommodate three unexpected diners. Cooking satisfaction is more than getting compliments; it's knowing you'd go all out whether you were cooking for the mayor and his wife or for your teenage son, who'll eat anything.

● *Do you enjoy cooking* enough *to devote the time and energy needed to do it for money?* You must be aware of what you're getting into. Tarna, for example, has to start making doughnuts by 4:00 a.m. to have them ready for customers at 7:30. Janet spends six to seven hours a day, six days a week, cooking the same things over and over. Most jobs are intriguing and fun for a while, but after weeks, months, and years of cutting the same crust, the intrigue could turn into monotony.

If you're still feeling positive about cooking or baking for money, now's the time to face the facts of your situation. For example, what facilities do you have at your disposal? Do you really have room to accommodate a pizza oven or a commercial-size dishwasher? Are your mixer and food processor heavy-duty, or will you have to buy commercial ones? Will making party plates for church doings require a second refrigerator? How big a venture can you realistically handle without deserting your family or having to re-do the whole kitchen?

And how much will it all cost? Your investment will depend on many things. If you decide to bake and sell birthday cakes, your expenses will be minimal, assuming you already own a standard stove and oven. You'll need mixing bowls, a mixer, pans, hand utensils, decorating gadgets, and ingredients; all should total less than $200. But if you decide to offer ten different fudge delights or fifty-eight varieties of soup to customers city-wide, you'll need lots more up-front money. For a soup business, you'd need large pots and stirring utensils, food processors and blenders, plus enough space to work and to store all your tools. Planning to spend $250 or more for the basics wouldn't be unreasonable. (These start-up costs are, of course, estimates and don't cover advertising, transportation, and packaging, or any miscellaneous expenses unique to your business.)

Whatever your initial cost, it's always wise to keep your overhead down. Be a bargain hunter. Look for discount warehouses and factory outlets for baking pans, candy molds, and other equipment. Buy supplies (flour, sugar, spices, chocolate, nuts, and cheese, for example) in large quantities. Check with restaurant supply houses, food brokers, produce dealers, and meat companies that offer discounts for quantity buying. Maybe you could join a food co-op in your community, toting your own containers and buying spices, grains, and other cooking ingredients in bulk. Use your bargaining skills to work out the best deals. If you can get it cheaper, you can pass along the savings to your customers.

What about pricing your homemade foods? One method is to estimate one-third for labor, one-third for ingredients, and one-third for profit. This might work for some businesses, but not all. One woman told us that if she used that formula, a loaf of her herb bread would cost $6, and no one would buy it. If you know your target customers, you'll soon know what they'll pay.

Pricing is determined by many factors—the area you're in, for example. If you could package a gourmet treat (maybe an elegant pâté) in New York City, it would probably sell for $10-$15 a pound. But in Alfordsville, Indiana, it might only go for half that, *if* it went at all. You must know what people in your city are eating.

Price will also be influenced by the way you plan to sell your food—through gift shops or restaurants, by mail, or in your home. If someone else must realize a profit from your treat, that has to be figured into the price. Another factor to consider is the price you pay for supplies. If butter costs you $2.50 a pound, your butter cookies will have to sell for a lot more than if you bought butter in quantity at $1.50 a pound. Don't forget to include packaging, mailing, transportation, and advertising expenses in your final selling price.

One more thing about pricing: Don't make the common beginner's mistake of overpricing your product because it's worth that much money to you. You have to win people over before you can capitalize on the "chip dip people can't munch without." Start out at a moderate price, and once your blackberry tarts become the rage in town, gradually increase the price to make a handsome, but fair profit. If people find pleasure in your cooking or baking, they'll be more than happy to pay for it.

Building up a loyal following is something that may take time. Make a list of places and people who would welcome your product (whipped hot chocolate for people who work outside in the winter, gingerbread cookies for day-care centers, hors d'oeuvres for caterers in town). These are the places to advertise. Send each a card or letter introducing your business. Visit them and give free samples to lasso reluctant buyers. But remember what we said in Chapter 1 about being taken seriously: You won't be flooded with customers for some off-the-wall idea like toothpaste-flavored taffy. Be reasonably sure you have a salable taste treat before you order ten thousand business cards.

Dany G. of California loved yogurt-covered and chocolate-covered citrus fruit rinds and hoped to sell them. She wanted to test-market them first to see whether others shared her taste for them. The services of all the professional marketing firms in her area were too expensive, so Dany decided to do some market research on her own. She made several boxes of her candy and took them to a large insurance company she used to work for. The manager knew her and agreed to let her use his employees and customers as a "tasting ground." The candy and a questionnaire about it were passed out to employees and placed at the cashier's and receptionist's desks. When Dany collected the questionnaires a week later, she found that many other people shared her enthusiasm for the treat and said they would buy it if it were readily available. They also responded to a question asking them to suggest a reasonable price. Armed with positive feedback, she concluded that her business was a good risk. It's been three years since Dany began her business, and she's currently making $8,000 a year from sales in her metropolitan area.

Since health and safety regulations vary from city to city, county to county, and state to state, be sure to check with the appropriate agencies for guidelines. To protect the public, the board of health sets up stringent requirements for food handlers. In some areas you must have a separate entrance to your business kitchen, which must be apart from your own kitchen. It doesn't have to be a large area; some spotless basements with only a sink, stove, and counter have passed inspection. Some areas only require that you have a stainless steel sink with two or three compartments. Inspections are usually twice a year, but this, too, can vary. Since health department officials will issue your food handler's license, don't even consider starting any type of food service until all their requirements have been met.

There are thousands of kitchen opportunities out there. And some room for catering and party planning, as well. We've divided our chapter into seven sections (candy and confections, baking, cooking, other kitchen products, catering, party planning, and teaching), each highlighting a group of jobs that could earn you—the good cook—some welcome cash.

Candy and Confections

Despite the bad press sugar gets, candy is still salvation for the sweet tooth. What would we do without fudge, peanut clusters, pralines, peppermint bonbons, toffees, and butter mints? We don't mean brand-name candies; we're talking about the homemade varieties that melt in your mouth.

There's something wholesome about sweets made in home kitchens. Maybe it's the flavor, or the care we know goes into fashioning chocolate hearts or butterscotch sticks. If you box your own special candy and sell it through your own shop or area gift stores, you could be more popular in your town than Hershey's kisses. Candy is a food for all seasons—and all ages. And the variety of shapes, colors, tastes, and sizes of sweet treats stretches the limits of your imagination. If you have the pots, pans, thermometers, and cooking space to make candy for an army of third-graders on Valentine's Day, maybe you have the ingredients for a candy business.

Candy making may involve cooking, baking, refrigerating, storing, and packaging. The specific needs of your venture will depend on what you plan to make, how much, how often, and for whom. Being able to get ingredients at low costs will be a consideration in determining the size of your business. The following in-a-nutshell moneymaking ideas are guaranteed to make you want to savor and share some of your candy products.

Make butter mints, chocolate-covered pretzels, and glazed nuts to **sell to catering firms, fine restaurants, and party houses**. Package them in attractive boxes or make up tray displays. Photograph the displays for a brochure describing all your candy varieties.

Starla R. is a talented cook, always on the lookout for new and different recipes. While vacationing in New Orleans, she and her husband dined at one of the city's best restaurants. She loved the dessert she ordered: a chocolate house (made from a mold) with hot strawberry sauce poured on top. When she went back home to Missouri, Starla tried to duplicate the dessert. She bought a house mold and experimented until she found "something close" and then served it at several of her club meetings. The compliments she got convinced her to sell the dessert to catering firms in town. One taste of Starla's chocolate strawberry surprise won over several caterers. Her now-famous dessert is served at dinners and conventions around her city and nets her $3,000 a year.

Sugarless candy can be made for diabetics as well as for people with weight problems. Many ingredients of this candy are the same ones you use in regular candy, but you'll also need things like artificial sweeteners, powdered milk, honey powder, fructose, coconut shreds, coconut powder, malt, carrot syrup, and fruit extracts. You will want to consult with a physician or dietician to be sure your candy is in keeping with the diets of most diabetics. Practice making your candy before you have people sample it. Then offer it to diet groups, drugstores, grocery stores, and health spas. If there are diet catering companies in your area, they might buy it, too.

"Natural" candy would be a hit in health food stores, exercise establishments, and college bookstores. All-natural sweets are more expensive to make than conventional candy, but there is generally more profit in a specialized product. You might barter with a health food store proprietor for ingredients in exchange for putting his store's name on the wrappers or boxes and selling the finished product in his shop (giving him a share of the profits).

April K. of Oklahoma believes that "natural" sweets are better for humans than "manufactured" sweets. Five years ago, when her daughter developed an allergy to sugar and chocolate, April tried a few recipes using concentrated fruit syrup and honey (instead of sugar) and carob powder (instead of chocolate). When her family tasted the new sweets, they were hooked, and so were many of her friends. She began making three different kinds: carob kisses, wheat germ honey balls, and health caramels. She offered the manager of a local health food store a commission to display and sell them. Together they set a price of $3.50-$5.00 a pound. Today April's candy line consists of seven varieties, including the all-time favorites, carob fudge and apricot leather. She sells through five stores now, including a major department store in her city. After expenses and commissions are paid, she averages a profit of $180 a month.

What about **popcorn balls and personalized lollipops**? These would be popular at children's parties or at family gatherings. Rita B. of Maryland loves the taste and nutritional value of popcorn, and thought others might, too. For years she has made balls by mixing popcorn with syrup, raisins, dried cereal, nuts, coconut, chow mein noodles, and granola, wrapped them in cellophane, and sold them for fund-raising projects at local schools and churches. She even made different colors by adding a few drops of food coloring into the syrup mixture. The popcorn munchies were always big sellers as TV and study snacks. When her husband's real estate job wasn't going well, Rita decided to get busy making popcorn balls for profit. She advertised them to local caterers and candy shop owners. Many of them had already sampled her treats at a fund raiser somewhere along the line, so they were quick to snatch them up. Her profits aren't grandiose—only $70-$100 a month—but the enjoyment she gets from contributing to the family till is more than worth the work.

Consider making **holiday or special-occasion candy**. Marzipan (candy made from almond paste) is popular around the Christmas season. Chocolate turkey mints would make an appropriate after-Thanksgiving-dinner treat. Advertise that you'll make holiday candy for people in town or mail it to their friends out of town. Hard-candy in assorted flavors would be good for mailing. These jewel-like sweets are festive-looking and fairly easy to make, and they're not likely to spoil or melt in transport.

Abby W. of Minnesota has always enjoyed making **hard tack candy**. Her friends especially liked her spearmint and anise flavors. To supplement her husband's income one October, she began selling her candy. She made several different flavors and colors and packaged them in quart and pint canning jars. She tied a holiday ribbon around each jar and began taking orders through an ad she placed in a regional magazine. She also sold the candy on consignment through a speciality gift shop. After the Christmas season, Abby continued selling her candy at fairs, bazaars, and festivals.

Candied and caramel apples are another favorite. Hard, crisp apples work best, like Jonathan or Red or Golden Delicious. Buying your apples from an orchard instead of a grocery store will save you money. A bushel of apples can range from $8-$11, but the price depends on your location and the year's crop yield. Caramel can be bought from candy wholesalers or cake decorating supply stores for about $7 for a five-pound block. Wooden sticks come from the same place for about $.85 for fifty. Caramel and candied apples sell for $1.00-$1.25 each at carnivals and bazaars.

Make chocolate **candy in the shape of motifs, emblems, coats of arms and symbols** of social clubs, political organizations, and sports teams. Make candy fezzes for Shriners, candy thermometers for doctors' organizations, elephant candy for the Republican party, and donkeys for the Democrats. The molds for these special sweets can be made from ceramics; some of the more common molds may be available at candy and cake decorating supply houses.

Baking

Home-baked goods are a part of our American heritage. Long before the days of Hostess Twinkies, women had the time to spare for baking, or they baked daily out of necessity. Today's woman is often forced to grab a loaf of Wonder bread or a frozen Sara Lee cake to satisfy her family's dinnertime pangs, because she doesn't have the time or energy to mix batters, knead dough, and whip cream. A good baker is worth her weight in cream puffs.

Bakers don't always like to cook; they prefer creating with flour and eggs instead of meat and vegetables. For whatever reasons, they find their satisfaction in warm kitchens filled with the aroma of banana bread. They take pride in serving more than the standard "three square meals" making nutritious whole wheat bread and a repertoire of tarts, cakes, and pastry at the drop of a fluted pie shell. The beneficiaries of a baker's skill salivate at the thought of a once-a-year cream nut roll or the autumn's first apple strudel. Even the most reluctant eaters usually melt at the sight and smell of a hot loaf of bread or a peach cobbler. Bakers are remembered for the extras they give to a meal—the unforgettable crust of the dinner rolls, the icing on the cupcakes.

If baking is fun for you, and if people always look forward to your contribution to the monthly bake sale, maybe you should consider expanding the range of your satisfied customers. You probably already have hundreds of tested recipes and all the hardware to turn them into dinnertime temptations or bedtime snacks.

Bake for restaurants. People frequent some places just for their light rolls, pumpernickel bread, or cherry cakes. Take samples of your special dessert to local restaurateurs. You could offer seasonal fruit pies, cream pies, cheesecakes, rolls, and different types of bread. You could bake the goodies in your home for a percentage of the menu price.

Wilma J. of Florida has always enjoyed baking pies and usually gets compliments galore for her citrus-flavored tarts. When she offered a sample pie to one of the better restaurants in her city, the manager hired her to bake them for his customers. She starts baking before daylight and takes the last load of pies out of her commercial-size oven at noon. The restaurant sends a van to pick up the tangy desserts in time for lunch and dinner clientele.

Offer to **bake bread** for a local health food store. Many breads use the same fundamental ingredients, with slight additions or differences in procedure to account for the many varieties. You could bake wheat germ, molasses, and soybean breads to sell, as well as the basics—white, rye, and whole wheat—and special breads like zucchini, applesauce, carrot, and pumpkin. One way to keep costs down is to specialize in one or two offerings.

Beulah A. of South Carolina has been baking bread to feed her family since she was twenty-two. When her five children were grown, she wanted to keep baking. She decided to supply bread to people staying at the campground adjacent to her yard. She and her husband Gus, who's retired, sell sourdough, potato, bran, and wheat bread. Beulah buys her ingredients at a discount through her son's grocery store. Last year she purchased a commerical bakers' oven. At five every morning she and her husband mix the dough and set it to rise. Gus punches it down and kneads it. Their loaves are all ready for the heavy customer flow from eleven to three. They sell around forty loaves of bread every day to campers, who delight in having the convenience of a bakery in their backyard. A monthly profit of $600 lets Beulah and Gus enjoy the pleasures of retirement, which include ball games and concerts.

Have **cakes** be your specialty. Bake them for birthdays, weddings, anniversaries, and parties of every kind. Your cakes might be noted for the moistness that's often missing from the products of commercial bakers.

Photograph all your cakes and show them to potential customers. Or offer to design cakes to order. If you offer special-occasion cakes, be sure to get at least one-third of the cost as a deposit before you bake the cake. Your time, the special ingredients you had to secure to make a one-time cake, and the intricacy of the project all count in setting a price. A three-tier anniversary cake serving fifty people would probably sell for $65-$75, depending on the amount of decoration. Make your prices competitive with the bakery down the street.

Betty G. and Stephanie K. of Delaware are a mother-and-daughter bakery team who "build" wedding cakes. Betty started this business many years ago by advertising on the church bulletin board. That notice got her a few cake orders, and since then, her satisfied customers have spread the word about the light texture, rich flavor, and home-baked goodness of the cakes. Five years ago Stephanie, a substitute art teacher, joined forces with her mom. Customers marvel that this duo will tackle almost any customer request and will bake any flavor—vanilla, chocolate, banana, strawberry, peanut butter, mocha, lemon, and more—a versatility that sets them apart from many commercial bakers. They recently made a cake large enough to feed one thousand people. It was actually five different-flavored cakes (each four tiers high) all connected by plastic bridges they bought at the wholesale bakery supply store. In the center was a champagne waterfall. It took Betty and Stephanie eleven hours just to assemble the cake at the reception site. It sold for $700.

Fruitcakes are a popular end-of-the-year dessert. Many fruitcakes can be baked ahead, wrapped in waxed paper, and stored in airtight containers in cool places. To keep them moist and fresh, wrap the cakes in cloth soaked in brandy or rum. Keep the cloth damp by pouring additional rum or brandy on it about every three weeks. You'll be competing with commercial bakers, so don't skimp on fruit and nuts, and use top-quality ingredients, like butter instead of margarine. Boxed in attractive tins, fruitcakes make a nice gift. They're also good shipping items. Start advertising for Christmas orders in September.

Bake **cookies, cupcakes, and brownies** for people who need a fast dessert. This would be a welcome service for working mothers whose children are asked to bring cookies for the class party on a day's notice. You can bake cookies in bulk and store them in your freezer for ready access in such emergencies. You could bake seasonal cookies to sell to people hosting luncheons, teas, children's parties, or business meetings. Another idea that might beef up your bank account is to bake cookies for special days or weeks set aside to honor groups or institutions. Design typewriter-shaped cookies for Secretaries' Week, book-shaped cookies for National Library Week. Advertise in related magazines and community flyers.

Linda J. of Montana is a **cookie portrait artist**. She was an art major in college, and when she isn't baking cookies, she's teaching oil portrait classes. She bakes sugar cookies in the shapes of people's faces and then decorates them to the smallest detail. She fashions heavy beards and bushy eye brows, dimples and fancy hair styles to match guests at a party, for example. Before a get-together, the customer gives her a snapshot of the guest of honor or some of the other guests, and she duplicates the faces in cookie dough. She also does houses, animals, objects, and even complete villages and farms. Her cookies have even been used to decorate store windows at Christmas and Easter.

Cooking

Cooking is as much a part of most women's lives as getting up in the morning. Some women have been preparing meals since they got married; others started long before that. For many, cooking is a chore, a someone-has-to-do-it proposition. But others enjoy the challenge and the call to creativity that cooking affords. We've already discussed the sense of accomplishment good cooks get from successfully preparing something new and the pride they feel when serving their family's favorite dish. These are the real chefs, who would slave in a hot kitchen for the pure exhilaration the experience offers them. They know all the tricks for success that are hidden between the lines of a recipe.

Cassie L. is a Pennsylvania teacher of home economics. During the summer and on weekends, she has an unusual cooking job. She **prepares food to be photographed** for the cover of a gourmet magazine. A few years ago her brother-in-law, Max, was hired to take food photos for the magazine. Once, when the regular magazine cook wasn't available, Max recommended Cassie. The editors were so pleased with her work that they now use Max and Cassie as a freelance team. Max and Cassie also work for food advertisers and for manufacturers of cooking pans and utensils who want to dress up their sales brochures with tantalizing cuisine. Cassie's job means that she might be preparing Christmas dinner in July, but she enjoys the summer work and the extra income it brings.

Advertise your availability to **prepare complete dinners** in customers' homes. Offer to cook for large or small groups, whichever you feel more comfortable with, featuring Chinese, Italian, or French cuisine. Start with small parties—four to six people—and work up to larger groups. Let your customers know you can cook plain old American food, too—a succulent roast beef or fried chicken, but don't try to cook anything and everything. Tout your forte—maybe omelets, German dishes, or Dutch cuisine. You'll have a stronger business if you develop a reputation as the best in a particular field. How many people can cook fabulous egg rolls *and* heavenly French onion soup?

Cooking complete specialty dinners takes a lot of energy and responsibility. You'll have to be able to plan a timetable for dinner, get the right ingredients in the right amounts, conjure up all the appropriate aromas and smooth over any possible snags. You'll also have to be honest with yourself and your customers about how much you can handle. Work with someone who prepares special-occasion dinners before venturing out on your own.

If you like informal cooking projects, have a **mobile hot dog stand**. Add your famous baked beans, potato salad, sauerkraut salad, and chips as side dishes. You could even offer hot dog specialties like coneys, creole frankfurters, bratwurst, and other sausage sandwiches. Advertise your hot dog stand on wheels for children's summer birthday parties, business grand openings, receptions, banquets, and community celebrations. One method of charging for your services at a party would be to set a per-person rate (say $3-$5) and establish the fee in advance, based on the number of people expected to attend.

Jeanne P., a New Jersey wife and the mother of four, has a small travel trailer that she and her husband converted into a hot dog stand on wheels. Shortly after she started the business, she ventured out without a spare tire, not heeding her husband's warning. Not ten miles down the freeway, she had a flat tire and sat there for four hours in the sweltering August heat before a suitable tire could be located. The worst part of the whole incident was listening to her husband say, "I told you so." Her inventory was intact, as her travel trailer's refrigerator runs on bottled gas, but her ego was deflated. Since that catastrophe, Jeanne never leaves the house without a spare. She confidently travels around her city, selling her famous coney dogs with the special tomato sauce. She's towed her trailer to horse shows and county fairs and was once hired to feed a wedding reception in the park.

Prepare a **weekly package of evening meals** that can be heated and served within an hour's time. You can plan the entrees, cook them, and freeze them, to be picked up by steady customers once a week. All your customers will have to do is pop them in the oven and prepare a salad or pour some wine. Mail your customers a menu every month, with choices ranging from baked chicken to barbecued ribs. Charge from $3-$7 per serving, depending on the meals selected. Working parents would eagerly respond to your advertisement if you also sold children's portions. The success of this job is in keeping your costs down, so you can charge reasonable rates. Buy fresh products in quantity. To avoid cooking too many meals, set a deadline on food ordering, e.g., noon on Friday for the following week, and charge a $25 deposit with each order. You could also take daily orders, to be placed before noon of that day. Any leftovers you have could be served at your own supper table. Know your physical and psychological limits and the limits of your kitchen. If your stove has only four burners, don't expect to cook two dozen different entrees in one day.

Start dinners for working people, who often come home after a hectic day only to be faced with preparing dinner for the family. Your duties could include putting a roast in the oven, preparing fresh vegetables, making a salad, setting the table, and even tidying up the kitchen to minimize after-dinner cleanup. The nine-to-five crowd would be happy to pay a dependable person to set the stage for hassle-free dinners. Arrange for your customers to defrost the pork chops or have a quart of milk handy for pudding on designated days. This is a word-of-mouth kind of job, and a good reputation can only be built on efficient, dependable service. This might be a sure-thing opportunity for you if you live in an apartment building or housing development and have easy access to your neighbor's kitchens.

Sylvia K. of Illinois is the mother of a toddler. She starts dinner for several families in her apartment building. That can mean frying some chicken legs, mixing a meat loaf and putting it in the oven, peeling potatoes, and making Jell-O. At three in the afternoon she begins her rounds to four different apartments, starting dinners that have been planned and shopped for by her customers. She empties the dishwasher, so it's ready for reloading, and sets the table. By five-thirty she's finished. She makes $60 a week without leaving her apartment building and without paying a babysitter.

Prepare **homemade soups** in your kitchen. Offer a variety— maybe seafood chowder, chili con carne, Russian borscht, and hearty minestrone. You can make large quantities and freeze them in gallon containers. Customers can pick them up after a football game or a day of sledding, or when company drops by unexpectedly. Fill thermoses with soup for people who work outside in cold weather. They can stop by at lunch for your warming concoctions.

Marilyn O. of Indiana operates a small business called **Soup du Jour**. Each day two of her delicious soups are featured for sale in pint or quart containers. Marilyn made the mistake of starting her business in the summer, and at first her family ended up eating most of the soup. But as the crisp fall weather set in, soup-loving customers flocked to her door. This year she plans to offer some cold soups, like gazpacho and vichyssoise, when summer comes.

What about **noodles**? Sell your homemade pastas—spinach noodles, ravioli, manicotti, etc. Be the last word in noodles in your community. Package them in plastic bags, freeze them, and supply them on consignment to grocery stores and delicatessens in your area. Not everyone has the time or skill to make good egg noodles; those who don't might buy yours to give their chicken noodle or beef noodle soup a touch of home goodness.

Egg rolls are a big hit for dinner, lunch, and snacks. These Chinese pouches of meat, fish, and vegetables are often bought ready-made, because most people—even those who like to cook—are intimidated by the thought of making them from scratch. If you have a secret recipe that always wins praise from your family and friends, consider selling your rolls to restaurants and caterers. Egg roll lovers will rally round. Throw in a few fortune cookies for some good publicity.

Start an **eating club** in your home. Teachers, secretaries, nurses, and others who work near you could come to your home during their lunch hour. You can offer tasty dishes at prices from $2-$5 and serve groups of five to ten workers who are tired of eating cafeteria or fast-food meals at noon. They might enjoy the relaxing home atmosphere, the change of scene, and the home-cooked lunches. Plan your menus a week ahead of the day they'll be served. Take reservations, so you'll know how much to cook. Advertise through local business publications and on bulletin boards in hospitals, office buildings, and teachers' lounges.

Tiffany K. of California is the proud owner of **Breakfast at Tiffany's.** She started the business in her own home five years ago, after some out-of-town visitors told her about a service in their city that served only breakfast food on a takeout basis. The idea appealed to her, as she'd always eaten a doughnut or a breakfast roll on the run. She started out small, limited her menu to only two entrees and preparing only enough food for ten customers. Word of her business spread through the corporate office buildings in town, and today the business has grown from a home kitchen venture to an operation that employs over twenty people. The menu is filled with every breakfast fast food imaginable: eggs, meats, pancakes, waffles, coffee cakes, sweet rolls, and a complete line of jams, syrups, butters, and jellies. Most of the dishes are Tiffany's own creations; a favorite is pancakes with passionfruit syrup. Breakfast can be ordered ahead or at the last minute. Some of the entrees are frozen, packaged in covered containers suitable for microwave or conventional ovens; others are sold ready for eating.

Other Kitchen Products

There's cooking, baking, and candy-making—and then there

are some culinary creations that don't seem to fit in any of those categories. For instance, does your family enjoy your **homemade preserves, jams and jellies, and pickles**? Others might, too. Why not sell them in specialty shops, at fairs, and at flea markets? You could bring back memories for people who once treasured mother's bread-and-butter pickles, brandied fruits, fruit butters, and corn relish, but haven't tasted them in years.

Preserving can be done in several ways. The amount of time and work involved will depend on the recipes you choose to offer. For example, strawberry preserves can be made from fresh berries and sugar, boiled together so that the fruits' natural pectin makes the jell (the long method). Or they can be made without cooking, by adding sugar and store-bought liquid pectin to frozen berries (the short, easy method). The same goes for pickles. In some recipes the cucumbers are packed and sealed in pickling brine in only a few hours, while other recipes take fourteen days for the processing cycle. Choose the method that suits your time schedule and your customers' tastes.

Cheese balls are a popular item at parties. Advertise several types, such as pecan, garlic and bacon, bleu cheese and ham, and cream cheese and spinach. Offer large, medium, and small cheese balls and have party trays of luncheon meats, cheeses, pickles, and olives as other options. Display your cheese balls around town. Donate a few to community groups at holiday times so that people will see and taste them. What about offering free samples in the grocery store? You can add a delivery service to reach a greater number of people.

Carol T.'s husband owns and operates a drive-through beer and wine carryout store in Kentucky. Many of his customers pick up drinks and snacks for parties. Carol got the idea of taking orders for **party trays**, offering customers a one-stop party shopping opportunity. She put up an ad next to the window where the customers paid for their beer and wine. The first week she got twenty-three orders, and now she gets so many that she's asked a friend to join her in making up the delectable trays. She buys her ingredients from a restaurant wholesale supplier. She charges $35 for an all-ham tray serving 16 people; an all-cheese tray the same size sells for $31. Her business is steady year round, but really booms during the Christmas season.

Make **edible party centerpieces**. They can be made in different shapes, forms, and sizes to fit the occasion. How about a candy Christmas tree, made from a cone-shaped piece of Stryofoam covered with gumdrops? Or a porcupine made from two cheese balls covered with black olives, nuts, and toothpicks. Buy or make pyramid or dome forms of wire or Styrofoam, and use toothpicks or other fasteners to attach candies, rolls, cookies, fruit, meatballs, or vegetables to make eye-catching treats. Sculptured food also makes a great centerpiece: a cauliflower lion, a button squash baseball glove, peanut puppets on stage, Cinderella's coach made from a pumpkin with grapefruit wheels. Have pictures of your centerpieces to show customers.

Ice sculptures are lovely decorations. A skilled artistic hand can take a block of ice and turn it into a person's head, a house, an animal, or an attractive abstract design. You can use colored water, made with food coloring, lemonade, Kool-Aid, or even punch, to make these interesting centerpieces. Molds for some sculptures can be purchased from culinary specialty shops. This moneymaking idea requires very little equipment—mainly a freezer (large enough to hold a big block of ice), a chiseling utensil, and a chest cooler in which to deliver the sculpture. These cold creations are hot items for today's party planners and caterers. The price you charge for each sculpture will depend on the amount of work involved in fashioning the melting masterpiece.

Catering

Catering is work for which a lot of women have informal training. Preparing good food and serving it efficiently and expertly is catering. It is an art and a skill that's often learned by the woman whose family all eat at different times. It can be mastered by the office worker who plans a romantic Friday dinner during the train ride home.

Sounds easy? What if you were catering a twenty-fifth wedding anniversary party, and the guests included people from six to sixty? Could you come up with a menu that everyone would enjoy? What if you were catering an affair where there was limited space? Could you devise a menu the guests would remember, even though they had to eat standing up?

Catering offers women a chance to show off their cooking and hosting expertise. If you're a born hostess, it will be apparent from the compliments you get from guests attending your dinner parties. Being a successful caterer requires patience and a love of preparing and serving delicious, appealing food.

Plain food can appear elegant when served on a lavish embroidered tablecloth, accompanied by a centerpiece made of fresh strawberries, baby's breath, greenery, and flickering candles. Sometimes it's not what you serve but how you serve it that makes the more lasting impression. The rewards are not only the substantial income you get from clients, but also the oohs and aahs you hear as their guests spot your scrumptious food displays.

Catering is a service that is used for any size affair, from a dinner party for 2 to a 350-plate wedding reception. We suggest that you start out on a small, informal scale, using paper plates and cups, plastic tableware, and disposable tablecloths and napkins. It's a good idea to go wading and see how deep the water is before you dive in head first.

Starting small might mean preparing sandwiches, hors d'oeuvres, and desserts in your home. These foods can be served at small parties or even at intimate wedding receptions held nearby. Prepare and deliver the food; if the customer desires, you can also set it up and even serve the guests. Make up a complete list of your hors d'oeuvres and desserts with a price list, and distribute flyers in your city; advertise in area newspapers and on neighborhood bulletin boards. When you've had experience, stress in your ad that no group is too small, and that you like to prepare for groups of eight or ten as well as for groups of one hundred. (But be sure you really *can* accommodate these groups; don't overstep your limits.)

After you've gotten your feet wet, decide whether it's more advantageous for you to rent or buy supplies such as tableware and linens. You may decide to buy some of the items a few at a time while you're still renting the others. Some catering services supply only the food and the customer supplies everything else; this, too, is an idea you might consider.

You don't have to buy the best. Considering the price of silver, stainless steel flatware is regarded as quite appropriate these days, and a service for twelve can be purchased for $50 to $100. For formal settings inexpensive china is sufficient. Service for twelve can be purchased for under $100. A nice selection of ordinary glassware can easily substitute for crystal and can usually be found for about $.50-$.75 a glass. Be sure to check around for discount stores, wholesalers, and factory outlets. Even seconds are often usable. National and regional bargain directories will direct you to stores that sell catering supplies at marked-down prices.

If you decide to do catering on a small scale, your start-up costs would reflect that fact. For about $100 you could stock paper plates and napkins, disposable cups and glasses, and plastic silverware to have on hand for small catering jobs. You should have a reserve fund for purchasing supplies for any unusual jobs you get.

Catering large affairs where you do the cooking on the party premises will cost you more to get started. If you're catering gala events and once-in-a-lifetime parties, expect your costs to be proportionately higher. First of all, a large refrigerator and freezer will be needed for storing perishable foods, and a cupboard, closet, or spare room for nonperishables, china, linens, silverware, and glasses. Large pots and pans are needed if you're cooking for a crowd. Your investment could be $2,000-$3,000, unless you decide to rent linens, china, and silverware. In that case your initial cost might be as low as $1,500.

Knowing and deciding how much to charge will take some thought and a few phone calls to local catering services. This is the best way for you to determine how to fairly charge your customer. The size and kind of affair, and especially the menu, can make a drastic difference, so be sure to get some prices on different menus for different numbers of people.

Before determining what your menu for a particular job will be, there are several things to consider. The first and most important is how much your customer wants to spend. Does she want to get by as cheaply as possible, or does she want a lavish affair? Decide on a menu appropriate for the number of guests, their age group, the atmosphere desired (formal or informal), the serving style (buffet or sit-down), and the location (indoor or outdoor). Do any of the guests have allergies to certain foods? Are they dieting? Are they on low-cholesterol or low-salt diets? Is the get-together a breakfast, luncheon, dinner, picnic, cocktail party, or barbecue? After all these questions have been answered, offer the host or hostess two or three different food ideas, and let him or her make the final decision.

The food for these catered affairs can either be prepared at your place and delivered or prepared on the premises. If you're hired to furnish only hors d'oeuvres, finger sandwiches, and relish trays, you could prepare and deliver them to the function for serving by the customer. But if you're hired to cook a five-course dinner with everything from hot madrilene to roast duckling with orange sauce, including a dessert of glazed pistachio ice cream and little iced cakes, it would be far better to cook it on the premises. Some menus would be impossible to cook and transport, unless you cared little about satisfying customers.

When you're approached for any job, be sure to get all the facts before giving an estimate of the cost. After you've figured it from every angle and have come up with a price you feel is fair to both you and the customer, then determine the conditions of a contract. For example, if you're catering a Japanese dinner where you cook an exotic feast while the guests watch, naturally you'll charge more than usual, because of the extra work. If you serve filet mignon garnished with artichoke bottoms and mushroom caps, you'll charge more because of the cost of the food. To protect you and the customer, these conditions must be spelled out in advance.

Be sure the contract clearly specifies the date and place of the affair, the number of guests, the desired menu, the way it will be served, the person responsible for cleaning up after the affair, the amount of deposit required, and the total fee or a method for determining it.

Make your business professional and ethical. Your reputation and future business depend on it.

The next few pages describe special kinds of catering businesses. Many of these businesses can be adapted to almost any occasion. Popular affairs for catering include:

anniversary parties	office parties
birthday dinners	retirement dinners
business meetings	surprise parties (for any occasion)
dinner parties	
fraternity or sorority parties	wedding receptions

Diet Catering. Statistics show that every year in the United States millions of people go on a diet, and less than half of them manage to stick to it long enough to lose the unwanted weight. If you've ever been on a diet yourself, you know just how hard it is when there's always so much fattening food at your fingertips. If you require a special diet for health reasons, you know the willpower required not to cheat. When you're cooking for a family, it's easier to eat the meals you prepare for them than to fix something special for yourself. And the working person who needs every extra minute just to manage a daily routine doesn't have time to spend fussing over a diet. You can provide a very helpful catering service for overweight people and for those on special salt-free and low-cholesterol diets.

Mary O., a retired dietitian from Minnesota, started a diet catering service in her city. She prepares some frozen dinners to be popped into the oven, and she usually sells a full week's supply at a time. She writes up menus a month in advance so that her customers will know what to look forward to. To a few of her customers she offers complete catering—delivering and serving hot meals nightly; others pick their meals up each day on their way home from work. Mary's customers are happy with her service; and they no longer have to count calories, because Mary does it for them. Her list of customers is always changing, but she averages fifty to seventy-five customers at any one time. She advertises at health spas, health food stores, and diet clubs and on community bulletin boards.

International Catering. This is an ingenious idea that can be more fun than work. If you know about or are interested in foreign foods and customs, this can be a profitable venture. A completely catered ethnic dinner should include not only the food and drinks but also the proper eating utensils, appropriate uniforms or costumes for the servers, and any decorations that are needed to create the atmosphere of Mexico, Italy, India, or whatever country you happen to be representing. Since this particular service could be quite expensive, you might make arrangements to secure the help of a local costume rental agency, food market, or travel agency to help create the atmosphere you need at a reasonable price.

Ruth W. of California is the wife of a retired army colonel. She has traveled extensively, and international foods, customs, and clothing are very familiar to her. When her husband retired, Ruth decided to start an international catering service. She began by catering small parties to make sure she really wanted to spend the better part of her free time this way. When she got requests to cater larger functions, she found that she needed to purchase more supplies. Besides making the food, she decorated the dining area, provided background music from the featured country, and hired people to serve the dinners dressed in national costumes. Import houses in the area supplied her with rental ethnic costumes and decorative items from the countries whose dishes she served. Cookbooks with foreign food specialties helped her to expand her menus. She offered everything, from Mexican, French, and Hungarian dinners to German, Italian, and Chinese food. She charged according to how many people she was serving and how expensive the ingredients for the dinner were. The meals ran from a low of $6.95 per person to a high of $22.50. Her service became such a hit that she was soon catering two or three nights a week. She started teaching a class in international catering. Ruth's catering service and her classes are both popular in her area, and she makes a nice income from her combined businesses.

Brown Bag. This is an excellent service for working people (students, teachers, construction crews) who prefer a tasty, well-balanced homemade lunch to cafeteria offerings or fast-food burgers. Vegetarian lunches and low-calorie specialties could broaden your menu. You can start on a small scale, catering to selected groups that support your brown bag experiment. If interest stays high, you could consider a lunch delivery service.

Specialized Catering. If you feel especially good in one area, then you might want to stay with it. You could specialize in wedding receptions, birthday dinners, or retirement parties. Maybe you want to do only children's parties. Be sure of yourself and your capabilities; don't pour out a lot of money on a half-baked notion. An advantage of specializing would be lower start-up costs for decorations, cooking equipment and supplies unique to your operation.

Linda W. of Florida is a young woman who loves to cater **picnics and barbecues** and any other outside affair. She began by fixing ribs with her special barbecue sauce for her husband's annual office picnic. She always served her homemade potato salad and fresh green beans with the ribs, and topped it off with her special chocolate picnic cake. After receiving several calls to do the same thing for other companies, she decided to run an ad in her local newspaper. Now she caters a barbecue almost every weekend, toting supplies—including food, grills, and serving dishes—in her Econoline van. She makes up all the sauces at home and cooks the ribs on a spit barbecue in her customer's yard or in the park. After trying some of her food, we understand why she has such a jam-packed schedule.

Party Planning

Party planning is a cooking-related talent of organized, perceptive women who know how to show people a good time. Does everyone seem to have fun at your parties? Do you have an eye for all the little details that go into planning a successful get-together? Are you entirely confident of your party-planning ability? If you can answer yes to these questions, then you're one of those women who could make extra cash turning someone's party idea into reality.

There are countless people who would like to entertain but don't have the confidence or ability to plan and carry out a successful feast or even an informal brunch. There are others who don't have the time, because of their busy work schedules, or who simply do not like the work involved in giving a party. There are people who keep going to parties given by others and keep feeling guilty because they don't reciprocate.

A party planner can make all the difference; your behind-the-scenes activities will do the host or hostess proud. The planning you do will keep guests from leaving early because the punch bowl ran out. Your knack for making the most of space will have party guests marveling at how the host or hostess ever managed to accommodate fifteen people comfortably in a garage for a rainy day barbecue. This job keeps you out of the limelight, but offers you both monetary and intangible rewards.

Parties flop for any number of reasons, and usually the food and entertainment themselves are not to blame. It may be that they're inappropriate choices for a particular event or a particular group of people. (Picture tuxedoed guests fumbling with barbecued chicken or hyperactive six-year-olds being entertained by a reading of *Treasure Island* at a birthday party.) It's often the little things that make or break a party: Knowing where coats will be hung, having enough chairs, opening windows to maintain comfortable room temperature, creating a traffic pattern that doesn't have guests stopping at the dessert trays before they get to the hors d'oeuvres. Party planning is a combination of natural talent (knowing what makes a group of people enjoy themselves) and skill (being able to create the atmosphere for them to do just that).

If you've engineered successful parties on your own turf, with a little more practice you could be hired to turn out a happening for someone else. Start small, planning for intimate groups of eight or ten, and build up to larger, more complicated parties. Advertise in church bulletins, to business and charitable organizations, fraternal organizations, and civic groups, and in newspapers. Advertise that you'll plan club luncheons and wedding receptions. Place an ad in the Yellow Pages under "Party Planning Service."

There's no big investment needed to embark on a party planning business. Most of the planning, after you talk to your customer and find out exactly what is wanted, can be done by telephone as you won't be responsible (in most cases) for actually cooking or serving the food. Keep careful notes of the details of every job. No two will be exactly alike. Settle with your client on a price range or budget for ordering everything from nuts and mints to roast beef and wine. You can also consider contracting to handle the cleanup after the guests leave.

A contract should be signed by you and your client, stating all details of the agreement, such as the rental of a hall when necessary, any special decorations that might be requested, the number of guests to expect, the cost and kind of food and beverages to be served. You should also specify whether you or someone else will secure each item and from where, as well as what the cleanup arrangements will be. If you're planning a party for fifty adult guests where you'll be ordering supplies for a spaghetti dinner, including salad, hot rolls, coffee, and spumoni ice cream, and planning seating arrangements and entertainment, a reasonable price to charge for your services would be in the neighborhood of $500.

Your planning could include selecting a site for the party at your customer's request. Maybe you own or could rent an old barn or other building that could be converted into a party house; maybe you have a large yard and swimming pool. If so, consider renting out facilities of your own and planning parties around them.

Camille S. of Louisiana is the widow of a prominent lawyer. Though she was left with a beautiful antebellum estate, she was also left with the monumental costs of maintaining it. She decided to take advantage of her reputation for giving some of the best parties in town; she turned her home into a party house. Each party is flavored with historical overtones: The entire setting, including the servants' costumes, looks like a scene from *Gone with the Wind*. She keeps a catering staff on hand to do the cooking and serving, but she plans the menus, decorations, and entertainment for the parties. She has almost all holidays and most weekends booked.

Humans, being the social creatures they are, love to party. The following are a few celebrations you might plan for customers who recognize the value of a skillful party planner.

Birthday Parties. How many parents dread the preparation and cleanup for a child's birthday party? Let them know you're available, and see how many will be happy to let you handle the whole affair. You can take care of the party hats and favors, decorate with balloons and crepe paper, plan the games for the children, and purchase and wrap the prizes. You can also prepare the food and bake or purchase the cake. You can hire the entertainment, maybe a clown or a magician. Let parents know you can be at the party to see that things run smoothly or you can do all the preparation and let them handle it from there. You can come back to clean up when the party's over.

Julie G., a West Virginia teenager, needed money to pay for a trip to Spain with her high school Spanish class. She asked all the neighbors for whom she did babysitting to call her if they needed anyone to do extra work. One of the working mothers asked Julie to handle her son's birthday party. The children enjoyed the party, and soon Julie began getting calls from other mothers to plan their children's parties. She earned enough money for her trip to Spain, and now, as a college student, she's still earning extra money planning parties for children. She spends three to four hours planning a party suited for its guests, and she charges her customers $25. She buys all the food, decorations, games, and favors, according to the customer's budget, and delivers them along with instructions for turning them into a fun party.

You may also want to handle birthday parties for teenagers or adults. They can be as simple or as fancy as your customer desires. They can be anything from a small dinner party to a large affair in a rented hall. As a party planner, you see that the drinks, food, and flowers are ordered and delivered, and that all the other details are taken care of.

Wedding Receptions. A notice on your church bulletin board or an advertisement in the local paper should put you in contact with many potential customers for wedding receptions. You can also talk to people who rent out party halls and houses and leave your name and telephone number with them. You decide what you can handle—anything from a small reception at the bride's home to a sit-down dinner for five hundred people, complete with music and dancing. Be ready for decorating the tables with flowers and preparing and ordering everything, including engraved match covers, the wedding cake, ice cream, and liquid refreshments. You may also be responsible for the invitations, the caterers, and hotel reservations for out-of-town guests. Contracting to handle the cleanup will be an extra incentive for the customer to hire you. What you charge will depend on how many hours' work you put in. A fee of $15 an hour would not be unreasonable, but check with your competition for the going rates in your area.

Georgette A. of New York started planning parties by volunteering her services at the church she attended. She lived near the church and could always be counted on to decorate the hall, make the punch, and hire parking attendants for the many social activities held there. Since many wedding receptions were held in the church hall, Georgette and two friends volunteered to decorate the hall and plan the receptions. When her three children reached high-school age, Georgette and one of her friends decided to capitalize on those years of experience and go into business planning wedding receptions. They discussed in detail with the bride and groom the colors, atmosphere, food, and entertainment for each reception. They planned celebrations that reflected the couples' interests and attitudes. They planned one reception in the park for two hiking enthusiasts. It wasn't long before they began getting calls from other churches to perform the same service. They were so busy that they had to hire additional people to staff their business.

Retirement Parties. Many companies give their employees dinners complete with gold watches when they retire. These events are usually thrown together by a committee of employees who don't really have the interest or the time. Contact some of the larger companies in your area and leave your card with them. They'll be happy to have a person they can call upon to plan a good party. Talk with the persons in charge and find out how simple or elaborate an affair they would like. Then you can do all of the preparations, down to buying the gold watch, if that's what they want. You'll make your customer happy, and the man or woman who's retiring will be impressed and flattered that the company cared enough to arrange for the very best.

Anniversary Parties. These parties usually start out simple and end up complicated. Advertising in church bulletins or newspapers should bring many responses. Children usually decide to give a party for mom and dad's anniversary without realizing how much work is involved. It often entails renting a hall, ordering a cake, arranging to have refreshments catered, sending invitations, making motel reservations for out-of-town guests, meeting guests at the airport—many of the same details that go into planning a wedding and reception. You can plan to have nostalgic background music for a fiftieth wedding anniversary—or music the anniversary couple danced to at their wedding.

Holiday Parties. Almost everyone *thinks* of giving a party around the holidays, but many never give one, because of all the extra work involved in preparing for it. After doing the Christmas shopping, cooking, baking and cleaning, many people are simply too tired to arrange a party. If they knew of someone who would make all the preparations, they would be greatly relieved. They could enjoy their own party instead of being exhausted after making sure everything was done. You could even help clean the house and prepare the food. They might even feel as though they were going to a party, instead of hosting one.

Many single men go to a lot of parties throughout the year and never have people to their places, which are sometimes less than presentable. They claim to know nothing about planning and giving a successful party. They might hire you to clean house, plan the party, and fix the food. There are also many women who would hire you to plan parties in their homes because they get tense and nervous at the thought of devising a menu or providing entertainment. You would be easing their tensions by ridding them of the details. Knowing you have things under control will free them to greet guests without wondering where they'll all sit in the living room.

Some of the other parties you could plan include bar mitzvahs, wedding rehearsal dinners, first communions, and theme parties. Parties don't go out of style, because people can always find an excuse to celebrate. Party planners aren't likely to go out of style, either.

Teaching

The skills (cooking, baking, and catering) mentioned in this chapter may seem simple to you, but there are countless people out there who feel inadequate when they're asked to bake for a cub scout meeting or plan a menu for a cocktail party. They rarely have parties or create desserts, because they're afraid of exposing their inadequacies.

Confidence is often what these people lack. You could hold classes for them in your home and teach cooking, baking and cake decorating, or candy making. Don't limit your classes to other women; there may well be children and men who would like to learn some of the secrets of the culinary arts. There's no limit to what or whom you can teach. We heard of a woman who teaches cooking to children aged two and one-half to five. Her classes of six to eight students make such delicacies as edible play-dough. She charges $18 for five thirty-minute lessons and enjoys answering the tough questions of those curious young minds.

To teach cooking in your home, you'll need ample space and equipment as well as proper food permits. If you have a stove in your basement, hold your classes for six or eight people there. If not, hold the classes in your kitchen, or you may be asked to give lessons at the YWCA or a local cooking store. Charge $3 per person for a one-hour class, or $25 for five longer classes. Have students bring their own ingredients (or the money to pay for ones you supply), and you provide the pots and pans. Have people work in teams of two on each project—a recipe for chocolate mousse, for example. Don't overlook teaching party planning too; lots of people haven't any idea how much hamburger to buy for a troop of hungry Little Leaguers. (That bit of information could prevent panic for many parents.) Whether you're teaching how to dress up turkey leftovers or how to curl radishes, oversee the entire operation, giving help and advice where necessary. When the class is over, everyone can taste the food and make comments.

If you like to cook and bake, and you're an organized person who enjoys communicating with others, you could be a success in teaching your culinary specialties. You don't need a license for this type of work, but you'll need lots of patience to survive the gamut of questions—from "How do you separate an egg?" to "What are the best uses for caraway seeds?"

If you're skilled in any of the areas mentioned in this chapter, by now you know that your skill brings not only satisfaction to you but joy to others as well. How about spreading that joy a little further and adding extra cash to the list of rewards you get?

Suggested Reading

Annechild, Annette, and Russell Bennett. *Recipe for a Great Affair.* New York: Wallaby Books, 1981.

Axler, Bruce H. *Profitable Catering.* Indianapolis: Bobbs-Merrill: 1974.

Betty Crocker's Cookbook for Boys and Girls. New York: Western Publishing, Golden Press, 1981.

The editors of *Bride's* magazine. *The New Bride's Book of Etiquette.* New York: Grosset & Dunlap, 1981.

Capon, Robert Farrar. *Party Spirit, Some Entertaining Principles.* New York: William Morrow, 1979.

Christensen, Lillian Langseth. *How to Present and Serve Food Attractively.* Garden City, New York: Doubleday, 1976.

Clayton, Bernard, Jr. *The Complete Book of Breads.* New York: Simon & Schuster, 1973.

Crookston, Stephanie. *Creative Cakes.* New York: Random House, David Obst Books, 1978.

Goulart, Frances S. *How to Write a Cookbook and Sell It*. Port Washington, New York: Ashley Books, 1980.

Hertzbert, Ruth, Beatrice Vaughn, and Janet Greene. *Putting Food By*. Brattleboro, Vermont: Stephen Greene Press, 1973.

Levin, Beatrice. *How to Win Recipe Contests*. Van Nuys, California: Creative Book Company, 1976.

London, Anne. *The American International Encyclopedic Cookbook*. New York: Thomas Y. Crowell, 1972.

Read, Jean B., and Mary Eckley, eds. *McCall's Book of Entertaining*. New York: Random House, 1979.

Reed, Marjorie, with Kalia Lulow. *Marjorie Reed's Party Book*. New York: Ballantine Books, 1981.

Weiss, Hal and Edith. *Catering Handbook*. Rochelle Park, New York: Hayden Book Co., 1971.

Dialing for 8
Dollars

(Making money with your telephone)

Your telephone could be a moneymaking resource just waiting to be tapped. Almost any articulate person with a pleasant voice can start a dialing service. It doesn't require a good car or expensive clothing. You usually won't have anyone looking over your shoulder while you work, and you won't have to punch a time clock or fight rush-hour traffic if you work from your own home.

No specific skills or previous experience are required to become a good "phone person." However, you must be patient and polite, speak distinctly, be a good listener, and be able to take messages accurately. A quiet place to work is helpful, as over-the-phone noise from small children playing or loud music blaring would detract from the businesslike atmosphere necessary for this job.

There are plenty of ways to make money by phone. Have you ever had several telephone calls to make and put them off because they were so time-consuming you just couldn't get to them between the time you left work and the start of your daughter's soccer game? Or maybe your calls had to be made during hours when you were on the job and away from a phone. Think about the person who works at a nine-to-five job every day and still must find the time to make, break, or change doctor and dentist appointments; place catalog orders; phone church, school, or girl scout groups; schedule repairs for the washer, dryer, or furnace. The list is endless, or at least it seems that way, especially if you are short on time. And some people have their lives so full that they can't even squeeze in a quiet sit-down meal or a hot Jacuzzi bath, let alone a call to the plumber about a clogged drain in the utility room.

Here is where you might be able to help put order into someone else's life and extra money into yours. Advertise your service in the newspapers or on neighborhood bulletin boards, and contact busy people you know who might need your service. Besides all those people who are too busy to handle the details of everyday life, potential clients include charitable organizations; political candidates; businesses too small to hire an employee to order supplies, take customers' orders, and set up or change appointments; and people who want regular calls made to check on elderly persons or convalescents. Let them know you're available twenty-four hours a day to make their calls. By prearranged schedule, they can call you during certain hours—say, 6 to 10 p.m.—to give you the calls that need to be made the following day and to receive any information you have for them from calls already made.

Nell M. of Idaho is a pert fifty-nine-year-old who needed to add to her income. She hadn't worked for quite a few years and felt that she had no skills. Since talking on the telephone was her favorite pastime, she got the idea of phoning for others. She called everyone she knew and had them pass the word that she was starting a **dialing service.** She also advertised in the daily paper and the neighborhood weekly. She charges her regular customers $10 a month and occasional customers $.50 per placed call. Business was slow in the beginning but has now climbed to twenty-seven customers, and she hopes to raise the total to about fifty.

You and your telephone can earn a steady income, but your success will depend in part on knowing what to charge. Check with similar business operations near you to get an idea of just what your service is worth. (You'll probably be surprised.) Determine your own rates, taking into account your time, the cost of the phone, and how you will handle toll calls. Have your regular customers pay in advance by cash or check. Offer them a flat monthly rate for an unlimited number of calls.

If you live alone, your home phone can be used for this service, but if there are several family members using your telephone, and your business gets off to a good start with several customers, you will probably need a separate line. The cost will depend on where you live and on whether you're required to pay business rates. Check with your phone company. Whatever the bill, it will be more than offset by the money that phone will be helping you earn.

One advantage of having a business phone is that you can advertise in the Yellow Pages. What better place to publicize a telephone service!

Making calls for other people isn't the only service you can provide with your telephone. Several more are described below. Which ones you consider offering will depend on where you live, your particular skills, your needs, and the needs of your potential customers. Be ingenious.

Wake-up Service

We all know people who simply cannot get out of bed in the morning. They might appreciate wake-up calls that wouldn't let them roll over for ten more minutes. People who live alone are likely customers. The monthly fee for a wake-up service usually ranges between $14 and $20, depending on the location. At that price, with only ten customers, you can earn $140 to $200 per month. Not bad, huh?

Rose Y. is a fifty-five-year-old widow living in a metropolitan area of California. Unable to do much physically because of a weak heart, and not wanting to impose on her children, she had to find a way to make some money from her home. She decided to start a wake-up service because it required no special talents and would put no strain on her health. She advertised in newspapers and on bulletin boards; she had flyers made for distribution in apartment buildings for singles. Within six months she went from a few customers to fifty-five. Before starting her business, Rose was depressed by her illness and her dwindling finances. Now her self-confidence has returned. And her bank statement looks a lot healthier, too.

Reminder Service

How many people forget their spouses' birthdays or their wedding anniversaries? How many more forget Grandma or Aunt Mary's birthday? Start a telephone reminder service. Advertise your reminder service on bulletin boards in busy office buildings. Men and women who spend hectic days on the job or travel a lot might take advantage of this service. Gear your advertisements to anyone who is busy or forgetful and tends to neglect important dates or occasions. Then set up two file systems: one listing all your customers alphabetically, and one organized by date. Go through your card file or your file drawers weekly and pull those files of clients who need a reminder call that week. Set your rates according to how many reminder calls must be made to each customer. Bill customers at a monthly fee for an unlimited number of calls or charge $1 per call for people needing only occasional reminders.

Jill C. of Rhode Island worked in a busy real estate office. Her job consisted of answering the phone for four salesmen who were in and out of the office constantly. Besides reminding her employers of appointments to keep and phone calls to return, she found herself helping them remember birthdays and anniversaries. When she quit her job to have a family, she missed the busy atmosphere of the office. She got the idea of a reminder service and began with only her ex-bosses as clients. She recruited several more clients by calling all the business people she had met in her former job. After about a year, word-of-mouth and newspaper advertising had built her small business into an interesting and lucrative work-at-home job.

Market Research

Have you ever been called and asked to remember what television show you watched at eight on Thursday night or to say what paper towel you like best? If so, you've been on the answering end of market research. Maybe you'd enjoy asking the questions. Advertise in newspapers, magazines, and periodicals, offering to do market research for companies, community organizations, and business groups. Explain your service and what you charge for it. Most people who do market research charge approximately $4 an hour.

Writers are also potential customers for this kind of work. They often need someone to conduct surveys and help gather research material for their work. You could conduct telephone research (calling libraries and resource people; conducting random sample surveys of people's attitudes, product preferences, etc.). Advertise in writers' magazines and related publications, offering to do **research and information gathering.** Because the work is often sporadic, helping writers with research makes a good spare-time business.

Billie G. of New York is an office worker who takes creative writing classes two evenings a week. Several writers spoke to Billie's class, and some of them complained that gathering research for their books was exhausting and tedious and slowed up their writing tremendously. She offered to help one of the writers who was really bogged down. Word got around and Billie was soon doing this work for other writers. She charges $5 an hour and now has eight regular clients who call her when they need her services. She finds the work educational, enjoyable—and profitable.

Message Service

Many people miss important messages because they are not at home to receive them. They may be at work, on vacation, working in the yard, or shopping for dinner. Anyone who is often away from the phone could use this valuable service. One way to set up a message service is to have your customers give your phone number to their associates and friends, the business establishments they frequent, the schools their children attend, etc. You can get their calls on your business phone, and they can then call you for their messages when they have time. In case of emergency you can contact them directly. You could also set up as an answering service (see page 126), but that would be more expensive.

Besides intercepting their messages, you can also deliver information your customers would rather not deliver themselves. Bob may want Sally to know he loves her, but be too shy to tell her himself. John may want to tell his neighbor to keep his dog quiet, but prefers to have you convey the message tactfully and anonymously. Sue may want to decline an invitation to an organization's dinner without facing the subtle pressure at the other end. If you go into the delivery side of the message service, there are several things to remember: be polite and speak in a friendly tone of voice; always give the message exactly as it was dictated to you; never give your name or your customer's name (unless, of course, the customer's name is part of the message). Let clients know that you'll deliver any message, as long as it isn't obscene.

Mary R. lives in a small town in Indiana and makes phone calls for her clients. Since everyone knows everyone else in town, it is often easier to have Mary convey anonymously any messages that might cause friction. Everyone knows that Mary does this job, but she is discreet and never reveals any details about her assignments—neither whom she calls nor who hires her to make the calls. She has telephoned people and asked them to cut their grass, turn down their stereos, temper their loud parties, calm their barking dogs, and stop taking their neighbors' parking spaces. She charges $5 for each call, and though she isn't getting rich, she enjoys the work and gets a few laughs from some of the people she calls. Of course, some of the people she calls are less than pleasant, but Mary has learned to take it all with good humor.

Phone-in Dictation Service

Business people, sales representatives, and others who travel often may not have convenient access to a business office. They could be your best clients for a phone-in dictation service. You will need a good typewriter and tape recorder for this business, as well as a supply of stamps and a ZIP code directory. Shorthand, typing, and proofreading skills are necessary if you are to do professional work. Let large businesses in your area know you are available and leave your business cards for them to give to associates. Leave some business cards at hotels and motels where business people from out of town stay.

Once your clients have supplied you with their letterhead stationery, they can phone in dictation for you to tape-record and then type and mail immediately. Your responsibilities will include making a carbon copy of each letter and sending it to the client's home or place of business. It's wise to keep a carbon for your own files too, in case one of the other copies is lost in the mail or you need to consult it for yourself or your client.

What you charge will depend of course on several factors, including your working speed, the value of your expertise, the amount of competition, and the going rate for such work in your area. A company letter may cost over $6 to be typed by an employee using a company typewriter. Your overhead will be lower than that of the typical business office, but be sure to take into account *all* of your expenses (equipment, supplies, telephone service) as well as your time. Don't forget to include the cost of postage for mailing the letters. You would charge more for detailed statistical charts, extra copies, and more complicated work, and you can charge less to customers with bulk typing orders.

Joyce L. of Minnesota is a homemaker who bowls every week with a friend whose husband owns a motel. She told Joyce that business people staying at their motel were always looking for someone to type business letters. Joyce told her friend she would like to try the job and shortly thereafter began getting occasional phone calls from the motel. She liked the work because it wasn't as confining as a nine-to-five typing job. She enjoyed being her own boss and, being a night person, did much of the typing while the family slept. Joyce called on several other motels in the area, offering the same service. She charges $2.50 for a plain one-page letter and now clears over $100 weekly with her phone-in service. She has learned how to budget her time to accommodate both her family and traveling business people.

Answering Service

This is another telephone service to consider if you live near your potential clients: doctors, dentists, police officers, and other people who are on call twenty-four hours a day. You would take their calls when they were unavailable. The cost to hook up your phone with a business or office in your area is approximately $10 a month and $5 to $10 a month for each mile between the client's phone and yours. You would pass this cost on to your client, along with a monthly charge of approximately $50 to $100. The rate you charge will depend on the number of hours a day you accept messages. These prices are approximate and may vary greatly depending on the region in which you live. For specific details on operating an answering service, contact your local telephone company.

The Bell System has begun to offer "call forwarding." This service allows a customer who pays a small monthly fee to have his or her calls automatically forwarded to another number. The customer can set up or cancel the forwarding any time, just by dialing certain numbers. If call forwarding is available in your area, it might be an inexpensive way to provide an answering service.

A telephone service is usually a very workable, profitable idea; so if you feel at home on the phone, don't hold yourself back.

Suggested Reading

Bury, Charles. *Telephone Techniques That Sell.* New York: Warner Books, 1980.

Gough, Vera, and B. R. Grier. *Better Telephoning: A Plan to Improve Your Telephone Technique.* Elmsford, New York: Pergamon, 1970.

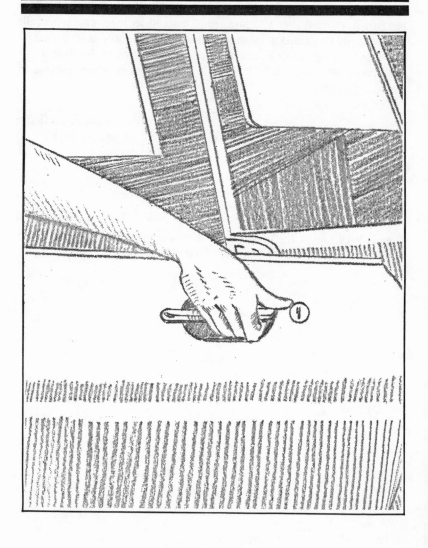

Put Yourself in the Driver's Seat

9

(Delivery, chauffeur and errand services)

Thanks to OPEC, inflation, high interest rates, and downturns in the economy, having private transportation at your fingertips is rapidly becoming a luxury. You know the liabilities of owning and operating a family car. Those same headaches are felt by businesses, community groups, schools—anyone who must transport products or people from one place to another. For many businesses, hiring a complete delivery service is cheaper than owning and operating vehicles themselves and having to hire qualified drivers. If you are fortunate enough to have your own car and a lot of time and energy, there are moneymaking opportunities waiting for you.

Businesses look for someone with a good driving record—someone who is cautious and drives defensively. Being punctual, responsible, patient, and cool in traffic is also a must for anyone contemplating this kind of job. The vehicle you will be using to perform various delivery services must be safe and well taken care of. Good tires and frequent oil changes are necessary for any car, van, or truck used daily for business purposes.

Delivery people generally enjoy driving. And they like the nonmonetary benefits of the job, including having no boss or set working hours. They also have a chance to meet a lot of interesting people, as their work location varies from day to day.

By keeping your eyes and ears open, you can discover which businesses would be glad to leave the driving to you. They won't be the same everywhere, of course; you will be able to profit by catering to your area's unique needs. Offices that sell show tickets might want you to deliver them; hospitals may need Xrays delivered to doctors' offices; city-wide businesses may need you to carry mail between branch offices. You could offer a shuttle service in parks or resort areas.

Keep in mind that the Internal Revenue Service allows a tax deduction of $.20 a mile for the first fifteen thousand miles and $.11 a mile thereafter to people who use their cars for business. If you are willing to keep careful records, you may be able to increase your business-driving deduction by keeping track of actual expenses. Deductible costs include depreciation, gas and oil, maintenance and repairs, parking and tolls, towing, washing, garage expenses, tires, license and inspection fees, taxes, insurance, and even motor club membership. If your car is used for personal as well as business driving, only the percentage of expenses attributable to business use is deductible; so be sure to keep good mileage records, too.

The cost of offering a delivery service is small if you already have a reliable car, truck, van, or trailer. A chauffeur's license may be needed, depending on the laws of your state. Check with your insurance agent before starting any type of delivery service, because transporting people, pets, or property may require some added coverage. Liability insurance can be costly, especially when you are carrying people or valuable merchandise. The cost will vary according to the vehicle used and the product transported, but you can generally count on about $100 a month for insurance. Accidents happen, and full coverage can soften the blow.

Knowing what and how to charge for delivery jobs is difficult because cargoes, vehicles, drivers, and destinations are so varied. Some workers who use a business's own car get an hourly wage and tips. (Pizza delivery drivers, for example.) Some people charge a percentage of the retail price of the delivered item. If possible, check prices of others doing the same type of work or contact businesses who offer these services. You should charge for your actual auto expenses, any special clothing needed, and the time you spend working; then tack on a certain amount for profit just to make it all worthwhile.

After you have determined which of our moneymaking ideas appeal to you most, advertise your services in places where people who might hire you are likely to look. Have some business cards printed, and mail them to people or commercial establishments that might need you. Advertise to reach the greatest number of potential customers. Because job experience is a good indicator of your record of reliability and service, be prepared to ask former employers to write references for you.

Carrying People and Pets

A **shopping trip** is a rare treat for elderly, handicapped, or disabled people. Advertise in local papers and post your business card in senior citizens apartment buildings and rest homes. Those who can't drive would gladly pay for transportation to and from grocery stores and shopping centers. You can set up a schedule to transport several people on a weekly basis to shopping areas, doctors' offices, and hair salons. If you have a van, consider equipping it with ramps or a lift so you can transport people in wheelchairs. There are thousands of people in this country who are stranded at home because of their lack of mobility. Some need transportation to and from hospitals for therapy and rehabilitation. Others would like to go shopping, to a movie, or to an exhibit. You will need a chauffeur's license to provide this service. If your vehicle has had ramps installed to accommodate the handicapped, you may be able to apply for a special license plate that will enable you to park in handicapped parking spaces.

If you live in a small town, a suburb of a large city, or a rural area, get a chauffeur's license and provide a **taxi service** for your area. Besides the added income, meeting new people would be one of the rewards of this job. There are a lot of people who don't drive or who don't always have a car available to them. Many areas don't have cab companies because there aren't enough people to warrant full-time service; you can be on call for the times when someone does need a lift.

Lena R. lives on the edge of a small town in Georgia. The town has a new shopping center, but the city can't supply bus service to it because there are not enough people to support it. Lena saw the need for a taxi service and placed an ad in the local newspaper, offering to transport people to the shopping area, to dental appointments—to anywhere they needed to go locally. Lena takes the calls at home and chauffeurs people around the town and the surrounding area.

Advertise an **airport taxi service** in your community, especially if no limousine service exists in your area. Take your customers to the airport and pick them up on schedule. Business people who travel regularly could become your steady customers. Holiday travelers, too, would welcome your service. Because long-term airport parking and limousine services are expensive, you could make extra money while your customer saves.

Children who are involved in after-school activities, such as sports, scout meetings, band practice, and dance lessons, have often had to give them up when mother went to work. You can pick them up and drop them off when their parents are not available. Your chauffeur's license will enable you to take them to doctor and dentist appointments, skating rinks, birthday parties, or any of the other places they need or want to go. Children in kinder-garten usually have school for only half the day, and parents who work might hire you to take them to school, then pick them up later and deliver them to ba-bysitters. A good piece of advice to anyone transporting children: Never over-load your seating capacity or your nerve tolerance.

Avonelle P. is a sixty-year-old grandmother living in Pennsyl-vania. While talking to her daughter, who works in a neighborhood day-care center, she learned that many of the young mothers whose children spent the day at the center were worn out and irritable by evening. Avonelle contacted the mothers and offered to transport the children to and from the day-care cen-ter every day for a fee of $12 per week for each child. She got a chauffeur's li-cense and now has a regular route set up; she makes three trips every morning and evening. The mothers are grateful; Avonelle feels useful and is making a nice income with her car.

Because some people are afraid to fly, they may have a diffi-cult time finding **long-distance transportation** when they need it. Run an ad-vertisement in the newspaper, offering to drive your customer to any destination. This is an adventurous job and can be very interesting, because you will meet fascinating people and have a different destination on every trip you take. People with emergencies in the middle of the night, families trying to get together during the holiday rush, and college students heading home for a break or summer vacation might welcome your service. To provide this long-distance transportation, you must have a vehicle big enough for any lug-gage your customer has to carry. You must also have good road maps and be able to read them.

Transporting animals can be another way for you to earn money. You must be a good driver and be able to tow a trailer if you want to carry large animals like horses. Horse breeders often move their animals hun-dreds of miles for breeding with other fine horses. Racehorses are transported to tracks during the racing season; show horses are taken to exhibit locations. Some animals need to be taken to state fairs for competitions. Others may travel to distant locations for medical treatment or surgery. Advertise in news-papers, at the racetrack, and in related publications.

Take pets to the veterinarian's office, to groomers for baths, haircuts, and nail clippings, to animal trainers for classes, and to kennels for boarding. Many pet owners, especially those who work, do not have time to run their pets all over town for these needed services. Run newspaper ads, and leave your business card with vets, dog groomers, and kennels; they will probably be delighted to be able to offer pick-up and delivery service to their clients. If you are transporting animals, large or small, be sure—for your safety as well as theirs—that they are secure in wire cages or other containers designed for the purpose.

Carrying Groups

Transporting groups of people can be fun and interesting as well as profitable if you like to drive and enjoy meeting new people. Almost any activity is more enjoyable if it can be shared with others. What you charge for the following services will depend on how many persons you transport, how far you are transporting them, and how much special care your clients need or want. You can either charge so much a mile or set a flat rate. You will need a chauffeur's license for this job, as well as added insurance coverage.

There are numerous **outlet stores** in our country where irregular but good-quality merchandise can be purchased. Sheets, towels, bedspreads, shoes, jeans, children's clothing, outerwear, carpeting, and glassware are just a few of the items that can be bought at a fraction of the retail price. Many people cannot take advantage of these excellent buys because the stores are too far away. Advertise shopping trips to these outlet stores. You will be swamped with calls from interested shoppers who want to reserve a seat in your station wagon or van.

Nina M. of Ohio made yearly trips to a neighboring state to shop at a famous bedspread outlet. She bought all the bedspreads and pillows for her home at a huge discount because they had minor flaws. Nina often had to limit her purchases because her car was full of friends who begged to go with her. She finally started charging $25 per person, plus expenses. She advertises in the newspaper and goes whenever she has enough shoppers to fill her car. Nina says she could now make the trip with her eyes closed.

Conduct **guided tours** to local attractions and points of interest in your community. Civic organizations, social clubs, scout troops, and groups of retired persons might be interested in this service. Contact these potential customers and submit a list of the places you think each group would be interested in seeing—or ask them where they would like you to take them. Museums, art galleries, antique shops, zoos, and concerts might be possible attractions.

Do you have an **outdoor theater** within a radius of one hundred miles? These "playhouses" stage Indian sagas, historical dramas, and other productions using either amateur or professional acting companies. This is a popular form of entertainment during the summer months. Advertise to escort small groups to these outdoor arenas. If you have appropriate vehicle modifications you can also agree to take groups of handicapped or disabled persons, who might otherwise miss out on this form of entertainment. Your responsibility will include making sure that access ramps and special restroom facilities are available at the theater.

Dining out is a treat we all enjoy. Serious food lovers might subscribe to a service that would escort them to **gourmet restaurants**. Visit a different restaurant each time: French, Italian, Chinese, German, etc. Schedule outings once a week or once a month, as they wish. People who might be interested in this service include cooking classes, gourmet clubs, church groups, elderly people, disabled and handicapped groups, and singles' groups. You can work as little or as much as you like, having one or several groups you usher periodically.

Escort **groups of children** to entertaining and educational sites. You can take them to zoos, amusement centers, movies, and picnics and for guided tours through government buildings, plants, and factories. Schools, both public and private, might hire you for this service. Hotel managers might also want to offer this service for children staying with parents at their hotels. Others who might be interested are day-care centers and parents whose children get restless and bored during the summer months. You'll need a van equipped with seats. If you plan to escort larger groups, rent a bus and get a chaperon to help with the children. Charge for this service according to how many people you take and how far you go. If your trip is more than two hours long, provide snacks for the children.

Contact large hotels and convention centers and arrange guided tours or shopping trips for the **spouses of conventioneers or business people** who are busy during the day. Husbands and wives might enjoy being escorted to shopping malls and points of interest in the area.

Dora S.'s husband was hosting his lodge's national convention in Chicago. Most lodge members brought their wives along, and there was nothing for them to do at the hotel during the day while their husbands were attending meetings. Those who weren't familiar with Chicago's offerings were reluctant to venture out alone. Dora's husband asked her to entertain the wives; so she made a list of places in Chicago that out-of-towners might enjoy. She presented the list to the wives and let them choose where they wanted to go. The hotel provided a bus and driver, and Dora was the tour guide. The hotel manager later called Dora and asked her to provide the same service for the hotel on a permanent basis. She now escorts conventioneers' spouses and other hotel guests to such places as antique shops, shopping centers, modeling show rooms, and theaters. Dora draws a nice salary and enjoys her work immensely. She has learned many new things about her hometown and has made new friends who come to see her when they return to the Windy City.

Use your van to escort hikers and outdoor lovers to **wildlife areas** for bird-watching, nature walks, backpacking, and camping trips. If you are knowledgeable enough to identify the birds, wildflowers, trees, and bushes of a particular region, you can share your expertise. Schedule your departure and return time in advance. A sack lunch that each person brings from home can be eaten leisurely along the way on day trips.

Angel P. of Washington is a college student who earns plenty of extra spending money by organizing and conducting wildlife and nature hikes through the beautiful Cascade mountains near her home. For years, Angel's father conducted similar hikes, and she accompanied him on these expeditions. When her father had to give up his hobby because of crippling arthritis, Angel decided to continue the trips herself and earn some money doing something she enjoyed. Angel is an expert when it comes to the out-of-doors, and she loves to share her appreciation and understanding of nature with others. Angel's van is equipped to carry eight people comfortably but has taken up to twelve on a group outing. She offers her services to schools, clubs and activity groups, girl and boy scout troops, and the general public; she advertises in newspapers until a group of nature lovers is formed. She never leaves without a first-aid and snakebite kit. Her trips have been limited to summers only because her winter months are occupied with ambitions to be a pediatrician.

Delivery Services

Start a professional **gift-buying service.** Advertise in the newspapers to become a personal or corporate gift buyer. Set up a file system that lists what your customer last sent to each person and his or her sizes, favorite colors, and individual preferences. Call to remind customers of their particular gift-buying occasions, or they can call you when unexpected business gifts are needed. Charge a fee of $20 plus 10 percent of the gift price.

Be a **shopper for hotel guests**. Contact the large hotels in your area, and offer to shop for guests who are rushed or who don't know where the best shops are located. A woman hotel guest might gladly pay to have you buy hosiery for her when she gets a runner in her last pair of L'Eggs; a man might need a rented tuxedo to wear because of an unexpected party invitation.

Leanne M. of Hawaii is a single woman with a bright future as a "go-fer." She runs an **errand service** for some of the hotels on the island where she lives. When a guest requests something that isn't in the hotel, Leanne goes after it. Her days, and sometimes nights, are busier than ever before. She has a mobile phone in her car so that she can be reached anytime, anywhere. Leanne has delivered everything from diamonds to boxing gloves; once she even delivered twenty-five pounds of pistachio nuts.

Comparison shopping is done by all of the big chain stores to determine if competitors' prices are higher or lower than their own. They also send **mystery shoppers** around to their own stores to judge how polite and efficient their employees are. If you own a car, this can be a good source of employment for you. Retailers usually send comparison and mystery shoppers to areas outside their own neighborhoods so they will not be recognized. The only skills needed for this job are the ability to look like the average shopper (Jane Public who wears everyday clothes) and the ability to observe and report on the quality of the operations.

Delivery is an important service offered by **catering firms**. They may want you on a part-time, full-time, or on-call basis for work during the day or evenings. **Bakeries**, too, offer such services. They deliver wedding cakes to wedding receptions. Call the bakeries in your area and offer to deliver cakes and other baked goods. To ensure the safe arrival of pies, strudels, and cream puffs, you might need to equip your vehicle with special equipment, such as boxes, stands, and cardboard dividers.

Small shops and other local **retailers** would take advantage of a delivery service if it were offered. They probably don't need a full-time person but might like to have someone on call. Contact owners of boutiques and specialty shops in your vicinity, and leave your business card. Antique shops, grocery stores, party supply stores, jewelry stores, and beauty salons (which may offer wig pick-up and delivery) would be potential customers. You could also offer to deliver office supplies for firms in your community. When these items are ordered by hospitals, businesses, and agencies, they are often needed immediately. You can be on call, or you can work regular hours.

Contact local **florists**. They often need extra delivery people at special times of the year: Valentine's Day, Mother's Day, and Easter, for example. They might appreciate having someone to call on during their busy seasons.

Lois B. is a fifty-five-year-old homemaker from Illinois. After her last child married, Lois found that her days were not busy enough. She didn't want a job because she enjoyed her new freedom after many years of raising a family. She saw an ad in the newspaper for someone to deliver flowers part-time at the local florist shop. She answered the ad and was hired immediately. Lois has a station wagon and has discovered that she can carry quite a few orders at once when she folds the back seats down flat. She works mostly around holidays, but she also gets called occasionally when the regular delivery person is off or when the florist has several weddings to do in one day. She enjoys earning extra money without being tied down to a regular job.

Once every year the phone company starts looking for scores of people to deliver **new telephone directories**, in both urban and rural areas. This would be good for the person who only wants to work occasionally. The work may require much lifting and carrying, so if you're considering this opportunity, be sure you are strong enough to handle the books with little effort.

There are advertising companies that deliver **grocery and department store ads** in plastic bags to homes once or twice a week. They have walking routes in the city and driving routes in the rural areas. Contact one of these companies to deliver ads by car in a rural or suburban area. You could net between $30 and $50 a week for delivering 450 advertisements on a driving route.

Call on pharmacies in your community and offer to deliver **prescriptions** for them. Pharmacies often provide a delivery service as a convenience to their customers. The service is especially helpful for elderly and disabled customers and those needing prescriptions on holidays or late at night.

Operating a **courier service** for businesses in your community can be quite profitable. Advertise to deliver rush items such as contracts, bids, supplies, and blueprints. Advertise to deliver anything, anywhere, any time. Potential sources of employment include doctors, hospitals, banks, insurance companies, architects, home builders, professionals' buildings, real estate salespeople, and lawyers.

Begin a **mail and parcel delivery service**, either on a regular or on-call basis. Some businesses can't afford to wait for regular mail service and would hire someone to pick up and deliver mail promptly as needed. You can advertise to pick up and deliver mail and packages to and from the post office, airport, bus station, or railroad terminal.

Advertise to **deliver books, candy, champagne,** and other treats to persons at airports, on boats, at railroad stations, or at college. A small, thoughtful gift means so much, and many people would give surprise presents if your service could deliver them.

Other Modes of Transportation

Remember that women are only limited by their imaginations—cars aren't the only way to go. Horses and buggies may transport sightseers and residents around the downtowns of some big cities---but what can you offer in suburbia or a rural area? There are other ways to travel. For instance, **boating** enthusiasts can have fun and get paid for it by taking groups of people out for fishing, partying, and picnicking. Place notices on bulletin boards at marinas, bait stores, beaches, and other places where interested people might look. Vacationers in the area and people who don't own boats may call you for a carefree day.

Flying is another popular form of travel, because it's fun and it gets you there fast. If you are one of the growing number of women who fly, you can transport people or cargo throughout your area or across the country by plane. Owning your own plane is not necessary because you can fly a leased airplane. A single-engine two-seater rents for about $29 an hour during the week and $30 an hour on weekends. You might carry pipe for gas companies, truck parts for trucking companies, newspapers for readers who want the *Times* in northern Minnesota, Maine lobsters for Kansas restaurants, or fishermen to remote fishing sites. Advertise this service at airports, and send your business card to companies that might want to transport their products by air.

Back on the ground, what about **trucks**? Tootie C. of Michigan stayed home for years while her husband, Ralph, an independent truck driver, traveled thousands of miles hauling cargo cross-country. After their children were grown, Tootie began to travel with Ralph and decided she liked it. She learned to drive the huge eighteen-wheelers, and they took turns at the wheel. When Ralph retired, the thought of leaving the road was unappealing to both of them. They started hauling Michigan's black cherries south, delivering them to several states. They would pick up a load of watermelons in South Carolina and head north, delivering melons along the way. Before long, they were hauling peaches and peanuts north from Georgia, and Michigan apples south. Tootin' Tootie, as she is known to her citizens band buddies, loves the traveling life with her husband. They've made friends while enjoying an interesting and profitable retirement.

Against the high price of gasoline your best defense could be a **motorcycle**. Consider delivering prescriptions for drugstores and small packages for area businesses. If you don't want to buy gasoline at all, how about a **bicycle** transport service? Especially if you live in a small, easy-to-get-around-in town, you could earn extra cash pedaling messages, lightweight merchandise, and odds and ends from one end of town to the other. You'd be getting both money and exercise for your work.

People are on the go. They, their pets and possessions need to get from here to there. If you get your wheels on track, you may be able to transport them and earn extra cash en route.

Suggested Reading

Davis, Geraldine H. *The Moving Experience: A Simple System for Organized Moving.* Virginia Beach, Virginia: Donning Co., 1980.

Eaken, Billy J. *How to Grow Rich Helping the Elderly and Handicapped.* Oakland, California: Bridgeport Publications, 1978.

Henke, Thomas R. *Managing Your Private Trucking Operation.* Washington: Traffic Service Corp., 1978.

Paulden, S. *How to Deliver on Time.* Brookfield, Vermont: (Pub'd by Gower Publishing, England), Renouf USA, Inc., 1977.

Reingold, Carmel Berman. *A Woman's Guide to the Care and Feeding of an Automobile.* New York: Stein & Day, 1974.

Sikorsky, Robert. *How to Get More Miles per Gallon.* New York: St. Martin's Press, 1978.

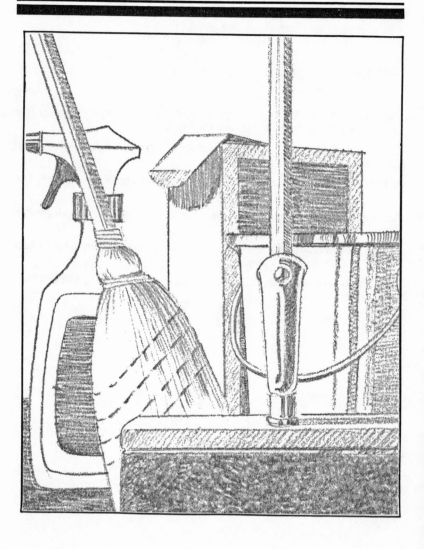

The Clean Machine

The Clean Machine

10

(Residential, commercial and specialized cleaning jobs)

A good cleaning person is always hard to find. Ask anyone who's hired help for cleaning purposes, and you will hear a lot of complaints—everything from housekeepers who don't show up for work to wall washers who harbor a fear of electrical outlets. One woman told us that she once had a housekeeper who was allergic to dust. If you've always prided yourself on keeping a clean home, and you get an adrenaline surge at the sight of a messy basement or dirt-streaked windows, you're probably a good cleaner. If you aren't afraid of hard work and can appreciate the satisfaction that comes from turning someone's scuffed and muddy floor into a spotless expanse of gleaming parquet, you may be a top-notch candidate for running a cleaning service.

Remember those little sayings we've all heard over the years about cleaning: Cleanliness is next to godliness; a clean home is a happy home; clean me, I'm yours. Regardless of how silly they may sound, the fact remains that sooner or later everything that exists must (or at least should) be cleaned. Thus the list of cleaning jobs is virtually endless and includes everything from cleaning velvet wallpaper in mansions to scrubbing soap-splattered walls in service station rest rooms.

One of the most ingenious ideas in our book came from Libby T. of Florida. A wife and mother of three small children, she explained to us that the price of a good child-care center stopped her from seeking outside employment. She decided to start an unusual cleaning service called **Drop It Off At My House**. Her newspaper ads say that she will clean anything that can be dropped off and picked up by the customer. She cleans cars, boats, campers, small appliances, typewriters, some furniture, and rugs. She scours copper pans, washes lawn mowers, cleans handbags, and has even cleaned a saddle with silver trim. A lot of her customers are working women who just don't have time for all those less-than-crucial but important cleaning jobs (one customer has a huge collection of leather-bound books to be cleaned and oiled twice a year). Often people need something cleaned at the last minute, such as tarnished silver. Libby manages to fit most drop-offs into her tight schedule.

There are three principal kinds of cleaning jobs available: general residential, specialized, and commercial. In the next few pages we will provide you with cleaning ideas in each of these three areas.

We've talked to a lot of women who do cleaning either part or full time, in commercial or residential establishments. They all seem perfect for the job: organized, neat, dependable, and intelligent. And they enjoy their work and their independence, as well as the added income. It takes a very "together" woman to fit a cleaning service into all of the daily activities she is faced with. But the cleaning businesswomen we talked to have definitely got what it takes.

All of them stressed the importance of using good, reliable supplies and tools, even if it means paying more for them. From stepladders and vacuum cleaners to window washing fluid and floor wax, the proper materials will give you better results and will help the work go faster.

Hanna J. is a longtime carpet cleaner from Indiana. When she first got started in the business, she tried to make her own "cost-cutting" cleaning solution from vinegar and what she thought was color-safe dry bleach. Her customer was left with a faded, vinegar-soaked carpet. It cost Hanna much more to replace the carpet than it would have to buy a good commercial cleaning product.

Good equipment and supplies also give your customers confidence in your ability to do the job right. Equipping yourself with the basics will cost you in the neighborhood of $200 to $250. If you buy your supplies in larger quantities from janitorial supply houses, you can often get a discount.

We came across many clever ideas in our contacts with women who earn extra cash with mop or sponge in hand. We've included some of them below. You may find a profitable notion that appeals to you, or your own inventiveness may lead you to a novel thought that has completely slipped by us. There *is* a place for you in the cleaning business if you're interested. The following suggestions may help you find it.

General Residential Cleaning

Many people call on the services of a cleaning pro, either occasionally or on a regular basis. Whether those services are needed every day or once a week, good residential cleaners are always in demand.

General cleaning involves such everyday tasks as dusting, sweeping, making beds, and washing dishes. Although it can be laborious, it can also be very profitable, because the few tools and supplies it requires are inexpensive. The basics—including a sweeper, mops, brooms, cleaning cloths, and various cleaning compounds—are often supplied by the customer, but some cleaning experts prefer to furnish their own supplies, because they enjoy using products whose performance they trust. The average rate for general cleaning help is $4.50 an hour, but rates vary, depending on the locale.

Almost everyone is a potential customer—male or female, married, single, widowed, or divorced. Some of the best customer prospects these days are working women, especially mothers. It's difficult to manage a home and family while holding down an outside job. Still reponsible for their families' laundry, cleaning, and cooking, most working mothers are more than happy to hire someone to relieve them of a few duties. Some elderly people no longer have the oomph necessary for vacuuming and other heavy cleaning. They could probably use some domestic help.

Watch your local papers, bulletin boards, or community news flyers for ads placed by people who need cleaning help, or place your own ad in one of these publications. Then wait for the phone to ring. It won't be long before you have as much work as you can handle.

Marge P. and Linda C. are two housewives from New York who teamed up and started **The Spring Cleaners**. They offer top-to-bottom residential cleaning. For each job, they give an estimate of the price and the amount of time the job will take. They make out a contract listing exactly what the customer wants cleaned. Their cleaning jobs usually include windows, walls, ceilings, floors, woodwork, cabinets, carpets, and upholstered furniture. They clean and polish light fixtures (even the very ornate ones) and make even the dirtiest appliances spick and span. The Spring Cleaners provide their own cleaning tools and supplies. Their work is excellent and speedy, and their schedule is always filled.

Lisa and Marcie G. are two teenage sisters from North Carolina. They earn extra money by doing **housecleaning** for working women in the area. High school is so demanding that during the school months they can work only on weekends, but their summer schedule is always jam-packed with customers. The girls do walls, windows, floors, carpets—even garages and basements. They are saving most of their earnings for college.

Specialized Cleaning

If you don't want to take on the engrossing task of whole-house cleaning, maybe you should limit your services to something specific. Word of "the best-scrubbed floors in town" travels fast. And if you can put the sparkle back into streaked picture windows, you could be in for lots of busy Saturdays.

Evelyn P. of Arizona is a middle-aged widow with a teenage son. She had been a secretary before she married, but after her husband's death a job with an adequate salary didn't seem to exist for a woman with her qualifications. She advertised that she would **clean and organize basements, garages, and attics.** At first the work just dribbled in, but when spring arrived, she was swamped with cleaning jobs—and has been ever since. Before tackling each assignment, she looks over the area to be cleaned and discusses with the customer the best method of moving, stacking, piling, or arranging the items. Her system is to sort out and clean the items and store them in labeled boxes. When she finishes any job, it's more organized than most offices. Of course, the amount she charges depends on the size and difficulty of the job. She usually bids a job by estimating the number of hours it will take and multiplying that by $5.

We heard about and met residential cleaners who specialized in almost everything. You can choose *your* specialty from any number of cleaning jobs around the home. Many are strenuous and difficult, but those jobs are the easiest to get, because many people would love to hire them out. They also pay a higher price than most other cleaning jobs. Cleaning specialties include **windows, floors, carpeting, walls, basements, garages, appliances, kitchen cabinets, linen closets, and curtains.** You may charge your customer by the hour, or before you begin work, you and the customer may agree upon a price for the total job.

You could even offer a regular service: **laundry and ironing,** for example. This age-old chore is dreaded by people from every walk of life; not even the latest easy-care, permanent-press fabric can change the fact that clothes have to be laundered. On-the-go men and women who work away from the home might welcome a laundry and ironing service in your area. Senior citizens for whom laundry has become too much of a chore and college students who can't seem to find the time between classes, work, and dorm life are also potential customers. Consider offering a pick-up and delivery service;

you might be amazed at the response. Pricing will depend on what other laundry services charge and on what you feel is a fair price.

Windows—Some people hate to do windows and would welcome the chance to hire out this tiresome chore. You could agree to do each customer's windows periodically (usually twice a year), or to be available whenever the client wanted them washed. Spring and fall will be busy times, especially if you clean, put up, and take down storm windows and doors.

Floors—Cleaning floors takes a lot of time and hard work. People who are just too busy to do it themselves will hire you if you advertise your services. Let them know you will scrub the floors in their kitchens, bathrooms, basements, and garages. You could also agree to remove the old wax from linoleum and hardwood floors, clean them, and then rewax and buff them until they glow. Stripping old wax away and replacing it is one of the most strenuous cleaning jobs on the home front, and it is also one of the most profitable. Doing a twelve-by-fifteen-foot room could earn you $20-$25.

Wall Cleaning—Spring cleaning would be a lot easier to face if someone would wash the walls. Advertise to clean walls and you will get many responses, especially in the spring and around the holidays when people want to freshen up the house. This is another highly physical cleaning job. If you have the stamina and agility for stooping, bending and reaching, consider washing walls for some income. You could earn $30-$35 for washing the walls in a large country kitchen. You might also advertise to wash aluminum and vinyl siding, especially after the spring thaw.

Carpet Shampooing—A good electric rug-shampoo machine is a must for this job. If you don't own a good one, you may want to rent or buy one of the new steam cleaners on the market. Steam cleaner prices range between $200 and $500. Small steam cleaning units can be rented for $12 to $15 a day. Make sure you go equipped with a good-quality shampoo and an effective spot and stain remover. This really isn't a seasonal job, as people clean carpets year round and you could earn 8¢-12¢ a square foot doing it for them. You can also offer to clean your customers' upholstered furniture with the upholstery cleaning attachment most steam cleaners have.

Specialized cleaning doesn't have to mean just houses. Depending on the economy and the lifestyles in your area, you might find yourself cleaning motor homes or mansions.

Kathy A. and Liza W. of Florida are two young college students who have been around boats and yachts all their lives, so it just seemed natural that they should earn their spending money working on them. These ingenious girls operate a **yacht-cleaning service.** Their business cards are on display at every local marina. When a docked yacht needs cleaning, Kathy and Liza are called by the marina owner. They clean the inside and sometimes put on their bikinis and go overboard to do some outside work like scrubbing the hull. They also clean and wax teakwood decks and handrailings and polish all the brass. On a busy day Kathy and Liza earn $100 each.

Kitty J. and Jackie W. of Ohio are young homemakers who add to their faimiles' incomes in a rather unique way. Since these ambitious women live near a large municipal airport, they decided to **wash and wax airplanes.** Kitty and Jackie contacted the airport's base operator and all of the local flight schools in the area. (A clean, shiny plane looks very inviting to a would-be flying student.) When a plane needs cleaning, Kitty and Jackie are called. They earn $25 for a two-place, single-engine plane. They charge between $100 and $150 to do a wax job. They are a dependable team who knew how to turn where they lived into a moneymaking advantage.

Commercial Cleaning

The commercial cleaning jobs available are too numerous to mention them all. We have listed some of them, though, just to show you the possibilities. We're sure you can add to the list, using your imagination and taking into account your skills, your inclinations, the equipment you have available, and the community you call home. Commercial vacuum cleaners, floor buffers, and a stock of general cleaning supplies and equipment for handling rugs, walls, and industrial machines are investments you'll have to consider if you're thinking of entering the commercial cleaning realm.

For many women one great advantage of commercial cleaning is the choice of hours. Offices are usually cleaned at night; entertainment establishments are often done during daytime hours. Edith L. of Virginia cleans **cocktail lounges.** She can work during the day and be home with her family in the evenings. If you take classes in the daytime, you may prefer to work nights. For couples who share a car or child-care responsibilities, opposite working hours can be a blessing. It should be easy to find a commercial cleaning job to fit *your* available hours.

Carla B. and Annie T. of Kentucky, both college students, earn their much-needed extra cash by working two nights a week. Their customers are two **automobile dealers,** and their job is to clean the huge showroom and the offices, lounge, and rest rooms at the dealership. It involves sweeping, emptying wastebaskets and ashtrays, scrubbing rest rooms, replenishing rest room supplies, and any other cleaning—such as washing windows, cleaning phones, venetian blinds—that needs to be done.

If nothing in the following list of commercial cleaning ideas interests you, then check through the Yellow Pages of your telephone book for other businesses. For commercial cleaning jobs, you should either apply in person or call the personnel manager of the business you'd like to clean. Is the business in need of a cleaning person at the present time? If not, ask if the personnel manager would please keep you in mind for any future cleaning positions that need to be filled. Every phone call should be followed up with one of your business cards and a list of references. If you apply in person, always leave your calling card. Commercial janitorial work often pays 5 to 8 cents per square foot. But check with other janitorial services before you determine your rates. You want to be competitive, fair—and a little bit richer.

Some of the best places to offer your commercial cleaning services are:

apartment complexes	mobile home dealers
art galleries and museums	office buildings
banks	professional buildings (doctors, dentists, lawyers, etc.)
beauty salons	
building contractors (for new homes)	
car and boat showrooms	realtors (for used homes)
funeral homes	recreational vehicle dealers
government buildings	restaurants
health spas	schools and libraries
hospitals and nursing homes	service stations (rest rooms, lobbies)
libraries	stores
	theaters

Jane K. of Idaho is a young schoolteacher who supplements her income by working three nights a week dusting and sweeping a **retail furniture store.** The store supplies her with the cleaning tools and other necessary equipment. She enjoys the work and the extra cash, and she gets a 10 percent discount on any item she purchases from the store.

Shirley K. and Barb T. are sisters from Pennsylvania who work for local **home builders.** Their job is to completely clean each new house that's built. The work is done in two phases. First they "rough-clean" the house, which means removing any paint or stain from windows, hardwood floors, doors, and cabinets and scraping basement walls and garage floors for cement and paint droppings. The second phase is to clean and shine the entire house except the freshly painted walls. When the women finish with a house, it is ready for the buyer to move into. This is one of the highest paying cleaning jobs available. Doing an average four-bedroom, two-story home pays around $200 and can easily be finished in three days.

No matter which area you choose or how much time you have to invest, you can clean up in the cleaning business.

Suggested Reading

Aslett, Don. *Is There Life after Housework?* Cincinnati: Writer's Digest Books, 1981.

The Book of Household Hints. Des Moines: Wallace/Homestead, 1980.

Consumer Guide editors. *The Fastest, Cheapest Best Way to Clean Everything.* New York: Simon & Schuster, 1980.

Grunfeld, Nina, and Michael Thomas. *Spot Check: How to Cope with Household Stains.* Los Angeles: Price/Stern/Sloan, 1981.

Heloise. *Hints from Heloise.* New York: Avon Books, 1981.

Johnson, Mary P. *Everything You Need to Know to Start a House Cleaning Service.* Seattle: Cleaning Consultants, 1979.

Moore, Alma. *How to Clean Everything.* New York: Simon & Schuster, 1978.

Wylie, Harriet. *420 Ways to Clean Everything.* New York: Harmony Books, 1979.

Young, Charmaine. *I'm Going to Clean Homes and Businesses.* Minneapolis: Burgess, 1977.

Color It Green

11

(Putting your green thumb to work)

If you have the knack of making plants grow, you've probably been told you have a green thumb. Of course, it's not really green—and not always clean, either, because you're known for digging in soil, trimming bushes, and pushing a lawn mower. A woman with a green thumb feels challenged by a droopy philodendron and is ambitious enough to figure out how to liven it up. She enjoys planning her garden months before the ground thaws. She's willing to work intensively at critical times: covering a half acre of pepper plants when a frost threatens in early June or saving dishwater to moisten parched cucumber plants in August. She takes great pride in her skills and the results of her labor. Sounds like you? Then get ready to think about how you can cash in on your expertise. Other people—those who've managed to kill a cactus plant or drown an air fern—rely on the green thumbs of the world to keep their lawns healthy, their vegetable bins brimming, and their vases full.

Many greenery hobbyists are knowledgeable about plant species and able to recognize diseases and pests that afflict their plants, lawns, and trees. They know when and how to effectively use insecticides, fungicides, and other treatments. They're often skillful with pruning shears and able to cut a straight line with a hand sprayer. Those less inclined to earthly pursuits are often willing to pay for jobs you *enjoy* doing.

Besides extra cash, you may find other benefits in working with greenery. Tending to the chlorophyll world is healthful, both physically and mentally. Outdoor gardeners find the sun, exercise, and fresh air invigorating. Time spent cutting lawns or cultivating flowers is time for communing with nature, getting in touch with your thoughts, and, for some people, relaxing. Indoor gardening offers some of the same peace and satisfaction without exposure to the elements.

Connie L. is a fortyish homemaker from Illinois with three grown children. When her kids were teenagers, they always took turns mowing the family's acre lot with a lawn tractor. After they left home, her work load eased, and she began to add inches and pounds to her body. One day she pulled the old rotary push mower from the garage and began mowing the yard. By the time she finished, working a few hours a day, it was nearly time to start over again. She kept this up all summer and succeeded in taking off the excess pounds, improving her muscle tone and getting a beautiful tan. Besides feeling better about her appearance, she takes pride in her manicured lawn.

We've divided this chapter into four moneymaking categories—produce sales, yard care, plant sales and care, and plant-related services—and discussed the requirements, rewards, and risks of each. There are, however, certain considerations in any plant-related business. You should be aware of these before you borrow even a hundred dollars to get started. You can't be overprepared.

Anticipate risks. Weather is unpredictable, but it's a serious concern in lawn and garden care, while temperature and humidity control is vital for indoor plants. (What happens when the light in your hotbed goes out in an electrical storm while you're on vacation?) You might encounter mechanical failures (your tractor, mower, or Rototiller breaking down), which could ruin your schedule for a week or more. Having backup equipment, or some place to rent it while yours is being repaired, is essential; customers don't want explanations in place of prompt, efficient service. Dealing with people is both a hazard and a reward of the business. There are those you will be unable to please, no matter how well you do the job. Others will be so appreciative of your work that you'll wish you could do more for them.

Another general consideration of going into any of these garden or plant care businesses is the cost of equipment and supplies. Some customers may provide the essentials, but others expect you to have your own. Inexpensive tools will do for most indoor plant care, but garden and lawn care might require an eighteen-horse tractor with mowing blade, tiller, and plow, which could cost you $3,000 or more. Top-quality tools are a must if you work on a regular basis. Cheaper tools won't hold up. They'll cost you more in the long run and will strain your patience as well.

Recognize your limitations. Taking on too much work or promising more than you can deliver is never good business. Your customer will be perturbed by your day-late mowing job, and you'll be exhausted if you try to book as many jobs as daylight allows. If you have a lower back problem, forget gardening and yard work. But if you're healthy and you're confident in your knowledge and skill, forge ahead. Know your strengths. You wouldn't promise a customer to grow Oriental vegetables such as Dai Gai Choi (Chinese mustard) and Choy Sum (flowering white cabbage) in a solar greenhouse if you had no experience in greenhouse growing. But you could probably make a profit with a vegetable stand if your garden has always yielded a bumper crop.

If you know nothing and want to learn enough to raise begonias to sell, or if you know a little and want to learn more about growing seasons or crabgrass, think about taking some classes. Keeping plants healthy, lawns green, and gardens thriving demands more than getting out the old watering can, mower, and lime spray. Opportunities to hone gardening skills and pick up lawn care tips are available through community college classes, community education programs, and co-op extension services. Working with a professional gardener or landscaper is also a good idea, especially if no classes are available in your area. Whatever interests you, there's a class or an expert somewhere to show you the ropes. We know two women who prepared for their plant businesses by different means. Although their first steps were not alike, they both ended up making money doing things they enjoyed.

Alice C. of Indiana took an evening horticulture class at the local university after years of failure with houseplants. It didn't take her long to learn that the Boston fern hanging in her west window was dying because of too much direct sunlight, and that she was killing her peperomia by overwatering it. After completing her classes, buying plant care books, and experimenting on her own, Alice went into the plant care business, tending plants for absent home owners and for small businesses that had plants in their offices.

Sally L. of Ohio went to work part-time at the local nursery to earn Christmas money. Even though she worked mostly selling craft items and decorations, she observed the special care the owner gave to the houseplants. When business was slow, she followed him around, asking questions about how to care for different plants. By the time Christmas arrived, Sally had learned a lot about basic plant care and especially about bromeliads, her favorite species. This foundation encouraged her to learn about outside plantings, and the next summer she planted annual and perennial strawflowers for drying. When she saw the beautiful centerpieces she was able to make with her everlastings, she started giving them as gifts and selling them at flea markets.

Even when you have the know-how, the equipment, and the time your plant business needs, don't expect it to go without a hitch. Your profits will depend on many things. Are people as interested in your work or service as they seemed to be in your survey responses? How are your competitors doing and what are they charging? Are your prices fair and in line with theirs? Is your energy for drumming up customers continuing? Are you willing to stick with the business? Are you building a reputation? Is your ad campaign reaching the right people?

There will be disappointments and setbacks (the customer who rented your Rototiller and burned up the motor by running it without oil; the week's schedule of yard work washed away with a week's worth of rain); but with some foresight, you can prevent the pitfalls from destroying your operation. Maybe your knees will hold up and your arches won't fall, and with a little awareness of how best to react, you'll be prepared to handle any problems that crop up.

Produce Sales

You can save money by canning and freezing home-grown fruits and vegetables. There's nothing like the taste of tomatoes and green beans grown in the heat of summer and savored on a cold January day—unless it's a handful of succulent cherries fresh off the tree or a freshly cooked serving of sweet peas. Although you may spend hours sweating and getting sore muscles, there's a feeling of satisfaction when you harvest those cucumbers for pickling or that sweet corn that melts in your mouth. Your produce might satisfy the appetites of people who enjoy the fruits of gardening but don't have the time, space, ability, or desire to wield a hoe or pruning shears.

Vegetable Gardening. Gardening is seasonal work that allows you to enjoy the great outdoors. Your profits include food for your own family, plus the cash you take in from sales of your crop.

You may live in the city and have only a twenty-by-thirty-foot backyard garden, or you might be a country dweller and have all the space you need. If you know how to make the best use of whatever space you have and if you're ready for the hard work involved in cultivating a garden, you can be an entrepreneurial gardener. Your profits will depend on many things, from the weather (over which you have no control) to the size of your plot and the amount of time you intend to spend with it (both of which you control).

To be a successful gardener, you must like working with the

soil, including giving it the preparation and treatment it needs to support a good vegetable garden. Samples of your soil can be sent to your county extension agent to be tested. He or she can tell you what nutrients you need to add for maximum productivity. Oftentimes, proper application of peat moss, well-rotted cow manure, gypsum, lime, and commercial fertilizer will insure a profitable garden. Then if you plan and organize your plantings, and spend a few hours a week hoeing to keep down weeds and loosen the soil, your plants should thrive. Of course, weather and insects are always risks. And you may have to learn how to deal with extreme temperatures or drought. If you find hornworms attacking your tomatoes, squash bugs infesting your zucchini, or beetles devouring your cucumbers, check with your county extension agent or a neighborhood garden center for the proper treatment or insecticide to use.

Basic Tools

Basic tools for raising a vegetable garden—a Rototiller, a hoe, a rake, a shovel, a hose, a sprayer or duster, and a few small hand tools—can be purchased for a total of $650-$1,000. If you plan on being a small-scale gardener, some of the tools can be rented for a reasonable daily or hourly rate. However, picking up and returning these tools can be a chore unless you live next door to the supplier. If you've ever tried lifting a Rototiller into the trunk of a car, you know it's generally a two-person job.

The vegetables most often asked for are tomatoes, sweet corn, green beans, onions, lettuce, green peppers, cucumbers, and some squashes. Knowing which ones you can best accommodate is important. Cucumber and squash plants require more space than any of the others because of their spreading vines. However, you can save space with any vine by giving it something to climb on (a stake, or wire cage, for example). Plant breeders have even developed squash, pumpkins, and cucumbers in bush form to take up less space.

Sweet corn needs a lot more space than many other vegetables. Several rows are needed to allow proper pollination. We recommend this crop only to people who have unlimited space.

Tomatoes and beans require less space, and they, along with cucumbers and summer squash, are high-yield vegetables. A single tomato vine grown on a wire cage can yield sixty pounds. (Think of that multiplied by a dozen plants!) A twenty-five-foot row of bush beans planted three to four inches apart will give you a yield of twenty to thirty-five pounds.

How to Sell Vegetables. If your garden produces a hearty surplus, you've got to know how to cash in on the windfall crop. The most common method of selling vegetables is to set up some type of temporary stand or booth. It can be a small picnic or card table piled with baskets or boxes of produce and covered with a canopy to minimize sun damage. You should have bags, baskets, and boxes for people to carry their produce home in; you should use an accurate scale for weighing; and you should have your prices clearly marked.

The appearance of any kind of business has an effect on how many customers will stop; a neat, attractive arrangement is always a good policy. Check the displays at farmers' markets in the area. How can you make yours more appealing? Don't forget the power of the newspaper to advertise your produce. In addition, post clear, attractive signs en route to your roadside stand or your yard display, giving price information and concise, accurate directions. You might also make use of local "swap and sell" radio programs to plug your business.

Before you advertise your produce to the public, be sure you have enough merchandise on hand to satisfy your customers. They probably won't return if you're always out of what they want. Don't promise "a truckload of cabbages" unless that's what you have. Be sure your prices are competitive; don't charge more for cucumbers than other independents unless you offer better service, bigger cukes, or free samples.

How about turning your home-grown produce into homemade products? You can sell them, or you can hand out small samples of them to stimulate produce sales. Pickles, vegetable breads, tomato sauce and other canned goods might sell well. Display a few freezer products, such as green beans, lima beans, or corn, keeping the actual frozen foods properly stored in your home or in a generator-run freezer under the canopy of your stand.

Sue L. lives on a farm and grows many vegetables including several varieties of squash (butternut, acorn, crook neck, zucchini, etc.). Squashes are her favorites because they're so easy to grow and pretty. When the squash are ready for harvest, she puts a "Squash for Sale" sign out front and sets up a salesroom in her garage. Each week she honors a different squash by using it in a tasty dish or baked goodie, and she treats her customers to samples. Some of the dishes she has prepared are squash and apple bake, nutty baked squash, and gourmet golden squash—a delicious dish using Hubbard squash, butter, sour cream, and chopped onion. From the beginning, customers loved the samples and began asking for recipes. Capitalizing on these requests, she compiled a squash cookbook one winter and sold it for $3 a copy the following summer.

Other places to consider selling your produce include campgrounds and mobile home parks. Get permission from campground directors and mobile home managers before you pack up your station wagon or truck, as many of them do not allow vendors on their property. When you get the go-ahead, display a sign on your vehicle-turned-produce-mart. Drive slowly through the grounds or park near the entrance, being alert for small children and darting dogs. Campers, especially those who are away from their own gardens back home, may welcome the opportunity to purchase tomatoes, cucumbers, corn, and other fresh vegetables.

Don't overlook the possibility of a "pick your own" operation. The two women whose case histories follow found ways to turn over some of their work to their customers. For more about the advantages and disadvantages of this kind of business, see the section on "How to Sell Fruit," later in this chapter.

Peggy's Pumpkin Patch in Ohio is a five-acre field of large-leafed vines and tall corn stalks. Peggy's husband, Jim, is a farmer, and he plows and disks the field and helps her plant and cultivate it. Besides pumpkins of every size and shape, they plant a variety of gourds and a huge patch of ornamental Indian corn. In autumn, newspaper ads bring people from all over who pick their own pumpkins and select gourds displayed on tables set up right in the field. Peggy has different-sized shelves, each labeled with a different price; if the pumpkin can fit on a particular shelf, the customer pays the price marked on that shelf. Her pumpkins, gourds, and Indian corn are also sold to local florists and arts and crafts shops for use in making centerpieces and decorations. The dried corn husks and silks are transformed into corn shuck dolls and flowers by the local seniors' group. Peggy's pumpkin patch profits help pay for the vacations she and Jim take every winter, when the farm work is slow.

Mary C. of Indiana makes several hundred dollars each summer with her sweet-corn enterprise. Her husband plows and plants a one-acre plot of ground for her, and she keeps the weeds down. Sixty to seventy days after planting, Mary puts a "for sale" sign at the edge of the field near her driveway, next to a locked tin box with a slot for money. She uses the honor system, and her customers pick their own corn, depositing $1.25 in the box for each dozen. Steady customers come by as early as July 1, asking when the sweet corn will be ready.

Sometimes the best way to sell your produce is in response to a specific need. Ruth V., a gardener and home canner herself, told us about the difficulty she had locating large, affordable quantities of vegetables, especially pickling-size cucumbers. When she could *find* the vegetables, they were so expensive that it wasn't economical to can them. Then she moved to a five-acre minifarm, and she decided to cater to people in her previous predicament. That spring Ruth and her husband plowed three acres and planted tomatoes, green beans, cucumbers, cabbage, and green peppers. They and their three teenagers worked in the garden regularly—hoeing, watering, pulling weeds, and spraying for bugs—and their vegetables flourished. Near harvest time, Ruth put an ad in the local newspaper, stating that she would have vegetables available for canning. Customers phoned in bulk orders, like two bushels of green beans or four bushels of tomatoes; Ruth would call them back when their orders were ready for pickup. Her teenagers set up a stand in front of the house to sell smaller quantities. The first year Ruth cleared $700, and her childred made $315 at the vegetable stand. She now has a flock of regular customers, many with standing orders for her vegetables every year.

Indoor Gardening. If you have a greenhouse, or decide to build one (see page 164), you can grow your own food year round. You can even raise exotic vegetables that would never survive in your yard. If your crop is large or much in demand, you'll be able to sell a lot of what you grow—and earn enough to pay for the greenhouse.

Vonda L. of Pennsylvania has always enjoyed greenery. Her husband, Bill, liked to grow flowers and kept their yard blooming with color all the time. When Vonda said she'd like a greenhouse, Bill didn't need much persuasion; it wasn't long before they had a twelve-by-fifteen-foot greenhouse adjoining their kitchen. Bill started growing orchids and joined the local orchid society, but Vonda's interest lay in unusual vegetable plants, because she loved to experiment, and she was bored with serving run-of-the-mill vegetables like beans and peas. She planted Chinese cabbage, leeks, Swiss chard, and the delicate, sweet Spanish and Bermuda onions that are so tedious to work with. She constructed shelves along the three outside walls of the greenhouse to save space for Bill's orchids, and she planted the tiny seeds. Once they started to grow, she spread the word about her extraordinary plants and began getting phone calls about her crop. She hadn't anticipated the great demand for her unusual offerings. Many people were disappointed when she ran out of vegetables, but she told them she would grow more the next year. Vonda only made $85, but she had the satisfaction of being able to serve and eat a variety of unusual vegetables.

We met Jane R., a woman from Ohio whose business is called

the Salad Bowl. She has a large greenhouse in her backyard where she raises salad vegetables year round, using a wood stove for supplemental heat during the cold weather. Among the things she grows are Buttercrunch and Tom Thumb lettuce, burpless cucumbers, leeks, potted chives, radishes, and peppers. To advertise her venture, she places a sign on her front door, runs a classified ad in the newspaper, and posts seasonal notices on the supermarket bulletin board. Her business started slowly but improved after a reporter interviewed her for a human interest story in the local paper. Jane saves on expenses by using nonhybrid seed (which costs less), buying seed in bulk, mixing her own potting soil, and recycling plant containers. She sells not only to individuals, but also to a local health food restaurant noted for its salad bar.

Fruit. If you enjoy growing fruit as a hobby, think about growing it for profit. Of course, growing to sell requires added space, as well as plans for facing contingencies such as blight, bugs, foul weather, and lean years.

Though fruit and vegetable gardening is always a risky, exciting undertaking, you'll have an advantage if you consult books and seek out veteran growers for advice on planting, cultivating, and selling your surplus crop. Weather extremes can ruin your crop. Interview people who grow fruit for a living and get their tips on dealing with cold weather, droughts, excessive rain, and other weather hazards. Fruit trees can become infested with aphids, slugs, scale insects, and diseases. Proper spraying and dusting are important to control this. It's also a good idea to keep areas where fruit is grown free of weeds, trash, litter, fallen fruit, and leaves—all of which draw insects such as wasps and bees.

Growing high output fruit trees requires pruning skills. Pruning controls the shape of the tree and secures the desired number of branches to regulate the amount of light that enters the center of the tree. It encourages bud development for fruit production and leaf growth. No matter how well you care for fruit trees, you must recognize that they seem to run in cycles of lean and productive years, and you have no control over this.

Some fruit grows on bushes, ground plants, or vines. Strawberries, for example, are a popular fruit that demands space and appropriate climate conditions. Since they are the "most wanted" fruit, you won't have any trouble selling them. Other types of berries in demand are blackberries, raspberries, and blueberries which grow on small bushes. Grapes, which grow on vines that can be trained to climb in arbors or on fences or posts, are also popular, for snacking, for wine making, and preserving. If you have a lot of space for ground plants, loose, well-drained soil, and a long growing season, you might try growing melons for sale.

Mary L. of Michigan loved strawberries and decided to grow them for herself. Farmers in the area never seemed to have enough, so she knew she had a ready market for any berries she didn't use herself. With the help of a book and a wise neighboring fruit grower, she planted six hundred plants (Sparkle, Fairfax, and Catskill), using the spaced, matted-row system illustrated in the book. She worked hard keeping most of the runners pruned to yield high-quality berries. She hoed twice a week, and once the plants were growing well, she mulched the patch with strawy horse manure. Mary and her husband spent the summer traveling through Canada, and the strawberries seemed to survive being left alone. She mulched them again in December, using clean straw, to keep them from heaving out of the ground because of ground freezes and thaws. The plants had borne no fruit the first year; Mary was eager to see what would happen when spring came. Once the new growth started in the spring, she removed the mulch, and the berries flourished. During harvest season Mary was in her patch every morning picking fruit. When she had plenty of berries for her own pies, shortcakes, and preserves, she placed the rest in the front yard on a picnic table to sell. She sold six hundred quarts of strawberries for $1 a quart, and could probably have sold four times that many if she'd had enough berries. Mary's husband will be retiring next year, and they plan to go into the strawberry business on a much larger scale.

You'll find that fruit is a perennial seller. There are more "natural food" eaters than ever before, and families buy fresh fruit not only because it's healthful, but also because it's delicious. So if you have fruit trees (apple, peach, pear, or plum), that have been sprayed, trimmed, and fertilized appropriately, don't hesitate to advertise your bounty.

How to Sell Fruit. If you have lots of fruit and don't mind people tramping about your property, how about setting up a "pick your own" system? Get tips from people who operate this kind of business. Plan for all the things that *could* happen (customers getting lost, falling from stepladders, or driving right up to the trees, leaving wheel ruts in your orchard). Don't forget to consult your insurance agent about increasing your liability insurance.

Letting customers pick their own fruit cuts down on labor costs for you. But be sure you have enough to satisfy all your customers. Provide sturdy ladders for them to use when picking, bags or baskets for carrying the fruit home, and ample space for parking, preferably in a paved or graveled lot. Insist that your customers pick a tree or vine clean before moving on to another. This practice makes picking easier for customers who come later. Insist that children behave and stay close to their parents. If you offer several varieties of a kind of fruit (apples, for example), post signs in the orchard indicating which varieties (Delicious, Winesap, McIntosh, Jonathan, etc.) are where.

What about selling fruit **products**, such as jams, jellies, and preserves? How about candy apples, apple cider, or dried fruits? Make fresh peach, cherry, or apple pies and sell them at your roadside stand. If you have surplus fruit but don't want to bother with a roadside stand or a "pick your own" setup, see if a local farmer's market (or someone with a booth at one) will sell it for you.

Yard Care

If you enjoy doing your own yard work and are experienced in planting, trimming, pruning, mowing, watering, fertilizing, spraying, and similar tasks, offer to give efficient, low-cost care to the trees, shrubs, flowers, and lawns of others. Being in good physical shape is important for this work, as it can be strenuous and as you no sooner get it done than it's time to do it again. Most people who hire you will expect you to show up every week or two, so being reliable is a must. Sometimes the weather will prevent you from doing work on schedule and will cause an overload for the next week. You may have to recruit extra hands to help you catch up.

The responsibilities of the job are many, but the joys of working closely with nature are attractive. As most of the work is seasonal, the sun, warm weather, and physical exercise are healthful and pleasing for outdoor lovers. This venture can be challenging, especially if you take over a yard that has been neglected for years and have to revive a nutrient-starved lawn or trim a shrub that hasn't been touched since it was planted. And what will you do if you're asked to save a birch tree about to be devoured by bagworms, or to grow plants uncommon in your area?

Since practical background and know-how are necessary, read books, take courses offered at local nurseries, and work with experienced people at tree farms or landscaping and lawn care companies until you feel qualified to work on your own. You'll learn that pruning doesn't mean whacking away with clippers. If you want branching, cut to a leaf node or, if the leaves have fallen, to a dormant bud. You'll learn when to prune, so you won't cut off next year's buds.

Spraying (for weeds, pests, and diseases) is another part of caring for trees, lawns, and ornamental plants. It can be used on entire lawns, along driveway borders, around trees, or for spot control of dandelions and similar weeds. From experience you may learn it's better to have one sprayer for herbicides, and another one for insecticides and fungicides, because even a slight residue of herbicide can injure sensitive trees and shrubs budding in spring. If one sprayer is used for all purposes, you'll know to rinse it thoroughly between uses. And you'll know to take care when spraying with weed killers, because the mist from high-pressure spraying can drift many feet on a windy day and can harm shrubs and kill flowers.

Start your business on a small scale, maybe by cutting lawns in your neighborhood. Call people who you know don't have the time, ability, or motivation to work in the yard. You might want to concentrate on cutting grass for home owners who are out of town on vacations. Burglars are often on the lookout for uncut lawns. And by regularly tending the yards of vacationing customers, you would actually be performing two services.

A good lawn mower and most of the other needed equipment, such as small digging tools, rakes, a hoe, a spade, pruning shears, a trimmer, and a sprayer, can be purchased for around $350. But if you have a yard of your own, you'll probably already have many of these. Big mowing jobs might require a riding mower, which would cost several hundred dollars. You would need a trailer or truck to take it from your home to the job locations.

Lois R. and Margaret C. are sisters living in the same housing development in Indiana. They're "yard freaks" who've learned through years of experience how to plant and maintain almost everything that grows. Three summers ago they went into the grass-cutting business in their neighborhood. In many households both husband and wife worked downtown, and they were pleased to have Lois and Margaret come by weekly and mow their lawns. Since both women had lawns of their own, the equipment was already in their garages, and no investment was needed. They work Monday through Friday, doing two yards a day, transporting mowers, clippers, hoses, lawn sweepers, rakes, brooms, trimmers, and electric cords in Margaret's station wagon. They charge $20 for each lawn they mow, including sweeping sidewalks and hosing off patios and driveways. They each make $100 a week, minus gasoline costs and equipment maintenance. Last summer they bought two new lawn mowers for their business.

Maintaining the grounds of commercial establishments might offer greater challenge and appeal. You need the same equipment whether you do residential or commercial work, but commercial establishments may be more insistent that you keep the lawn manicured at all times. A neighbor may be understanding about your sick child, broken equipment, your abscessed tooth, or the bad weather, but if a national insurance company president is coming to visit the local office and your mower is kaput, no amount of explanation will make up for the shaggy lawn. Many days you won't talk to a soul from the company or building that employs you. These customers just want the work done, and if you don't do it, they'll get someone who will. Be prepared with backup equipment, and have extra people on call to help you if you get behind because of rain or illness.

Retirement communities, mobile home parks, and any other multiple-dwelling developments would be good places to advertise your services. Condominiums are good potential customers. The managers will hire you and then charge each resident a monthly fee for the upkeep of the grounds.

Laura M. lives in a mobile home park in Georgia. Her elderly neighbors next door were unable to tend their yard, so Laura cut their small plot of grass every time she did her own. They insisted on paying her for the work, and it wasn't long before other neighbors asked Laura if she had time to mow their lawns. Besides mowing and trimming lawns, she plants and tends flowers for those unable to do so. She now has several regular customers and makes $22 every week for about six to eight hours work.

Contact real estate companies and building contractors with unsold homes or condominiums or vacant apartment buildings. To attract potential buyers or renters, they must keep the lawns cut and yards landscaped. You could do it for them. Land developers, too, need someone to maintain the acres of land they have bought for future development. Most cities and counties have ordinances that require the developers to mow these parcels at least twice each summer.

Dorothy B. of Arkansas is a widow with a teenage son and daughter. Spiraling inflation made Dorothy's income from her husband's estate no longer adequate for raising two children. When one of her neighbors, a home builder, mentioned that he was looking for someone to mow the lawns of his model homes, Dorothy agreed to do the job with her own lawn mower. When school let out for the summer, she bought a second mower, and her son and daughter began helping her. She now works for several builders, not only cutting lawns but also cleaning the new houses before they're put up for sale.

Other promising commercial customers for your lawn service include:

banks	professional buildings
churches	restaurants
funeral homes	schools
hospitals	shopping centers
nursing homes	

Indoor Plant Care and Sales
If you're one of those lucky women who have small greenhouses at home, have you ever thought of turning your plant or flower hobby

into a moneymaking business? As a greenhouse enthusiast, you've probably equipped your structure with wooden benches that have slotted bottoms to insure good drainage and raised sides to hold soil in place. You set many of your plants in pots on a bench. And you've also reserved some floor space (without benches) for growing tall plants that need headroom.

But what if you want to raise plants to sell, and you don't have a greenhouse? You can still make a go of it. Some gardening books and magazines give directions and illustrations for constructing hotbeds and coldframes from scrap lumber. The price of a greenhouse can vary from $300 to $3,000, depending on its capabilities, complexity, and size. If you are into building, polyethylene structures can be put up inexpensively. Some greenhouses are heated almost entirely by solar heat, with a supplemental heater for wintry days when the sun doesn't shine.

As an alternative to buying and constructing a greenhouse, many gardeners raise their plants under artificial lights. For under $30 you can erect a chain-hung fixture with a fluorescent grow light. Four to five flats of seedlings can be started under each light, at the distance necessary to produce optimal growing conditions.

As a green thumb, you've undoubtedly learned the proper soil mixture for your plants. A basic mixture for most plants might consist of equal parts of garden soil, German peat, and clean river sand. To work the soil, you use a few hand tools; to enrich it, you use fertilizers; to control diseases and pests, you use effective fungicides and insecticides. You probably use plastic or clay pots for your growing plants. (If you intend to sell your plants, you might want to invest in some decorative pots.)

If you plan to turn your hobby into extra cash, you might consider starting with hanging plants that spill down from baskets or trail and dangle from pots. Swedish ivy, wandering Jew, philodendron, and many ferns are popular. Cacti are also good sellers; many produce splendid flowers in the spring. In recent years, dish gardens and terrariums, which group plants with similar needs in one container, have become quite popular. You may want to visit other greenhouses to see their specialties and their bestselling plants. Your home greenhouse could offer varieties not grown by your competition. Start with your favorite plants, and grow a few new ones each season. After a while you'll discover which plants move and which don't.

Some plants, such as coleuses, geraniums, begonias, and the asparagus fern, you might want to start from seed. Others, like verbenas, fuchsias, and ivies, start well with cuttings taken with a sharp knife. This is the least expensive way of building up a collection of fine plants. Dividing clumps is still another way to start new plants. Varieties such as ornamental asparaguses and airplane plants develop clusters of crowns. A cluster can be broken into three or four pieces, each with stems and roots. You could use all three ways to increase your plant inventory.

Some people prefer attractive foliage plants, such as ivies, asparagus fern, airplane plant and wandering Jew. Other people would rather buy blooming plants like fuchsias, lantanas, and geraniums. You will have customers for all types, so grow both foliage and blooming plants in your indoor garden.

For best results buy your seeds from a reputable seed house. Some of these are W. Atlee Burpee Company, Park Seed Company, Stokes Seeds, and Buell's Greenhouses. When selling your plants in winter, protect them from the cold by wrapping them in tissue paper. With each plant purchased give the customer a card that has tips on keeping the plant healthy, and let customers know you're available to answer any questions regarding the plants they buy from you.

You probably recognize the advantages of working with plants indoors, as opposed to gardening or doing lawn work. It can be done anytime, day or night, in any kind of weather. Since you do most of the work in your own home, you can enjoy the side benefit of living as well as working in the tranquil atmosphere greenery provides. You should know the disadvantages, too. You'll probably have higher electricity, heating, and water bills than you had before you added the greenhouse. And when you plan to be away for more than a day, you'll have to get someone to come in for routine upkeep of the plants.

Place your hanging or potted plants in gift shops in your area, or put a sign outside and sell them directly from your home. Managers of gift shops will charge you a commission if they sell your plants, but you may be willing to pay this to avoid having strangers wandering through your home or bothering you at inconvenient times.

If you decide to sell the plants from your own home, you'll be saved the bother of transporting them to another place, as well as the risk of plant shock from a change in the environment. Your customer can come right into the greenhouse to pick out that gorgeous piggyback or jade plant. If you don't have a greenhouse or don't want customers in it, you should have a separate room in your home where you can keep the plants in controlled light, temperature, and humidity. A room full of different specimens will be a pretty picture, and your customer may go away with more than he or she originally intended to buy.

Donna J. of Maine loved to see flowers in bloom, but she had to contend with a short growing season. So that she could enjoy her flowers year round, she got a loan to build a greenhouse. Then she had to figure out how to pay off her debt. Since hanging baskets of flowers seemed to be big sellers in area flower shops, Donna decided to grow the plants herself and arrange them in attractive baskets for sale. She sells many of the traditional flower baskets, such as vining geraniums, begonias, and petunias, plus some unusual ones like herb baskets—spearmint, lavender, and sage—which are becoming big hits with her customers. She gives the customers tips on how to turn even the most shadowy nook in their home into a growing space. She gives them the benefit of years of trial and error.

Besides selling plants directly from your home or in a local shop, plant parties are another way for you to cash in on your green thumb. Start by having your friends host parties where you can display and sell your plants and give tips on their care. You can also advertise that you'll host plant parties for local community organizations and clubs. Exposure is important; people who see your plants and hear your instructions on their care are likely to come by later to look at your full selection.

Plant Rental and Maintenance. Most banks, offices and professional buildings have plants in their lobbies, hallways, and other public areas. If your greenhouse accommodates tall, full-bodied plants (figs and corn plants, for example), start a service in which you furnish the plants for such buildings and go back every few days to care for them. One of the most popular is the heart-leaf philodendron, which is very slow growing but will become enormous if given average care. Other popular plants are the Norfolk Island pine, which grows well in sun or bright indirect light, but will survive in dim light as well; palms, which have distinctive foliage and are very easy to care for; and, of course, the many hanging plants. If a building or office doesn't need any more plants, offer to provide regular, expert maintenance for the ones already there. Greenery is often used in model homes, condominiums, and apartments to make them more attractive to the prospective buyer or renter. Talk to contractors and apartment owners; offer to furnish and care for decorative plants until someone moves in.

Jeanne L. is a Missouri housewife and a self-taught plant expert. One day during a dental check-up, she was chiding her dentist on the sad state of the potted palms and hanging plants in his office, and he jokingly asked if she would like to care for them. Before she left his office, they reached an agreement, and in no time, Jeanne made the sick plants well again. On the basis of excellent references from her dentist, she got the job of caring for plants in other nearby professional buildings. She now has a steady income from work she enjoys. She gets paid according to how many plants there are in each building; last year she cleared $950.

Dried Arrangements. Indoor plants include a lot more than scheffleras and jades. Experimenting with dried flowers and herbs can be very exciting, and a treasure chest of new ideas awaits you when you grow them and discover the many ways they can be used.

Grow different varieties of strawflowers, everlastings, and grasses that can be dried for attractive flower arrangements and decorations. These floral deocrations withstand heat and the dry indoor atmosphere and will last for months or years without ever needing water. You can throw out your artificial flowers and replace them with natural dried flowers picked for free from fields of weeds. Use dried flowers to decorate a table, brighten a corner, frame a mirror, dress up a shelf, or fill an empty fireplace. You can incorporate seed pods, nuts, fruits, grasses, rushes, cones, leaves, and branches into your arrangements. Classes in fashioning dried flower arrangements are offered as noncredit courses in community education programs, and many tips can be gleaned from books on the subject.

Look through seed catalogs under "Strawflowers" or "Everlastings" to choose seeds for annuals and perennials to plant in the spring, so you'll have them in late summer and fall for drying. Common types of annuals include the everlasting sand flower, globe everlasting, everlasting daisy, immortelle, candlewick static, love-lies-bleeding, and African daisy. Common perennials are the pearly everlasting, sea lavender, gypsophila, feather grass, and cloud grass. Seed catalogs will describe the varieties and offer tips on planting and raising them.

Proper drying is important, because if any moisture remains, the plants will become moldy during storage. There are three ways of drying: *natural means* (tie small bunches at stem ends with florist's wire and hang in a cool, airy, shady place—maybe a basement or crawl space); *dry heat—room temperature in a dark place* (tie florist's wire around stem end and hang in a closed cupboard); *using desiccants* (bury flowers for three or four weeks in one part sand mixed with two parts powdered borax or silica gel).

In addition to growing and drying the flowers and making arrangements for sale and display, you could even have a workshop in your home to teach others how to dry the flowers from their gardens and how to make flower arrangements, plaques, calendars, swags, garlands, and other decorations. To accommodate your students, you'd need a spare room for drying, as well as boards, glass, urns, picture frames, and tweezers.

Herbs. Many people keep chives, caraway, thyme, oregano, parsley, and other herbs in their kitchen windows, bringing them in from the garden to enjoy all winter in their cooking. To do this, select the plants you want to bring indoors in August, and make sure you have a window that gets sufficient light (at least five hours of direct sun a day). Use pots of plastic or clay, filled with any good organic potting soil. Then transplant healthy plants from your garden into the pots, or start new plants from cuttings or seeds. Once a day give the herbs a breath of fresh air by opening a door or window in an adjoining room; a cold draft in the same room might be too much of a shock. Herbs like high humidity while they're growing, so water them and spray their foliage frequently. An occasional taste of weak manure tea will keep the herbs well nourished. Herbs can be grown completely indoors—in your greenhouse or in your house—but they won't get as bushy as they would with the benefit of some outdoor growing. If you grow lots of herbs, you can sell them in little pots for other people's windowsills.

Besides using herbs as cooking accents and windowsill decorations, you can use them to add a scented, soothing touch to a relaxing bath. A combination of eucalyptus, sage, lavender, and pine in the tub is invigorating. Take your favorite blend of herbs and oils, such as mint, almond oil, comfrey, and wheat germ oil, tie them in a handkerchief, and toss the bundle into the tub.

Make potpourris and sachets to sell. The ingredients are the same for both, but the consistencies of the mixtures are different. Potpourris are made from coarsely broken herbs, spices, and flowers, while sachets are made of flowers crushed to a fine powder and spices and citrus peels finely ground. Some ingredients you may need, such as vetiver root and tonka beans, won't grow in your garden and will have to be bought from herbal, botanical, or pharmaceutical outlets. Look in the Yellow Pages under "Herbs" and "Pharmaceutical Products—Wholesale and Manufacturers."

Sell dried herbs, bath mixtures, potpourris, and sachets year round at flea markets, gourmet food shops, craft bazaars, bath specialty shops, and gift shops, or—when the weather's good—at a roadside stand. To determine prices, check with stores selling similar items, and price yours accordingly.

We interviewed Lynn Q., an Iowa woman who grows culinary, aromatic, and healing herbs outdoors (in season) and sells them. Lynn has always been interested in herbs, their uses, and their history, and she enjoys sharing her knowledge with others. Her favorite cooking herbs are basil, caraway, chives, cumin, oregano, parsley, and marjoram. Mint, lavender and tansy, sage, pennyroyal, sweet flag, and horseradish are a few of the many others she grows. Her customers can buy them freshly cut, or dried and sealed in plastic bags. To dry the herbs, Lynn ties them in small bunches and hangs them in a warm, dry place for about two weeks. With each herb, she furnishes a mimeographed sheet of information about its history and uses. She also supplies recipes with her culinary herbs—for example, anise and banana bread, poppy seed cake, and caraway fruit dessert. She also sells seed and starter kits (small pots containing starter medium and seeds) for the beginning herb gardener, and she supplies fresh and dried herbs to a local health food store.

Bedding Plants. Some avid gardeners grow the plants for their gardens from seed, but most people buy bedding plants. Bedding plants include flowers and vegetables. The most popular are tomatoes, cabbage, peppers, melons, and any flowering plants (such as petunias, pansies, and begonias) that cannot be started easily outdoors. The advantage of growing your plants from seed is that you have no big cash outlay. There's little danger of failure from the weather, because the plants are raised in a hotbed or greenhouse. They're started in late winter and early spring and kept at a temperature of seventy-two degrees day and night.

You may want to investigate further the idea of growing bedding plants for your own use or for sale, as you won't need a lot of expensive machinery to get started. And we all know how expensive they are at the nursery. To avoid unanticipated problems, take courses in greenhouse growing or work with a grower to learn tricks for starting seeds, preventing disease, controlling insects, transplanting seedlings, nurturing the soil, and scheduling your planting. Check with the Department of Agriculture in your state. Commercial growers that sell plants are usually required to pass inspections and receive certificates.

The profits you make will depend on the size of your operation. The price of bedding plants can vary anywhere from $2.00 a dozen to $.50 each, and the space required to grow them is minimal. When the plants are three to four inches tall, they can be sold either in plant packs or in individual containers. Individual pots are generally used for tomatoes, onions, squash, peppers, and melons.

Another type of plant that might bring in extra cash is the less common vegetable: for example, the leek, asparagus, or kohlrabi. These vegetables add nutritious variety to our meals, but some of them are hard to find in supermarkets. People might grow their own if they could readily buy the plants.

Since so many people have become devoted dieters and salad lovers, a complete line of salad plants (like those grown by Jane R., mentioned earlier in this chapter) is a good moneymaking idea. Kale; Swiss chard; New Zealand spinach; Boston, leaf, iceberg, and red lettuce; and table, Spanish, and Bermuda onions might sell well. There are also many delicious Chinese vegetables that can be sold as started plants. Good asparagus crowns are usually available in nurseries. You could start the seeds one year and sell roots the next.

Other plants to consider are rare vegetables, from amaranth (a hot-weather substitute for spinach) to tomatillos (a basic ingredient in the mildly hot green sauce often served with tacos and other Mexican dishes). Some of these plants may not be in demand where you live, so you must study the market thoroughly before investing your time, energy, or money in raising them. Foods do run in fads, so check gourmet, specialty, and health food stores in your area to find out what people are buying or asking for. Be careful not to buy outdated seeds, and make sure the plants you start for sale will grow in the climate of your customers' gardens.

And plant sales don't have to be limited to vegetables. What about fruit? Strawberry plants are always big sellers.

Plant-Related Services

There are a lot of services that can be offered to gardeners, landscapers, and weekend mowers. Every community's needs are different, so it might be a good idea to try new ventures on a temporary basis first. Survey your neighbors, talk with local nursery owners—become attuned to the kinds of services your community would support. If you get a green light from your preliminary research, and if your first efforts pan out, greater financial investments won't seem like such a risk.

If you live in a tourist area where cottages are leased for the summer, consider renting mowers and trimmers to the seasonal occupants. Or rent equipment to year-round residents who don't have their own or who can't wait for their broken tools to be fixed. Hedge trimmers, grass catchers, and Weed Eaters are convenient, timesaving devices that amateur yard workers might welcome. If you own unused land, you may want to rent garden space—especially to apartment dwellers and people whose yards are only big enough for a picnic table.

Rental Gardens. With today's escalating food prices, many families feel that they could benefit from raising some of their own food. Other people simply enjoy the challenges of gardening. Besides the vegetables to be reaped, gardeners get a bonus of fresh air, sunshine, and exercise. If you have an acre or more of vacant land, think about providing your neighbors with individual twenty-five-by-forty-foot garden plots for about $25 a summer. Some communities already have rental gardens, but there's usually room for more of a good thing.

You can prepare the soil for planting by plowing and disking, or you can hire a farmer with a plow and disk to do the job for about $35 an acre. People who rent the plots can plant and tend their gardens in their spare time, using their own tools. Know your own community before starting a garden rental service. Rural residents, who have plenty of garden space, wouldn't get excited over rental gardens. But in a suburban community of small yards, apartments and duplex housing, there might be many people who'd jump at your offer, especially if your acreage were nearby.

Tool Rental. Renting garden and lawn tools could be a great aid to part-time gardeners and to house owners or renters who find yard equipment a low priority in their budgets. Hoes, rakes, shovels, wheelbarrows, Rototillers, lawn mowers, weed trimmers, and hedge clippers are just a few of the tools that gardeners and yard workers frequently need.

If you rent out tools, expect to lose some small ones, and be prepared to repair, service, and replace many others. Give customers clear directions for the proper use and care of the tools they rent, especially Rototillers and other machinery. Such instructions not only help the customer but can lengthen the life of your equipment. Evaluate the long-term prospects for your service. Even if communities consisting of postage-stamp lawns initially support your tool rental service, they might eventually find renting and returning tools a hassle.

If you decide to try a rental service, check around for the best deal on the equipment you need to start with. Buy tools in the fall, when stores mark them down to sell quickly, or watch newspaper ads and buy good used tools from people moving or breaking up housekeeping. To obtain the needed inventory for a small-scale tool rental business, expect an initial cash outlay of about $1,500.

Rose K. is a middle-aged widow from New Jersey who started a garden rental service. She owns a large empty lot next to her house, and renting it out for garden plots seemed better than seeing it grow knee-high weeds or having to mow it regularly. Her son plows and disks the land each spring, and her customers rent garden plots of whatever size they want. When Rose first started renting the plots, she noticed that several of her customers were using tools from a local rental company. The second year Rose invested in some extra hand tools and one Rototiller, and she rented them out by the hour. Today she also sells vegetable plants and seeds. Her customers can get everything they need in one stop. She operates her business from May to October and clears about $750 each summer.

Garden Tending. In Chapter 6 we discussed opportunities for earning extra cash by caring for houseplants while their owners were away. Garden tending is a more strenuous version of plant-sitting; the physical demands and time requirements are greater. But gardens don't flourish on their own, and if you enjoy doing your own gardening, you may want to take up the challenge of staking up the tomatoes or bringing in the harvest around town.

In order for any garden to produce to its maximum, hoeing, weeding, and dusting for bugs must be done regularly. These jobs are time-consuming and can be hard work, especially on hot days. They'll often leave you sweaty and thirsty, with a sore back and callused fingers. There are a lot of people who would be happy to hire someone to tend their gardens on a regular basis. You could have a standing day for doing a certain garden, barring rain or storm.

Prime customers for your garden tending service are people planning vacations; gardens and trips to the beach just don't mix. Early vacations interfere with the very important weeding process: It's vital to keep young plants as weed-free as possible. Late summer vacations, when vegetables are starting to bear, aren't in the garden's best interest, either. If you're planning on a bumper crop, you must harvest the produce as it ripens so the plants' energies can be used to develop new fruit. (Cucumbers, for example, must be picked every two or three days.) You can charge either by the hour or by the job for this kind of work. To charge by the job, you'll have to estimate how much time it will take.

Marilee P. is a Maryland woman who tends gardens for vacationers during June, July, and August. She hoes and weeds the gardens, suckers the tomatoes, and dusts the plants to keep bugs off. If the produce ripens and her customers will be back in a few days, she picks and stores it for them. When her customers plan to be gone longer, they sometimes arrange for friends or relatives to have the produce. If not, Marilee is free to take it home. She charges $5 an hour for tending gardens, and her work is appreciated. Regular customers call her every year as soon as they pick their vacation dates, to make sure she'll be available to care for their garden plots. The money she makes goes into a special savings account to help update her wardrobe and buy Christmas gifts.

We hope this chapter has inspired you to put your green thumb to some money-making use. Not everyone enjoys working with plants. Whatever your area of greenery expertise, you'll find people willing to pay you for doing work you love.

Suggested Reading

Abraham, George. *Green Thumb Book of Fruit and Vegetable Gardening.* Englewood Cliffs, New Jersey: Prentice-Hall, 1969.

Abraham, George and Katy. *Green Thumb Garden Handbook.* Englewood Cliffs, New Jersey: Prentice-Hall, 1977.

Abraham, George and Katy. *Organic Gardening under Glass.* Emmaus, Pennsylvania: Rodale Press, 1975.

All About Growing Fruits and Berries. San Francisco: Ortho Books, 1977.

Bartholomew, Mel. *Square Food Gardening.* Emmaus, Pennsylvania: Rodale Press, 1981.

Crockett, James U. *Crockett's Flower Garden.* Boston: Little, Brown & Co., 1980.

Crockett, James U. *Crockett's Indoor Garden.* Boston: Little, Brown & Co., 1978.

Crockett, James U. *Crockett's Tool Shed.* Boston: Little, Brown & Co., 1979.

Genders, Roy. *The Complete Book of Herbs and Herb Growing.* New York: Sterling Publishing Co., 1980.

Genders, Roy. *Mushroom Growing for Everyone.* London: Faber & Faber, 1969.

Gilbertie, Sal, and Larry Sheehan. *Herb Gardening At Its Best.* New York: Atheneum, 1980.

How to Build and Use Greenhouses. San Francisco: Ortho Books, 1979.

Jankowiak, James. *The Prosperous Gardener.* Emmaus, Pennsylvania: Rodale Press, 1978.

Logsdon, Gene. *Successful Berry Growing.* Emmaus, Pennsylvania: Rodale Press, 1977.

McCullagh, James C. *The Solar Greenhouse Book.* Emmaus, Pennsylvania: Rodale Press, 1978.

Moon, Doug. *Gardening for People.* Santa Fe, New Mexico: John Muir, 1975.

Schuler, Stanley. *The Gardener's Basic Book of Trees and Shrubs.* New York: Simon & Schuster, Fireside Books, 1973.

$*#(¢@&$ 12

(Typing and secretarial services)

Typing is a skill many at-home women have. They picked it up along the way in high school or college but when they stopped doing friends' term papers or left the office job downtown, they quit typing, too. The skill is usually still intact; it's just buried under cookie dough, last summer's paint supplies and a layer of uncertainty. Typing is like riding a bike: once you learn, you never forget. And you never forget the pride that comes from pounding out a crisp-looking page. At first you may be a little rusty, and your fingers will probably feel like cubes of lead, but with practice and perseverance you'll soon be back to your old level of speed and accuracy. And you never know when the skill you've been stashing in the closet with the portable typewriter may be just the way to earn some extra cash.

While her husband was out of work recuperating from a heart attack, Ada L. of Pennsylvania earned extra money typing **income tax forms** for local Certified Public Accountants. Because of her enterprising skill, she didn't have to worry about unpaid bills. By the time the tax season rush was over, Ada's husband was back at work. And though she didn't need to work anymore, one of the CPAs recognized her good work and asked her to stay on part-time. If you're in a financial pinch, and going back to a nine-to-five job is impossible for whatever reason (small children at home, illness in the family), typing at home to earn extra cash is a job worth considering. And even if you've got enough to get by, you may want to add a few pennies—better make that dollars—to the old cookie jar, especially with a pair of jeans costing between $20 and $50.

When Edith L. of South Carolina retired after thirty years as a medical secretary, she wanted to keep active and decided to put her clerical skills to good use. Each weekday she goes to a different retirement complex in the city and helps with residents' correspondence, including business letters, insurance forms, and letters to relatives. She carries her portable typewriter and all supplies (typing paper, envelopes, dictionary, ribbon, carbon paper) with her in a briefcase on wheels. Even though she charges only $1.50 per letter or insurance form, Edith makes enough for spending money. She likes helping people with their business chores and enjoys visiting with her clients.

If you own a typewriter, get it out and blow the dust off the keys. If not, borrow one from a friend or rent one from a typewriter rental agency. It doesn't have to be the latest model with all the fancy gadgets; for practicing, any typewriter will do. Using an old manual typewriter may even help your fingers limber up more quickly. If you've been away from the keyboard for a while, you'll probably have to work on building the self-discipline that's needed to turn out the work on schedule. Set practice deadlines for yourself. And keep them. If you agree to have a term paper completed in twenty-four hours, failing to do that could be disastrous for the student. Stick to a practice typing schedule. Borrow typing books from the library. After practicing for a month, you should have your speed and accuracy back. When your skills are polished, *then* is the time to invest in the best-quality typewriter you can afford.

Talk to a typewriter salesperson and have him or her explain the difference between a machine costing $250 and one costing $500. The more expensive machine may be the best buy, because it will last longer and give better service than a less expensive model.

You'll need a few basic supplies before you begin accepting work. They are: 25 percent rag bond paper, envelopes, carbon paper, correction materials (correction tape, fluid, eraser), typewriter ribbons, paper clips, pencils, stamps, a file cabinet, and, of course, a good dictionary. As a typist, you're a proofreader too, even though the writers are ultimately responsible for the spelling and grammar of their letters, memos, and manuscripts.

Have some business cards and circulars made up, or make them yourself with that fancy new typewriter. Advertise your home typing service and include your prices. Knowing what to charge for your service is important. Call other typists in your area to find out the going rates. A rough estimate is $.04 to $.05 a line, or $.75 to $1 per double-spaced page. Of course, you should charge extra for carbon copies and more difficult jobs, like charts, theses, or screenplays. Other special charges might be: rough draft **transcribing**—$.06 a line; **specialized transcribing** (legal or medical)—$.06 a word. There are several books on the market with pricing information. We've listed some of these books at the end of this chapter.

Potential Customers

If you live in a city with a college or university, place your card on every bulletin board you can find there, and don't forget laundromats, grocery stores, taverns, and any other place frequented by **students**. They always have things that need to be typed (theses, term papers, reports), and they'll keep coming back, especially if you can do work on short notice.

Noni P. of Ohio is a sorority housemother at a small university. She took this job after retiring from an executive secretarial position she held for seven years. Never having been married, Noni thinks of these girls as her own daughters and takes much pride in their schoolwork. To supplement her salary and to help the girls, she began typing their papers. Her work was excellent, and word of her abilities spread around campus. Students flocked to her door. Noni's been doing college typing for several years now and has saved enough money to pay for her upcoming trip to Europe.

If you don't live in a university town, gear your advertisements to small businesses, civic clubs, churches, and schools. Many businesses and organizations have sales, social events, or fund-raising functions several times a year, and they need someone to type leaflets or correspondence.

Writers are also a good source of work. These creative people are always looking for someone to type their query letters, manuscripts, and articles, and they often need the same material typed several times. (Write and rewrite is the story of life for any writer.) If you can line up several writers as regular customers, they can provide a steady flow of income for you. Besides earning extra cash, you could meet some interesting people and enjoy the fringe benefit of reading their material before it's published. Place advertisements in your local newspapers, the Yellow Pages, and writers' magazines.

At certain times of the year, such as the end of a fiscal year, inventory time, income tax time, and annual report time, even **large companies** are inundated with more paperwork than their employees can handle. If you call and leave your name with the office manager of such a company, maybe he or she will call you the next time the typing work load gets too heavy. Some firms will let you do the typing in your home because of lack of space in their offices. Home typists usually have the work brought to them, but there are times when it is better for both parties to have the typist pick up and deliver the work. Make sure you secure the name of someone to call if you have any questions.

A good point to remember when you contact any of these companies is that hiring you to do the work is less expensive for them than paying a temporary employment agency for a daily typist. Also point out what an advantage it would be for them to use someone whose competence and reliability they were familiar with, rather than having to break in someone new every time they need extra help.

Ellie D., a Connecticut divorcee in her early forties, typed shipping invoices, billing statements, payroll checks, and correspondence for a small company. When she remarried, she quit her job to stay at home. Her employers asked if she would continue to do their typing if they furnished her with a typewriter. She agreed and has organized her time so that she can also do typing for another small company. These home-based jobs finance Ellie's twice-a-year jaunts to Las Vegas with her new husband.

Audrey G. of Minnesota does typing at home for one of the nation's largest **insurance companies**. When her sister, who is a secretary for the firm, asked if she would like to do the reports that had to be sent to the home office, she agreed to try it. The insurance company furnishs the typewriter, and Audrey is very happy with the job, since she can do the work at her leisure. Although working was not a necessity for Audrey, she has used the money to buy custom draperies for the living room, a dishwasher for the kitchen, and patio furniture—extras she could never before afford.

There are many **business people who travel** extensively and need correspondence typed when they are out of town without a secretary. These people usually stay at motels, and the managers would probably be glad to offer this service to their guests. Contact several motel managers and offer to do secretarial work for people staying at their motels. People who need letters typed can call you and dictate the letters over the telephone. (See Chapter 8.) If your clients use dictating machines, you can pick up the tapes for typing. Or you could pick up their rough, hand-written drafts. Then, according to their instructions, the completed work would be either mailed or returned to them at the motel or their home office. Many of your customers will probably be on tight schedules, so you could offer quick pick-up and delivery service.

Nelda E., a young wife and mother in Arizona, was alone most of the time because of her husband's traveling. She decided to fill her time with a skill she had used in her last secretarial job: typing. With telephone and typewriter, she set up an office in her home and began looking for work by calling motels in her area, offering to do secretarial work for the business people who stayed there and to pick-up and deliver the typing assignments. She charges $2.50 for a letter and $1 per page for straight copy work, plus $.20 per mile for traveling to pick up and deliver the work. She charges extra for mailing and carbon copies.

Jobs You Can Do with Your Typewriter

Addressing envelopes is always a good way to make money with your typewriter. Think of all the junk mail that is deposited in your mailbox (furniture store ads, jewelry store ads, bargain days flyers from your local department store, etc.); someone had to type your name and address on every piece of it. Of course, many large companies have computerized mailing lists for this work, but small companies, because they have less mail and slimmer budgets, find it more economical to hire someone to do this typing.

Beware of the advertisements you read in some newspapers and magazines, promising you big profits for addressing envelopes. Most of these ads instruct you to send them money, in return for which they will send you materials to get you started addressing envelopes for astronomical fees. Almost all these ads are hoaxes, and their sponsors profit from naive people who send in money hoping for a convenient at-home job.

Lee A. of Oregon is a widow who lives alone. Although she had enough income to get by, she didn't have enough for the trips she likes to take to visit old friends. Her son-in-law, who manages a large furniture store, asked Lee if she would type addresses on several thousand envelopes for flyers advertising the store's annual sale. She enjoyed the work as well as the money. Since then, she has contacted other stores in town and offered to address their advertising mail. She does occasional typing for several other businesses now, too. From her part-time earnings, she is able to budget for yearly vacations with her friends.

Résumé typing is also in demand. Many of today's ever-mobile business people need résumés typed on an almost regular basis. Others who might take advantage of this service are schoolteachers, retirees looking for jobs as consultants, people changing careers or returning to the work force after several years' absence, and students fresh out of college seeking their first job. If you have experience **writing résumés,** you might consider offering that service as well. So much the better for your pocketbook.

Real estate contracts often need to be typed on weekends or at odd times of the day or night because home buyers who are moving from out of town or who work late hours have little time to look for a house. Once they find a place, they usually want to sign the contract immediately and complete the deal. Advertise to be on call twenty-four hours a day to type those contracts. Make appointments with the real estate firms in your community to discuss your emergency typing service. Individual real estate salespeople may want you to type their correspondence, too, if their businesses are too small to support full-time secretaries.

All restaurants change their **menus** occasionally, some more often than others. Often they just add a typed list of the daily specials to their regular menus. Talk to the restaurant managers in your vicinity and offer to type their menus. You need not be a speedy typist for this kind of work, but accuracy is important.

Gail M. of New Mexico needed to earn some extra cash. She and her husband have six children, two of whom are in college, and though her husband earns a good salary, their budget was strained. While they were dining in a restaurant one evening, Gail noticed how dog-eared the menus were. Later at home Gail thought of asking the restaurant manager if he would hire her to type new menus. The next day she went to see him and showed him samples of the typefaces she had: Delegate, Courier, and Advocate in the pica size; Letter Gothic, Prestige Elite, Light Italic, and Script in the elite size. She even had Spanish and French characters and accents in the Advocate type. She had bought the typewriter with the special typefaces at an office supply sale. The restaurant manager was delighted and hired her on the spot to furnish him with 60 new menus done in the Script face on quality bond paper. He would insert them later in leather menu holders covered in clear plastic. He agreed to pay her $1.50 per menu. Gail typed one menu and had one hundred copies made at $.10 each. The restaurant manager paid her $90 and was pleased that she had given him 40 extra menus. Gail made a profit of $75 after expenses. She soon got the job of furnishing El Adobe, a popular Mexican restaurant, with 125 menus done in Spanish type. She made a profit of $160 on that job. Before long, Gail had a portfolio of menus to show and is presently typing for 45 restaurants; she types only the weekly specials for some and entire menus for others. She averages about $3,800 a year with her typing.

Most lawyers have secretaries to do their typing during the day. There may be times, though, when they need typists after regular office hours to meet them at hospitals or jails to take **depositions** from their clients.

Court reporters who record depositions on machines may need freelance typists to transcribe the statements quickly and efficiently. Providing either service might require being on call twenty-four hours a day and having shorthand or speedwriting skills. Legal secretaries may also use their skills in other ways.

Tondalyia K. of New York, for example, was a legal secretary who took a one-year pregnancy leave. During that time, so as not to get rusty and out of touch, she took a job **transcribing court proceedings,** which were delivered to her and picked up by a court messenger. Tonda managed to share her baby boy's first year and add to the family till as well.

Start a **billing service** in your home. Businesses too small to require full-time office help might welcome someone on a part-time basis. Offer to pick up, type, and mail their bills. Some of the people who might be interested in this service are doctors, optometrists, dentists, plumbers, electricians, television repair specialists, shop owners, lawyers, and funeral directors. You can work as few or as many hours as you want, according to the number of clients you take on.

Jean L. of Iowa works for an insurance company and lives in an apartment complex near a shopping plaza that houses several small shops and a number of professional offices. When she called her dentist, whose office was in the shopping center, to complain about a mistake in her bill, he told her that the agency that handled his billing had it all messed up. On her next trip to his office, she offered to do his billing cheaper than the agency was doing it. They agreed upon a price, and Jean started immediately. Since she already owned a typewriter, the only equipment she had to buy was a calculator and a small filing cabinet. In several month's time, she was doing the billing for the doctors and lawyers who kept offices in the same plaza. She charges $10 an hour. She works about ten evenings a month and adds about $160 to her monthly income.

Other Clerical and Secretarial Services

Besides typing, you may have other secretarial skills, such as filing, bookkeeping, order filling, and shorthand, that you could get paid to do at home. Maybe you learned them in school or by taking extra courses while employed by an office, or maybe you added to your clerical skills in order to get a promotion. If you learned the basics once, the skills are still there, though they may be dormant.

Take inventory of your skills and find out how you can polish or improve them. High schools and universities often offer courses in beginning or advanced typing, shorthand, bookkeeping, accounting, and other business-related subjects, including how to use the newest business machines. Brush up, practice—and maybe learn some new business procedures. Adult education courses offered through the public schools are relatively inexpensive. The evening classes usually last between ten and fifteen weeks. Registration fees run from $35 to $50. After some refresher courses, you may be ready to cash in on your knowledge.

A home **filing service** can be another good business to start. Many small companies don't have enough work for full-time office help and would welcome someone to keep their filing up to date. They could deliver the papers needing filing to you once a week. You might also do their telephoning and monthly billing.

Nell S. of Georgia is seventy-one and lives with her daughter and her son-in-law, Pete, who operates an auto body and repair shop next door to his home. Before Nell moved in, Pete's business papers were strewn around the shop and the house. Every time he had to file a tax form, the whole family was in an uproar because of Pete's sloppy record keeping. Nell changed that fast by having Pete put his business papers and incoming mail in a box every day. Nell goes through the box, makes out bills for work done, records payments that come in the mail, and files correspondence and invoices. Pete pays Nell $50 a week and loves her for bringing order into his life. Nell, in turn, feels useful and has extra money to spend on her hobbies and to spoil her grandchildren with.

Bookkeeping is another service that a lot of small businesses might welcome. Being neat, organized, accurate, and conscious of details will make you a good bookkeeper. You must be able to record debits and credits and to balance the books, and you should know the laws relating to filing tax forms. If you are good with figures and have had any experience with bookkeeping, advertise to keep the books for small businesses, especially for the person who runs his business from home and doesn't employ a staff.

Mary R. of Tennessee spent World War II in England, cutting through red tape, ordering supplies, and keeping books for Uncle Sam. After thirty years' service in the army, she returned to her hometown to reacquaint herself with relatives and friends. The adjustment to civilian life was hard, since she was used to military life and its many responsibilities. Being an experienced accountant and bookkeeper and wanting to keep busy, Mary put an ad in the local paper, offering to balance the books and complete tax forms for individuals and small businesses.

Freelance **shorthand reporting** is a service often needed at conventions, conferences, and meetings of all kinds. Freelancers record events and type reports, letters, and memoranda. If shorthand is a skill in your secretarial repertory, advertise it in news and trade papers. To find out what groups are booking conventions, contact the Chamber of Commerce in your city and the managers of the hotels where conventioneers stay. Have your references ready to present when these groups seek out your expertise. If you live in a rural area, call on community organizations, banks, hospitals, etc.—anyone who might benefit from your quick pen. The prices you charge will vary according to the going rates in your area.

An accurate typist who can complete work on deadline is always in demand. Sit down at your typewriter and start practicing now.

Suggested Reading

Drouillard, Anne, with William F. Keefe. *How to Earn $25,000 a Year or More Typing at Home.* New York: Frederick Fell Publishers, 1980.

Glenn, Peggy. *How to Start and Run a Successful Home Typing Business. 2nd rev. ed.* Huntington Beach, California: Pigi Publications, 1980.

Heller, Jack. *Typing for the Physically Handicapped: Methods and Keyboard Presentation Charts.* New York: McGraw-Hill, 1978.

Kozlow, Stephen G. *How to Start Your Own Secretarial Services Business at Home.* Northfield Center, Ohio: SK Publications, 1980.

Liles, Parker. *Typing Mailable Letters.* New York: McGraw-Hill, 1980.

Moon, Harry R. *Typing from Rough Drafts.* New York: Milady, 1978.

Temple, Mary. *How to Start a Secretarial and Business Service.* New York: Pilot Books, 1978.

Don't Sell Yourself Short

13

(Jobs for saleswomen)

Seal a deal, land a sale, corner the market—these are familiar slogans in the business of selling. From the caravan traders of ancient times to the chic Madison Avenue marketers of today, the goals are the same: Come up with a product that people will want; devise a method to sell it to them. This chapter focuses on how you, the home-based woman, can make money by selling—a skill that may come naturally to you. It may be something you already do nearly every day—from selling the boss on the idea of leaving early to make a World Series game to selling your husband on new carpet for the den or the kids on a new liver recipe.

But don't be fooled into thinking that selling is easy. It's an art that demands time, hard work, and a willingness to take risks. Since no one can predict the whims of human beings, it's impossible to count on a sale until it's final. There are few guarantees in the business, but one thing is certain: The more you understand about what's involved in the selling game, the better chance you have to win.

Some women have so much natural sales talent that they could probably sell hand warmers in Miami. Most of us, though, have to work at it to be successful. There are many ingredients involved in effective selling, not the least of which is a woman's own enthusiasm for an item that has value for her. The successful saleswoman *believes* her products better her customers' lives. A time-saving mop, half-price designer jeans, energy-saving cloth window shades—the "selling" woman is proud to offer these to her public.

A saleswoman is an assertive, inventive individual whose creativity and perseverance are complemented by a head for figures. She's probably blessed with the gift of gab and a genuine interest in people. A successful salesperson has a feeling of pride and achievement at the close of a sale.

Products and Methods

If you are a saleswoman at heart, your first job is to think of a product that you can readily and inexpensively make, buy, or find—a product that people in your area might want or need. Research the interests, lifestyles, and needs of your community. Observe which are the busiest stores at the mall; ask your neighbors if they'd support a fabric outlet in town; talk to your PTA—would its members frequent a stationery store featuring the work of local printers, artists, and lithographers?

Find a product, an angle, and a method of operation that can't miss in your city. Popcorn at Little League games, produce at the end of the driveway, Tupperware at a home party, wooden toys from a garage showroom—these are a few examples of how a home-based woman can earn extra cash by selling. Follow the classic sales commandment: Find a need and fill it.

Bonnie H., a vivacious Maryland homemaker, has done just that. She makes money with her weekend business while enjoying her favorite hobby: flying model airplanes. She and her husband spend many weekends at a rural **flying field.** Since it's the only place hobbyists are allowed to fly their model planes in that area, there's usually quite a crowd. Bonnie suggested to her husband that they drive their camper van to the site so that she could **sell snacks:** hot dogs, potato chips, candy bars, coffee, and soft drinks. Her initial outlay was $100, and the first day she sold everything. Her business has grown; she clears several thousand dollars a year, and she spends more time selling than she does flying.

When you've hit on a product you believe in, you have to find an appropriate way to sell it. What sales method appeals to you? Selling can be done over the phone (see Chapter 8), on a college campus, or on a chartered bus en route to a sporting event. The ingenious saleswoman headquartered at home and armed with know-how and energy has options galore for exercising her selling ways. You can sell your product directly from your home if local zoning laws allow. You can use your barn, garage, shed, or basement or even a room in your house. Some things can be sold at roadside stands, flea markets, trade shows, craft shows, fairs, or gift shops (on consignment). Party-plan and mail-order sales are popular these days, and there's always that old standby: selling door to door. Select a method that fits your product, your situation, and your intended audience. Selling flowered bookmarks through a local gift shop might work; selling them over the phone probably won't. There's usually more than one way to take your product to the public. (See Chapter 3 for the pros and cons of various selling methods.) You might like to sell miniature dollhouses at local flea markets, but if you have no transportation, you can sell them from your enclosed porch. If you're selling quilted jackets to neighbors in Iowa, you might consider a mail-order business so you can reach potential customers in Alaska and Maine.

Eleanor J. lives in Ohio, thirty miles from the nearest city. Clothing in the local specialty stores is expensive, so most people travel quite a distance to shop. Five years ago Eleanor and her husband went to Cincinnati to attend a baseball game and discovered a men's clothing outlet store that sells famous brands of **men's suits and accessories** at a discount of 50 percent or more. Eleanor bought twenty-five suits in popular sizes, took them home, and sold them from a vacant bedroom that she transformed into a showroom. Besides the convenience of shopping in town at reasonable prices, her customers enjoy the benefit of her quality alterations. She now makes several trips a year to Cincinnati to buy men's suits which she sells at a $25-$40 profit.

How important is timing in starting your venture? Being aware of what people are in the market for at different times of year is helpful. Spring, when many people do cleaning and redecorating, is the best time to sell cleaning tools and supplies, from companies such as Amway, Fuller Brush, and Stanley, or home decorating needs like carpeting, drapes, and bedspreads. The Christmas season is a great time for holiday goods: toys, party clothes, fancy foods, flowers, fruits and nuts, and gift items. Seasonal clothing, such as swim wear, down vests, mufflers, and fishing caps, should be introduced at appropriate times. Few people will be looking for warm mittens in March. Many holidays call for their own special treats, for instance, candy, flowers, and cards for Valentine's Day. Some items, however, are always on the "wanted list" of the buying public: T-shirts and jeans, cosmetics, jewelry, tobacco, and food and drink are year-round stock.

Licenses, Money, and Marketing

Before starting any business, obtain a vendor's license required by law for any retail seller. As mentioned in the marketing chapter, a vendor's license number also permits you to buy from wholesale dealers without paying sales tax. Contact your county licensing agent for further details.

Also check with state and local sales tax offices for information concerning the collection of any sales taxes.

Getting started in selling requires some up-front money; how much depends on what you're selling and what scale you plan to do business on. Starting small always makes sense. A good general rule is: Never invest more than you can afford to lose. Though some have succeeded with less, it's a good idea to have a six-month operating reserve of available cash.

Pricing is important, and there's no single formula that will work in every situation. You need to know your market and what it will bear, as well as any seasonal variations. The two basic pricing rules, according to the Small Business Administration, are: (1) Realize that the market, not your cost, sets the price at which a product will sell; (2) figure the lowest price at which you can sell your product and still make a profit. Trust your consumer sense and good judgment. Sometimes you can add 25 percent to the usual price (the highest that people will normally pay), and the item will still sell. If you get a shipment of glittering party dresses in your shop the week before Christmas, the dresses can usually be marked up with no harm to sales. If the product is something you make yourself (a stuffed giraffe, an original cable-knit sweater design, a metal initial key chain), a standard pricing rule applies: one-third for labor, one-third for material, and one-third for profit.

As long as your business is on a small scale, all customer payments should be in cash. Checks are often considered cash, and you should consider accepting them. It's frustrating to lose a sale because you're afraid to take a check, but a few bad checks can make a big dent in a small business. Unless the customer is someone you know and trust, use the same policy as most stores: Ask for identification in the form of a valid driver's license and one major credit card.

As your business expands and comes into direct competition with other stores in your area, you should consider other methods of payment. Bank cards, such as Visa and MasterCard, are good means of extending credit. Each will cost you a monthly fee, based on how much the service is used. The price is set by the sponsoring bank, so it varies. Check with local banks for further details.

Once you have chosen a product or products to sell and a method of selling, advertising becomes important. When you first start your business, there may not be enough funds to hire an advertising company, so do the next best thing: Become advertising-conscious. Try to analyze the difference between the successful ads you see—the ones that cause you to remember products—and those you hear and see *once* and promptly forget. (Does anyone remember the name of the product in the commercial with the huge fist emerging from the washing machine?) Read about advertising. There are many books published on advertising techniques; some are listed in the bibliography at the end of Chapter 3.

Bulletin boards, flyers, community newspapers and local magazines, business cards and letters, and word of mouth are all good means of advertising. The amount you spend depends entirely on you and your business, but remember that good ads in the right places can do a lot for any business. Local newspaper and magazine advertisements can usually be bought for under $100. Before you post your hours or buy a neon sign, refer to Chapter 3, where we discuss advertising and marketing in more depth.

Selling Ideas

We will list some ways for you to make money selling, but the list is only a beginning. After reading our suggestions, think through all the angles of one that tickles your fancy. Or look around and come up with an original idea that's bound to make money. The following case history describes a woman who did.

The Customer Comes to You. Lorna D. of Florida has always been captivated by **containers.** She has collected boxes, jars, and other receptacles since her childhood. Today she owns and operates the Container Boutique, a little shop that specializes in containers of every type, shape, color, and size, all handmade by craft people in the area. Lorna sells them on consignment in her shop and through her catalog mail service. The containers are made of plastic, wood, metal, basket materials, glass, fabric, leather, rope, bamboo, shells, pottery, and even bone. They'll accommodate everything from perfumes and jewelry to tobacco and spices. Lorna has turned her fascination into a moneymaking business.

Open a **gift shop** in your home. Give it a name: Sherry's Boutique or Gifts 'n' Such sounds like a real business. Remodel that extra room, after checking with the zoning board to make certain it's lawful to operate a business in your neighborhood. Or consider renting space in a nearby shopping center. Look through other shops and see what merchandise is moving. Unique gifts, metal jewelry, handmade wooden animals, or hand-knit sweaters may be available in your own community. You can also buy your products from wholesale gift houses in your area or from craft fairs and shows that draw artisans from far away. Consider offering gift wrapping and hand or mail delivery for the gifts you sell.

Vicki G. and Sara L., two California friends, put to work a terrific selling idea. They both love needlework; making baby clothes has always been their favorite hobby. They decided to use it as the theme in their business venture. They started New Arrivals, an elite gift shop specializing in **handmade baby gifts** for ages up to one year. Everything in their shop is purchased from top-quality craft workers in their area. New Arrivals has everything from clothes and toys to furniture.

A **toy resale shop** can be set up in your garage or any unused space around your home. Accept toys that children are tired of or have outgrown. Sell them on consignment, keeping 50 percent of the sale price for yourself. The price you charge will be determined by your customers' readiness to buy and guided by your knowledge of fair selling prices. If you are handy at repairing toys, accept broken ones for resale. (You would keep a larger percentage of the sale price for yourself if you sold a toy you repaired.)

Rent a **motel room** in your city for one or two days, and sell your product from there to keep overhead down. (This is often cheaper than renting shop space.) You can sell on discount such things as jeans, brand-name skirts, blouses and tops, outerwear, and bathing suits. Consult the *Thomas Register of American Manufacturers,* found in most libraries. This book lists the names of many wholesale dealers in the United States. Write to one that carries a product you wish to sell, and ask if they will sell directly to you or will send you their local distributor's name and address. More specialized publications (e.g., *Profitable Craft Merchandising, Souvenirs and Novelties, Toys and Games)* can also be helpful in locating a salable product. Advertise the dates and hours of your motel sale in local newspapers and magazines. This kind of selling can be especially profitable around the holidays, since many people are buying gifts then. Should you need extra fitting rooms, free-standing portable privacy curtains can be rented for about $5 a day. In any case, you should arrange for exchanges in case there are any size problems.

Roxanne P. of Arizona used to be a sales clerk for a major department store in New York City. She is very much in tune with the latest fashions and decided to earn some money with her knowledge. She figured that many women in the smaller cities of the Southwest would enjoy seeing and buying the latest New York fashions, so she contacted an East Coast wholesaler and ordered a shipment of women's clothes. She made arrangements with several motel managers around the state to hold one-day sales at their motels. Then she placed newspaper ads. Her first selling trip covered four cities in four days; her initial cash investment totaled about $3,300 for the fashions, a vendor's license, motel rooms, food, gasoline, portable privacy screens (which she bought), advertising, long distance phone calls, and miscellaneous expenses. Her gross income came to just over $6,500, giving her a profit of more than $3,000. Roxanne has been conducting these selling trips three times a year for several years now. Women in the Southwest have never been better dressed.

If you live anywhere near a popular fishing spot, you might want to consider selling **live bait.** Gather night crawlers, crickets, grasshoppers, and minnows and sell them from your home. You'll need an old refrigerator, cooling tanks, bait tanks, reliable containers, and plastic bags. You can also consider growing your own night crawlers for sale. Printed how-to information on worms is available from companies listed in the classified sections of many outdoor magazines.

Dessie Ilene J. is a homemaker who lives near a popular fishing site in Tennessee. She needed to earn some extra cash, so she decided to take advantage of her location. She got some information on growing worms, and since it didn't sound too difficult, she decided to try it. With the help of her husband, Ed, she had their basement half-full of worm beds in two weeks. These tall, stackable units hold many shallow drawers filled with loose dirt and ground-up rotted leaves. The worms multiply in the drawers. Dessie converted her garage into a salesroom and installed an old refrigerator there to store the worms for sale. During the summer she also kept a large tank full of minnows. In her second big season, Dessie responded to fishermen's needs by adding to her inventory other types of bait, fishing lures and hooks, as well as soft drinks and snacks. Because she grows her worms indoors, there is never a weather problem, and since the big lake rarely freezes over, she has year-round customers.

If you have a passion for **purses,** start a home-based business selling designer purses, fabric purses, evening purses, shopping-bag-size purses, and suit-pocket-size purses, along with purse accessories such as wallets and key chains. Handbag wholesalers are listed in the *Thomas Register of American Manufacturers*. As a home-based entrepreneur, you won't have much overhead, so your prices can be at least 20 percent lower than those found in stores. Designer purses, for example, usually retail for $50-$200. There's often a 100 percent markup from the wholesaler to the retailer (that's you). So you can sell them for 20 percent less than most retailers and still have an 80 percent markup.

The Product Goes to the Customer. Sell **pet accessories** to animal lovers. Locate distributors of pet collars, toys, dishes, and name tags through pet magazines, journals, and clubs. Attend dog, cat, and horse shows, peddling such items as blankets, coats, brushes, and grooming aids.

You could also sell your products to boarding kennels and veterinarians or to the general public via newspaper ads.

Louise L. of Kentucky raises and breeds registered Morgan horses. She trains them to appear in shows near her home and in neighboring states. She and her husband own a truck camper and love traveling with their horse trailer in tow. With skyrocketing gasoline prices and rising inflation, Louise knew she had to find a way to earn some extra income—or give up her horses. Though she had won lots of ribbons showing her horses, those ribbons didn't pay the bills. For several months she had been feeding her horses a new high-protein feed that made their coats shiny and seemed to help them perform better. She asked the feed distributor if she could sell the feed in her area; in no time at all she was in business. Her route includes horse farms and feed stores to which she delivers once a week; she is currently expanding her range of customers. Louise pays $1,020 for a ton of feed and sells it for $1,440. She usually sells more than three tons a month. The money she earns allows her to continue showing her beloved Morgans.

Start a **craft-supply shop on wheels.** If you own a van or station wagon, stock it with items commonly needed by hobbyists, such as yarns, thread, needles, glue, and new craft kits. Take your store on wheels to nursing homes, retirement centers, hobby and craft shows, rural areas, and other places where supplies are hard to come by. Since you'll buy your items in quantity from wholesalers and thereby get a discount, you may be able to charge your customers less than stationary establishments (which have to pay rent and utilities) and still come out ahead. The convenience of your mobile service will encourage craft enthusiasts to buy. Your investment will include the costs of the products and of gasoline, insurance, repairs, tires, and possibly shelves for your vehicle. Be sure to consider these expenses when you are pricing your products.

A **mail-order business** can be an exciting, profitable venture. Millions of dollars in checks, money orders, and credit card transactions are spent each year by people who appreciate the variety and convenience that shopping by catalog affords, and who love the thrill of getting a package in the mail. Selling by mail is a way to reach people in big cities and in the middle of nowhere. Your customers are people who enjoy the lure of a tempting catalog or an inviting ad. Indeed, advertising is crucial to a mail-order business. It's all you have to convince your public of the worth of your product.

Just about anything can be sold by mail: food, toys, clothing, stationery, books, recipes, advice, teaching methods, records, camera equipment. You might already have a product at your disposal that you could market with minimal effort: ash fallout from Mount Saint Helens or seashells from your beachfront property. There are a few mail-order enterprises, however, that are illegal: (1) selling pornographic literature, pictures, or films, (2) operating lotteries and direct gambling setups, (3) selling any new drug without the approval of the Food and Drug Administration, and (4) sponsoring chain letters or pyramid schemes.

When you find a mail-order product you think others will benefit from buying, take a hard look at your finances. Your initial starting cost again depends on the product. If you decide to sell that volcanic ash, it shouldn't cost over a hundred dollars to start packaging the historic dust; cameras would require much more upfront money. To run the business, you need a headquarters to sell from. The amount of space required will depend on what you're selling. Tiny bottles of perfume can be stored in a closet, but huge floor cushions need more room.

You needn't be a college graduate for mail-order selling, but you do need plenty of good sense and determination to build a successful business. Educate yourself to the ins and outs of the enterprise. There are several published books fully explaining mail order businesses; one is listed for your reference in the bibliography at the end of this chapter. Mail order selling requires a vendor's license obtainable from your county licensing department. You should be brimming with questions about mailing laws, regulations, and prices; the post office supervisor can be very helpful in answering them. You may also want to subscribe to a government publication called *Domestic Mailing Manual*, costing $17 a year. The booklet is updated and revised by the post office as needed to cover mailing procedures and postal regulations for all classes of domestic mail. Check the post office; it's well worth the money.

When your business plan is set and you've decided on a target market, it's time to advertise. Buy mailing lists broken down into categories or occupational groupings (e.g., homemakers, merchants, teachers). Check the Yellow Pages under "Mailing Lists," or consult *Direct Mail List (Rates and Data)*, a directory listing brokers of specialized mailing lists. Advertise in selected magazines. For instance, monogrammed scarves and hats might do well in runners' magazines in the autumn months.

Nell B. loves candy, especially fudge. For years she has collected and experimented with fudge recipes. One day, when she was gathering all the recipes to keep them together in one place, she hit upon the idea of printing them and selling them through the mail. She typed and mimeographed them, stapling the pages together to make a small booklet. It took Nell about a week to complete the work, and her costs came to $.50 a copy.

She put ads in four different newspapers, offering her fudge recipes for $4. The response was so good that she assembled two more booklets, one of hamburger recipes and one of cheese dishes. Since her recipes are selling beyond her expectations, she plans to add a new recipe booklet to her line each year.

Check the newspapers to find out where major **events** such as parades, festivals, rock concerts, celebrities' personal appearances, political rallies, trade shows, and conventions are being held. Make or buy related items, such as badges and T-shirts, and sell them to people attending these functions. Other items that can be keyed to particular events include hats, glasses, mugs, scarves, pennants, and posters.

Larrilyn K. is a California kindergarten teacher who is such a sports fan that she fills up every weekend traveling to sports events in her state. Realizing that she was spending too much money on her tickets, food, lodging, and transportation, she decided to help fund her passion by selling souvenirs before and after each game, match, or meet. She ordered her products from a company that advertised in *Souvenirs and Novelties*. She converted her van into a **rolling souvenir shop,** hiring her brother to build shelves to hold breakable items like mugs, ashtrays, and glasses. Beneath the shelves are drawers for T-shirts, sweaters, jackets, and blankets appropriate to sell to fans of various teams. She bought plastic bins (the kind you store potatoes in) for badges, postcards, and pens. Umbrellas, pennants, and flags are carried and displayed in a detachable overhanging rack. Larrilyn sells her sports memorabilia near stadium parking lots and makes nearly as much money selling as she does teaching.

Door-to-door selling can be done in your spare time. You can sell encyclopedias, magazine subscriptions, Avon cosmetics, Fuller brushes, Watkins flavorings, Amway products, or furniture polish. Many people set up a route, and their customers look forward to regular visits and to new products on their doorsteps. Look in the Yellow Pages under the product category that interests you for companies that sponsor door-to-door selling ventures.

Selling by the **party plan** is big business today, and many women thrive on this type of work. Some of the products being sold at "parties" are: Tupperware, Mary Kay cosmetics, toys, pots and pans, plants, jewelry, and clothes. Many women love these informal get-togethers, because they can shop and visit with friends in the comfort of someone's home. The hostess usually receives a prize for giving the party, and if her party is a success, she may be offered employment as a company spokeswoman. Check your phone book or look through Moody's *OTC Industrial Manual* (available in most libraries) for the addresses of these home party companies. Write to them for further details.

Sidewalk selling can be an exciting challenge. Many people—such as homemakers, students, and downtown employees—sell part-time from street corners and parking lots because of the low overhead (no advertising costs, no showroom, no rent or utility bills). Check with your city license department for full details on what you can sell and where you can sell it. Then pick a heavily trafficked spot, and get permission to occupy the space from the owner or renter of the location (usually the merchant nearest to it). When traffic, both automobile and pedestrian, stops for a light or a sign, your potential customers have a chance to view your wares. Products sold on the street are usually items with universal appeal—plants or bouquets of flowers—or articles that trigger impulse buying—paintings or exotic trinkets. These goods can often be purchased from wholesalers in your area. The price you charge depends on what you have to pay for the products. Since you will probably have little or no competition, profit can range from 50 percent to 100 percent. But remember: Grossly overpriced items usually go unsold. Customers in cars have only until the light turns green to make up their minds about stopping at your display. Attractive signs and careful arrangement of your merchandise will encourage them to park and browse.

Marsha M. is a high school senior in New York. She's involved in so many extracurricular activities at school that she can't squeeze in even a part-time job. She began making flowers from crepe paper and selling them, for $1 singly and $5 in bouquets, on a busy downtown street corner on Saturday afternoons. Working from noon to five p.m. once a week nets Marsha enough money ($20-$25) to pay for school supplies, clothes, and cosmetics. She has so much fun that several of her friends have begun selling paper flowers on other street corners.

With some hard work, a little capital, and a lot of enthusiasm, you can turn a selling personality and a bright idea into a very profitable enterprise.

Suggested Reading

Friday, William. *How to Sell Your Product through (Not to) Wholesalers.* San Francisco: Prudent Publishing Co., 1980.

Garrison, William E. *Selling Your Handcrafts.* Radnor, Pennsylvania: Chilton, 1974.

Girard, Joe. *How to Sell Anything to Anybody.* New York: Warner Books, 1977.

Hyman, Henry A. *The Where to Sell Anything and Everything Book.* New York: World Almanac, 1981.

Simon, Julian. *How to Start and Operate a Mail Order Business.* New York: Mc-Graw-Hill, 1976.

Sims, Dennis C., et al. *The OK Saleswoman.* Palo Alto, California: TACL, 1977.

Standard Rate & Data Service, Inc. *Direct Mail List Rates and Data.* Skokie, Illinois: Standard Rate & Data Service, Inc., 1981.

Wage, L. A. *How to Use the Telephone in Selling.* Woodstock, New York: Beekman Publications, 1974.

Walters, Dottie. *Never Underestimate the Selling Power of a Woman.* New York: Frederick Fell Publishers, 1978.

Wood, Jane. *Selling What You Make.* New York: Penguin Books, 1973.

The Art of Extra Cash

14

(Jobs for the artistic and craftsy)

Arts and crafts are a stab at immortality—a way to say, "I was here." A unique brand of genius goes into every crocheted afghan or impressionistic watercolor, and a ceramic pot may well "live" long after the potter does. Years from now your grandchildren may remember you by the visual expressions you've left behind. There are few forevers when it comes to people-made products, but it's heartening to know you've contributed to the beauty of someone's home by painting a mural there or to the memories of a youngster by building a dreamed-of dollhouse. Maybe you can touch people with your artistic skills and talents—and make money in the process.

Arts and crafts opportunities for the home-based woman appear endless. You might be inclined to weave a colorful basket, dye and cut wool for a hooked rug, cross-stitch hospitality samplers, paint water-resistant designs on fabric, or sculpt a coffee-table figurine. There's a public out there waiting to buy what you make. Handcrafted merchandise is appreciated by young and old, rich and poor.

We're not about to try and solve the age-old, ongoing argument about whether craft is art (or the other way around) in this chapter, because we recognize that there is no clear-cut answer. Some people think of crafts as functional creations fashioned with manual dexterity (cloth games, enameled trivets, lettered invitations). If that's so, art is represented by purely aesthetic objects created mainly as expressions of the artist's attitude and feelings and born from her talent, taste, and imagination (a sketch, a paper sculpture, a clay statue). But artists may practice a craft (a caricaturist using lettering in her work), and craft workers create art (a basket weaver designing her own containers). The distinction is vague, and whether you consider an idea in this chapter an art or a craft is up to you.

Somewhere along the way you got hooked on arts and crafts. Maybe you loved the original creations of others and sought lessons to "do it yourself." Or you found the items you coveted most so expensive that you knew you'd have to make them or do without. Maybe you were lovingly taught by a grandmother who was rarely without a whittling knife in hand, or by a girl friend in high school who took you to an art camp one summer.

Your interest has turned you into an at-home artist or weekend craftworker, and you're curious about whether you can earn extra cash to feed your hobby or your family. Maybe you're a natural—someone who's always had her fingers in paint or is up to her elbows in clay. (You designed your senior class emblem and painted flowers on the window boxes at the church sale.) Or maybe you want to polish a skill or brush up on an artistic technique you picked up as a hobby in college or while babysitting on weekends. You're wondering whether you could make money by refining your skills, doing something you've enjoyed in your spare time. Whether you're a rainy-day painter or an after-the-kids-are-in-bed enameler, you recognize that the necessary levels of skill, involvement, time, and energy vary among the many creative ventures available to you.

If you flipped directly to this chapter in the book, it's safe to say you enjoy the creative process. And you would probably continue to find pleasure in it even if no one ever saw your work, bought it, or extended compliments on it. With that as a given, what this chapter is really saying is, "If you can make some extra cash doing something you enjoy, what are you waiting for?"

If you want to learn a new craft or polish one you already have, particiapte in workshops or courses offered at a craft supply store, the YWCA, or your public school's continuing education program—or find a master of the craft with whom you can work. You'll refine your technique and benefit from the creative stimulation of working with others. If you get compliments on your doodles, consider taking drawing classes. If you'd like to illustrate your town's centennial brochure, take a course to refresh your memory about color, design, and perspective—the fun things you took as electives in college. Community colleges and extension services often offer courses in particular techniques on evenings and weekends.

Before You Start

When you've developed the ability to create something you'd like to share, you've laid the foundation for an at-home business. But there are some important questions to ask before proceeding further.

How do you know you have a salable artistic skill?

Pamela D. knew when she made her mother a jute wreath, decorated with dried flowers and a rust-colored bow. Several people who saw it hanging in her mother's home called and asked her to make wreaths for them. If you get compliments on your handmade objects, and requests for more of them, chances are that people will be willing to buy them. There's never a guarantee, but informal surveys of people in your neighborhood can give you a fairly accurate picture of general public response.

Your competition in the marketplace may well be more vigorous than you imagine, with everyone trying to make extra money these days. Therefore, it's more important than ever to take a businesslike approach to your ideas. If selling knit slippers in a Montana town means joining ranks of slipper boutiques, you should probably choose another product. Do some market research to discover who your potential customers are, how to reach them, how large the market is, and how long it could support your business. (Once everyone in town has a dried-flower wall hanging, then what do you do?) Start out with a few sample pots or drawings; see how they sell before you invest a lot of time, effort, and money in building a huge inventory.

Why would the public want to buy your art or craft? There could be many reasons. People love the idea of handmade items and are drawn to individually designed products such as ceramic Christmas ornaments or coffee mugs with a different name on each one. One-of-a-kind items, like that blue bird you molded from clay or the necklace you made from shells, are popular: we all enjoy owning "the only one on the block." Basically, your customers will buy a product if they like it, if they can't make it themselves, and if the price is right.

How much time are you willing to devote to your craft or your artwork? If you dabble in some artistic endeavor, you know the time required to do a good job. If you're thinking of selling your work on a regular basis, you must be willing and able to dedicate a good part of each day to getting the sketch finished or the stencil made. Don't underestimate the time needed for each project. Keep track of the time it takes to complete a product—from the birth of the idea to the signature in the corner. This will help you determine what size operation you can best handle.

What about pricing your work? Keeping track of your time will also help you price your work. If it takes hours to produce an item and, for whatever reason, you can only charge a small price, that craft is a less-than-optimal choice if you hope to make much money. Consider your time, the cost of materials, and the price customers might be willing to pay. Be concerned about keeping costs down. Be alert for chances to use your environment for ideas and supplies. That old red barn in the country may be perfect for your watercolor painting, and those pinecones and berries would make a beautiful Christmas decoration. If you sell the product yourself, the price of materials multiplied by two might be a fair selling price. But since there is art whose labor value far outweighs the cost of materials (*beadcraft,* for instance), you must decide on a price that is fair to you and your customers. But if you offer your pottery or party hats on consignment, you will have to raise the price, since most shops charge one-fourth to one-third of the selling price for each stained-glass sun catcher, beaded jewel box, or crocheted lace doily they sell.

Observe your competition and find out what is selling where, to whom, and at what price. Compare your products with competing ones and see how yours rank with others in price and design. Watch the market for new trends, as some products sell all the time and others lose their popularity after only a short time. Items like mood rings and pet rocks come and go quickly, but hula hoops are still being sold in the stores.

Do you have a specific place at home where your craft supplies and equipment can be left without disturbance from the dog or the kids? Space is of utmost importance if you are going to spend a part of each day with your craft. Clear out that spare bedroom and make it into a workroom; turn a corner of the basement into a studio; rearrange the walk-in closet downstairs and throw out the junk—you may be surprised how roomy it is. If you have no available nook in the house, maybe you can use a part of the garage. Allow for plenty of ventilation if you're painting with oils, spread lots of newspaper on the floor if you're making pulp for papier-mâché, and be sure to keep little feet outside when you're cutting glass.

Do you have the ability to meet order deadlines? Only you can answer that. If you go into a frenzy every time the house needs to be cleaned, you need to shop for groceries, and the dog has to go to the veterinarian all in the same day, forget it. You must have the ability to look ahead and schedule your time in order to meet deadlines. Stay calm, and recruit help from family members when needed. Above all, be realistic about the number and complexity of orders you can deliver. Irresponsibility is promising to deliver two hundred handwritten wedding invitations in twenty-four hours. Your professionalism and your reputation are built on quality and consistency. Be honest with yourself and your customers: Make realistic deadlines, and accept only those jobs you *know* you can do well.

Do you know how to copyright your original designs? If you are a craftsperson who has spent many hours giving birth to new items, consider getting a copyright to protect your creations. A copyright is legal protection for an original work and that protection begins when your creation is completed. From that point, only you (or someone who has your permission) can reproduce, display, or distribute the work. But to ensure protection of your work, be certain that the copyright notice is easily seen on your art or craft. Use the symbol © or the word, copyright, along with the year it was created and the name of the creator. If you foresee that others could copy your design or infringe on your rights to it as its creator, register your copyright with the Copyright Office within three months of the time you make your work public. Write to the Register of Copyrights (Copyright Office, Library of Congress, Washington, D.C. 20559) indicating the type of work you wish to copyright. On receiving the appropriate forms, complete and return them with a required fee to the Copyright Office. You will also forward a copy (or in some cases, a photograph) of your creation for the Library of Congress collection. In return, you'll receive a certificate of registration which gives your work in-depth protection.

For more information about the copyright law, regulations, etc., write to the Copyright Office for a free Copyright Information kit. Be prepared, if you register with the Copyright Office, to act on infringements to your work; you can't ignore some infringements and fight others. The Copyright Office doesn't provide legal advice, so if you ultimately decide to bring suit against someone, recruit the services of a lawyer knowledgeable in copyright law and be prepared to prove that your registration was the first one filed.

Do you know when you can sell a craft based on an idea you get from a book or magazine—and when you might be violating someone else's copyright? Only the artistic content of the copyrighted work is protected. Anyone can use the same source material and give his or her own artistic impression of it. You and your neighbor can paint or photograph the same scene, the Statue of Liberty, for example, because it's in the public domain; you are not violating a copyright. But you can't sculpt Donald Duck or do a spin-off of someone's copyrighted design for a new game. You will know that something is protected by the copyright line on the work. If you try to sell a design that even resembles a copyrighted design, you're stretching your luck. For example, you cannot copy Miss Piggy, Mickey Mouse, or Snoopy, even with small changes. And, even though your work may give Snoopy hair and blue eyes, if your creation is still publicly recognizable as Snoopy, you're infringing on someone's copyright. Lawsuits have been brought against craft workers who copied or made minor changes in copyrighted designs and sold them as originals. The best advice about deciding whether selling your work is an infringement of copyright is: When in doubt, don't use the design.

You can sell your original handicrafts at art fairs, flea markets, garage sales, craft shows, and gift shops or through the mail. You may exhibit your artwork in galleries, community buildings, and regional art centers. Specific information on how and where to sell your art and crafts is available by consulting the *National Directory of Shops/Galleries/Shows/Fairs: Where to Exhibit & Sell Your Work,* listed in the Suggested Reading following this chapter.

A smattering of springboard ideas follows, to whet the appetites of existing and potential artists and craft workers. To turn the ideas into reality, count on doing plenty of research and spending a lot of time planning. Reference books and mentors can teach you many things. The most valuable lessons are learned, however, when you're up to your wrists in glue or on your knees cleaning up a mess you've made with india ink.

Today's marketplace supports originality and style. Regardless of how long your craft has been practiced, your ingenuity can invent new ideas and find creative ways to give life to age-old ones. As long as people see beauty in artistic creations, there will be an audience for your work.

Ornaments and Decorations

Decoupage is the art of decorating surfaces with applied paper cutouts. Your basic supplies include: colored pencils or other coloring media, curved scissors, containers for glue and water, a sponge, a lintless cloth, a tape measure, a ruler, varnish or lacquer, brushes, turpentine, sealer, sandpaper, steel wool, and finishing compound. To prepare an object for decoupage, you'll sandpaper it, then paint or stain it. Apply a sealer; then glue on a cutout design. Varnish it and rub it down several times, waiting twenty-four hours between each coat. Finish by rubbing down the surface with steel wool until it has a soft, dull glow. You'll need lots of arid storage room for best drying results.

Stained glass has become a popular craft in this country. Once you've mastered the procedures (usually by taking lessons at workshops), there are endless possibilities for you to earn extra income. Stained glass is used in windows in homes, restaurants, and churches, as well as in lamps, mirrors, clocks, and chess and checker boards. Sun catchers hanging in windows are also very appealing. Working with stained glass requires a lot of patience, time (it may take as long as forty hours to assemble a Tiffany-style lamp from a kit), and special knowledge, especially if you create original designs and cut your own glass. When possible, work for a while with an expert, who can give you tips learned through years of experience.

Jill B. is an ambitious young woman from Massachusetts. After a government cutback, she was left unemployed as a social worker. Jill decided that while she was waiting for another job, she would try to sell some of the lamps and other stained-glass items she'd been making and storing away. She had taken lessons for almost five years at the shop where she purchased her stained glass, and she'd learned how to cut the glass and how to design her own ornamental pieces. After selling most of her stained-glass work in only a few months, she realized that her hobby could probably earn her as much as her former job—about $15,000 a year. Soon she opened her own shop and began teaching classes, selling the glass and other materials needed by her students. She now spends a lot of time studying the "Tiffany era," and as a result, her designs match that period. She sells her merchandise through the mail and in other shops, as well as in her own. A few of her lamps and windows are in elegant homes in Boston.

Shell art is lovely and easy to do, and it has a wide range of uses. If shells are not readily available to you, check the Yellow Pages under the following headings: Arts and Crafts Supplies, Hobby and Model Construction Supplies, Jewelers' Supplies, and Shells—Marine. Shells can be transformed into flower arrangements, jewelry, lamps, picture and mirror frames, wind chimes, and beautiful wall plaques. The supplies you need will depend on what you make, but some common ones found in craft supply stores are resins, epoxy cement, wire cutters, chain-nosed pliers, and paint brushes.

With **papier-mâché** you can become an artisan for the price of glue, cord, acrylic paints, and a batch of newspapers and paper towels, plus discards you don't know what to do with. There are several formulas for working with papier-mâché, but the most common is the homemade paper pulp method. You can shape the pulp into many different forms before painting. A large worktable covered with clean newspapers is needed to ensure that your work will dry undisturbed. This craft is often messy, but the results can be delightful: a colorful piñata or a coal mine for a model-train display.

Alice M. of Maine got interested in papier-mâché when she had her cub scouts using the pulpy mixture and cutting festive shapes with cookie cutters to make Christmas tree ornaments. While she was snowed in after Christmas, she began experimenting with other papier-mâché projects shown in the library book she had borrowed. She began covering plaster-of-paris owls with newspaper squares, using heavy cord for the eyes, beak, wings, and tail. She painted them gold, finished them with acrylic gloss varnish, and began giving them as gifts. When summer came, Alice placed her owls in a nearby gift shop that tourists frequented. They sold out fast, and she furnished the store with more. Alice sold twelve dozen owls at $8 each. Since her materials (mostly newspaper) were so cheap, she cleared about $800.

Found objects, such as cones, pods, and cattails, can be transformed into centerpieces, ornaments, wreaths, candle holders, wind chimes, mobiles, and jewelry. There are many flowers and leaves to press, wild fruits to preserve, and nuts, cones, and seeds to make into natural home decorations. To kill any bugs, cone artists heat their supplies in a 150- to 200-degree oven for an hour before they use them. Basic supplies for many of these craft ideas are inexpensive. They include wire, Elmer's glue, clear acrylic spray or paint, ribbon, Styrofoam, and Masonite Peg-Board. Books showing how to make the decorative keepsakes offer valuable tips and can be used as stepping stones to experimenting with your own ideas.

Judy S. of Michigan is an expert craftswoman and has been involved in everything from tole painting to making jewelry from polished rocks. One of the crafts she enjoys most is working with **pine cones,** which are plentiful in her part of the state. A favorite project is the American eagle she makes from cone scales. She glues the scales with linoleum paste onto wallboard cut into an eagle shape. The eagle's wings are made from large scales and its head from smaller ones. Judy sells these decorative eagles (as well as other cone crafts) for $15 each at her frequent garage sales and at church bazaars and flea markets.

Ribbon art is fairly simple to master and requires no special knowledge other than a basic understanding of hand sewing and, for certain projects, a grasp of the rudiments of knitting and crocheting. It involves using ribbon to macrame, weave, and braid unique decorations. Many items can even be made by children, and materials are easily found in craft supply stores. All widths of ribbon may be used, according to what you are making.

Beth R. of Texas likes to make **bookmarks** from ribbon scraps, giving them to friends and selling them at church bazaars and craft shows. Her favorite ribbon art, though, is making free-form **wall hangings** by weaving different widths and textures of ribbons in lines and blocks to form an all-over pattern. Although each hanging takes fifty-six yards of ribbon and two wooden rods, Beth profits by buying her ribbon on sale. Her hangings are so unusual that she sells them at shows throughout the year for $50 each.

Beadcraft uses a variety of beads strung on sturdy thread (nylon fishing line works well) to create jewelry, wall plaques, centerpieces, ornaments, wreaths, small Christmas trees, handbags, room dividers, and boxes and other containers. To practice beadcraft, you'll need wire cutters, long-nosed pliers, a small ruler, and a few thumbtacks. Florists' supplies are needed for "planting" flowers if you design beadcraft centerpieces. Both your hands and your eyes will get a workout with this craft, as will your patience to see an intricate project through to completion.

Lois R. of Maryland stopped at a craft shop one day to buy "just a few beads" she needed to complete a wall hanging. Since she was getting the beads at a wholesale price, she decided to stock up on other supplies and ended up spending $300. She soon realized that her budget couldn't accommodate her spending binge, but the store refused to take any of the beads and supplies back, because she had purchased them wholesale. Determined to salvage some good from this predicament, Lois bought some fishing line and made three necklaces. She wore one to a meeting the next day, and one of her associates loved it. The associate bought one of the necklaces for $25. In a restaurant later that day a waitress asked about the necklace; Lois knew she was on to something. She now makes one-of-a-kind jewelry and her work has been featured in several magazines. By capitalizing on a situation she couldn't change (a mountain of bead supplies), Lois has turned her creativity into a lucrative business.

Stenciling is an art form that uses an impervious material, such as thin cardboard or woven fabric, perforated with a design. Paint is forced onto a surface through the perforations in the stencil. Stencils can be bought at art supply stores and are light enough to be held in place with masking tape. Stencil designs can dress up fabrics, wood, paper, clay pots, walls, windows, doors, and furniture and can even be used to edge wooden floors. After taping a stencil in place on a piece of smoothly sanded wood, for example, use a stencil brush in an up-and-down tapping motion to apply the paint (usually alkyd enamel). After the paint is dry, the stencil is removed, and a protective coating of polyurethane varnish is applied to the wood. A steady hand, a strong arm, and patience are a stenciler's traits, as this work can sometimes be tedious. Knowing what looks good on a drab door frame or a bare wall will set you apart from those who know the stenciling procedure but lack the artistic flair to create unforgettable work.

Ellen M. of Oregon saw rooms decorated with stencil art at a home decorating show. She asked questions about it and found that an area home improvement store would be giving lessons in stenciling. She signed up for the classes and learned the techniques of applying and brushing a stencil and sealing it in place. She tried the process on furniture and window shades in her own home. Friends who saw her work asked her to do stencil art in their

208 Extra Cash for Women

homes, and before she realized it, she was in business. She began advertising to do decorative stenciling of her own designs. After years of experience, Ellen began giving stenciling lessons to other "weekend artists." She charges $10 an hour for her stenciling work and about half that for an hour lesson.

Useful Objects

Candle making is a hobby that can be turned into a money-making venture. If you have made candles for yourself or your friends, begin to take orders, and build your business gradually. Make candles for everyday use and for special occasions and holidays, such as Christmas, Easter, birthdays, weddings, and anniversaries. Be cautious while working with the hot wax, and if you have small children around, be sure they stay clear of your work area. To make candles on a regular basis, you'll need a well-defined, fully equipped workshop. This is not a craft whose equipment you can put in a drawer at day's end or carry around in a suitcase.

Caning chairs can put money in your pocket. Many people with beautiful old chairs in need of reseating have difficulty finding someone to do the job. Chair caning is not difficult, but it requires care and patience. You can start caning chairs inexpensively, as the basic tools needed are a penknife, a hammer, pliers, scissors, a small stiletto, and a clearing tool (a flat-topped instrument used with a hammer to clear the holes of old cane). You can learn the craft by taking workshop classes at the YWCA or by finding someone who does caning to teach you. There are also instruction books on caning at libraries and craft supply shops. If you are already adept in this art, you might consider teaching others who would like to learn.

Lacy A. of Mississippi has always had great admiration for almost-forgotten arts and crafts, like chair caning. She learned this craft when she was only nine years old from her great-aunt Tac, and she's been practicing it ever since. About ten years ago she had mastered four different forms of seating—rush, willow, seagrass, and cord—and figured she could earn some extra cash with her skill. She made several design samples—the standard octagon cane design, a Scandinavian rush design, a diamond cord design, and others—which she showed to local antique-shop owners, asking for repair work. She also contacted some of the small furniture craftworkers in her area. Over a period of two years, her business really boomed, and now her schedule is booked weeks in advance. The standard octagon cane seat takes Lacy approximately two days to complete and nets her $90.

Quilting is another age-old art that testifies to the industry and thrift of women in America. We'll discuss quilting in Chapter 15, but to whet your appetite to its money-making possibilities here's a look at a quilt maker who combines her artistic talent with a love for history.

Drucilla P., a North Carolina homemaker, makes historical handmade quilts. On each quilt she embroiders a story about a specific event in American history. Her Civil War quilt is by far the most popular, because it tells the story of the Civil War from beginning to end. It takes her about two months to complete one quilt, and each sells for$250-$500, depending on the kind of material she uses. The quilts cost her approximately $50 a piece to make. Drucilla's history quilts are sold in gift shops and through the mail from ads placed in regional magazines. One was sent as far away as Australia to an avid American-history buff.

Basket weaving has become quite popular these days, mainly because of the hundreds of new and revived uses for attractive basketry chairs, tables, planters, decorator pieces, room dividers, headboards and picture and mirror frames. Tools required for basketry are not expensive—shears, round-nosed pliers, a knife, and an awl. Most basketry is made from cane or willow, which can be bought in craft shops. Two kinds of material are used: Firm lengths called warp serve as spokes or ribs of the basket; lighter, more flexible pieces called weft are woven around the warp. Basket weaving is slow and time-consuming. Try this craft if you are patient and have nimble fingers and quite a bit of leisure time.

Barbara M. of New York got interested in basketry when she was home-based with two small children. She took some evening classes at the YWCA to learn the basics and went on from there with the aid of some instruction books. Because she soon had too many baskets around the house, she tried to think of something she could make and sell. She decided on dog and cat beds made from willow, with colorful cushions to fit inside. She asked pet shops in her city if they would carry her pet baskets. Fourteen owners agreed. Though Barbara isn't getting rich, she sells between fifty and sixty pet baskets a year at $50 each. It usually takes her twelve to sixteen hours to hand-make a basket and her profit is $32 on each one. Because she enjoys her part-time craft, Barbara is thinking of expanding her line to include baby bassinets.

Gourdcraft is quite uncommon, but very handsome and useful. Gourds can be grown in the backyard. They have long running vines similar to those of cucumbers, melons, and pumpkins. After they are harvested and allowed to dry, they can be fashioned into canisters, bowls, jewelry, birdhouses, and centerpieces. If you're a city dweller, you can buy gourds at farm markets or grocery stores.

Charlotte M., an Arkansas homemaker, is a gourd lover. She grows gourds of all shapes, sizes, and textures. In 1974 Charlotte and her parents took a trip to India, where she discovered **musical instruments** made from gourds. The vina, the sitar, and the tamboura are all stringed gourd instruments. Charlotte dreamed of making one herself. A few years later, when she was married, she managed to interest Jon, her husband, in the same idea. After much study into gourds, they decided to grow them in their small yard and to try making the instruments. Screw hooks were put into their roof, and thin wires running from the roof hooks were fastened into a wide, flat board on the ground to give the gourds something to climb on. The plants grew beautifully. Some of the gourds were molded into desired shapes by putting bands around them as they grew. Hanging from the eaves, they were definitely a conversation piece for friends and neighbors. Once the gourds were picked and dried and cut, drilled and fastened appropriately, they became violins, guitars, and lutes. Both Charlotte and Jon have learned to play instruments; they enjoy playing them as much as making them. They sell about six instruments a year for $200-$500 each—nearly all profit because, though the craft takes time, it doesn't cost much money.

Needlework is probably the most popular of all crafts. Crewel embroidery, needlepoint, crochet, knitting, and bargello (a vertical needlepoint stitch) are just a few of the needle crafts that can be used to make pictures, wall hangings, afghans, shawls, coats, and rugs and to decorate pillows, clothing, accessories, seat covers, and cushions. Needlework requires patience and the ability to do close, detailed work with small finger movements, using various needles, hooks, and stitches. One of its most appealing features is its portability: You can do it anywhere. (You'll find more information on moneymaking needlecraft options in Chapter 15.)

Making **pottery** by hand remains one of the most satisfying and fascinating arts. Earthenware is the oldest and most common pottery type, although stoneware and porcelain are also popular. Different pottery products require different kinds of clay, which can be bought in powdered prepared form. Many objects can be shaped by hand, but a potter's wheel can help a crafts person transform a shapeless lump of clay into a hollow pot in what seems like a matter of minutes. The pots can be decorated with designs, either by pressing molded glazing to the surface in a relief treatment or by painting them with enamels or other inorganic paints and inks that won't burn out during firing. Many potters have their own kilns, either electric or gas, to fire their pottery. Equipment and supplies can be expensive for this hobby, and you should learn well the many techniques of the craft before investing in tools and undertaking the trade as a moneymaking venture.

Wanda A. of South Carolina has been kneading and throwing lumps of clay for years, making decorative pots, teapots, jugs, mugs, and dishes. Since she lives on a major street of a popular tourist spot, her pottery attracts passing motorists like an automobile showroom when the new models come out. She became interested in pottery many years ago when she and her late husband took a vacation through the Southwest. She learned to appreciate the many different colors, designs, and symbols and learned to read the stories told in pictures on the pottery. She was so inspired by what she saw that she enrolled in several pottery classes on her return to South Carolina. Her part-time fascination soon became a full-time occupation. After her husband's death, she was especially glad to have a meaningful activity. Today her monthly pottery earnings add over $200 to her social security check.

Not Just for Kids

Edna M. is a North Dakota wife and the mother of two children. She is also a longtime collector and lover of **dollhouses.** She buys handmade dollhouses from a retired man in her town and makes all the furnishings herself. Some of her materials come from a craft supply house, and some articles, like the tiny toothbrushes in the bathrooms, are improvisations of her own. Edna is showing a good profit from her orders for fully decorated and outfitted dollhouses, especially at Christmas.

Soft-sculpture toys bring all kinds of shapes to life: the exotic (giraffes, elephants, camels, spiders, dragonflies, bumblebees, ostriches, peacocks, and flamingos) and the common (horses, hens, pigs, roosters, and, of course, teddy bears). The materials used to make these toys are found in many homes—scraps of cloth or felt, yarn, pipe cleaners, and buttons. Patterns are needed to make the toys, but be sure not to use someone else's copyrighted design. If you are making stuffed creatures to sell, design your own pattern and copyright your work (as described on p. 203).

Betsy Jo K. of Missouri is a very busy woman. She is not only a preschool teacher, but a wife and the mother of an energetic five-year-old son, Aaron. Betsy Jo has enjoyed making dolls and stuffed animals since she learned to sew in high school. She makes them for her nieces and nephews at Christmas. After Aaron was born, she started making them in the shapes of characters from his favorite bedtime stories and nursery rhymes, such as the Three Little Kittens and Hansel and Gretel. Her son loved the creatures so much that she began selling her creations. One of her best customers is the hospital gift shop; her stuffed dolls and animals bring cheer and smiles to kids trying to get well.

The Art of Pens, Pencils and Brushes

Be an **illustrator**. Drawing is a special talent, nurtured through practice. Many drawing enthusiasts began their practice on grade school desks and later drew for high school newspapers. They may or may not have had formal training, but they continue drawing because they enjoy it. If you have often been asked to draw for others and have accumulated sketches over the years, make up a portfolio of your work and include examples of your various styles—humorous line drawings, sketches of commercial products, still lifes, portraits, etc. Let these be your calling card to book publishers and printers, art studios, advertising agencies, agents, greeting card firms, and magazines who use freelance artists. Or you may decide to sell your artwork directly through the mail, at bazaars, art and craft shows and fairs. *Artist's Market* is an excellent source for finding potential buyers and learning how to query them. Sending the right work to the right buyer is very important, so do some homework before applying the postage to your envelope. Knowing how to submit sketches to a potential client, how many to include, and what kind to send establishes your professionalism and could be an important factor in landing an assignment. You won't get the chance for an illustration credit (and some cash) if you never share your work.

Cutting **silhouettes** means scissoring a profile of someone or something out of black construction paper. To make following the outline easier, the subject is often placed behind a thin screen with a bright light focused on it to form a sharp silhouette. Some people can do one in five to ten minutes. Once the silhouette is cut, it is mounted on a white background and framed. Offer to do silhouette portraits of youngsters at a birthday party. Think about "cutting" the same people at some high school activity years later. What you charge for a silhouette will depend on your materials and your expertise.

Hire yourself out as a **caricaturist** for parties, and draw pictures that exaggerate the characteristics of the guests. This unusual idea, popular with guests, will appeal to the host who wants his or her party to be a little different from the ordinary get-together. If you enjoy drawing, take art classes from the YWCA, evening classes at your local high school, or a noncredit college course. Learn how to refine the characters you've been drawing for years during telephone conversations. Practice. Then charge the host a flat fee for attending a party and drawing the guests.

Helen D. of New Hampshire is a self-taught caricaturist who began in high school, amusing her teachers with her humorous character sketches. After she married, she penciled caricatures of her friends' children and started getting requests for her funny drawings at parties she attended.

When the family income was reduced because of a slowdown in her husband's selling job, she set up an easel in the neighborhood shopping mall and began drawing the shoppers. She did quite well, especially on weekends. As a result of advertising in newspapers and trade magazines, she began working at conventions, fairs, and trade shows, making a nice income from her ten-minute cartoon drawings.

Calligraphy is the art of beautiful or elegant handwriting. If you have a steady hand and the time to practice the flowing calligraphic strokes (with fine-, medium- and broad-nib pens dipped in rich black ink), advertise to reproduce famous quotations and poems, inscribe invitations and announcements, and design posters for community events. Few people have the time or inclination to master the tricks of a smooth line and evenly spaced, perfectly slanted letters. Yet many appreciate the elegance of the finished product.

Mary Ellen P. is a schoolteacher in Iowa. When the local high school needed someone to hand-letter diplomas, she got the job. She enjoyed it so much that she wrote to high schools and colleges all over her state, sending them samples of her work and offering to do their diplomas. She's been lettering for years now and finds the work relaxing, even though it's time-consuming and the pay doesn't reflect the time involved. Mary Ellen earned $900 last year in her "after-school job."

Do **oil or watercolor paintings** if you have the experience and training. A lot of people would love to own your originals. You could do a painting to match the decor of a room; offer to paint an accent scene to go above a customer's rust-colored couch. You could paint customers' personal possessions—boats, airplanes, favorite musical instruments. You might do watercolors of their children or pets. Advertise that you can work from a photo if that is most convenient for your customer. The best way to paint from a photograph is to enlarge it with an opaque projector. This speeds up the work while ensuring that you get precise details and dimensions. Project the image onto the size of canvas you plan to use; trace the lines, and your picture should be perfect. Then you're ready to paint. Charge from $50 to $500 for your watercolors, depending on the design, complexity, and size of the paintings.

Draw and paint original cartoon characters or colorful scenes on **children's playroom or bedroom walls.** Day-care centers, preschools, and other places where children romp might hire you for this colorful work. Some people have a natural ability to do this work, and others take art classes to learn the basics of figure drawing, perspective, and other necessary skills, or to refine the techniques they've been using in their just-for-fun drawing sessions. Know your customers before you begin, as some people are hard to please. Find out what the customer wants on the wall, and be honest about whether you can do the job. Give an estimate of the cost and of the time you'll need to complete the project. Let customers know whether the paint you use is washable, how long it will take to dry, and whether it can be touched up if it becomes damaged.

If you have success with wall-painting for children, you might advertise to paint **landscape murals** on commercial and residential walls. As you complete each job, take a photo and build a portfolio to share with potential customers. Much practice and an ample supply of confidence are needed to paint an aesthetically pleasing composition with the right dimensions and an appropriate subject and color scheme. You could land a contract to do all the wall murals in that new professional building in your town.

It takes talent, taste, and skill to turn an art or craft hobby into a moneymaking enterprise. But most of all it takes confidence. If you're lucky enough to have the first three qualities, don't hide your work in a desk drawer or an old trunk. Let it be a source of pride and, we hope, of cash.

Suggested Reading

Bodger, Lorraine, and Delia Ephron. *Crafts for All Seasons.* Englewood, New York: Universe Publishing, 1980.

Brabec, Barbara. *Creative Cash.* Milwaukee: Countryside Books, 1976.

Davis, Sally Ann, ed. *1982 Artist's Market.* Cincinnati: Writer's Digest Books, 1981.

Davis, Sally Ann, ed. *1982 National Directory of Shops/Galleries/Shows/Fairs.* Cincinnati: Writer's Digest Books, 1981.

Dyer, Anne. *Design Your Own Stuffed Toys.* Newton Center, Massachusetts: Charles T. Branford Co., 1969.

Frederick, Filis. *Design and Sell Toys, Games and Crafts.* Radnor, Pennsylvania: Chilton, 1977.

Jaffares, Katherine. *Calligraphy: The Art of Beautiful Writing.* North Hollywood, California: Wilshire Book Co., 1978.

Marsten, Barbara. *Step-by-Step Dollmaking.* New York: Van Nostrand Reinhold, 1981.

McCall's Needlework and Crafts Magazine editors. *McCall's Needlework Treasury.* New York: Random House, 1964.

Ossin, Archie and Myrna. *How to Start and Run a Profitable Craft Business.* Fern Park, Florida: Ossi Publications, 1977.

Parry, Megan. *Stenciling.* New York: Van Nostrand Reinhold, 1977.

Reader's Digest editors. *Crafts and Hobbies.* New York: Norton, 1979.

Switkin, Abraham. *Hand Lettering Today.* New York: Harper & Row, 1976.

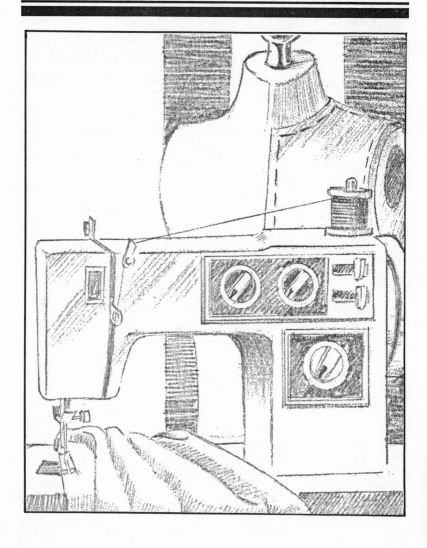

Sew & Sew & Sew   15

(From sewing machine work to hand needlework to alterations)

Sewing is power—the power to dress yourself and your family and to outfit windows, beds, and couches, usually at a fraction of the cost of buying ready-made items in local department stores. Besides going easy on the family's finances by "making it yourself," you can use your sewing skill to beef up the bank account by making things for others. If sewing clothes isn't your forte, your skills may lie in a variation on the needle-and-thread theme: knitting, embroidery, quilting, tatting, or hand sewing. Whether functional or decorative, sewing and other needle arts are money-making opportunities for the home-based woman.

Because many people don't have the time, talent, or inclination to cut out a pattern or replace a zipper, you, the ambitious seamstress, can usually find more work than you might have imagined. But before you agree to make your niece's graduation dress or the drapes to match your neighbor's bedspread, be confident of your ability to do a good job. Sewing for others isn't quite the same as whipping up a Halloween costume for your four-year-old, who couldn't care less whether the seams matched.

Be Prepared

Your customers will expect faultless work (they're paying you for clothes and home furnishings that are a reflection of them). You must have the patience to see a job through, the ability to measure for a perfect fit or to match a color not found in nature, *and* the skill to sew it up. Other times you may be asked to do alterations on ill-fitted clothing; this requires being able to recognize a problem fit and knowing how to correct it. You may be under a deadline, working to finish a project in time for a ceremony or class play. If you measure up in all these categories, you could build a lucrative business. But expertise, good intentions, and lots of customers don't always ensure a successful business venture.

Dotty W. of Indiana is a wife and the mother of four children. A few years ago, she started a clothing repair and alterations service for some of the local dry cleaners. She also offered her expertise to the public through well-placed newspaper ads. It wasn't long before Dotty was swamped with stacks of mending work. On top of that, her own family had ripped seams, lost buttons, and raveled hems of their own. But she needed the money desperately; the paying customers had to come first. Her house was always cluttered with piles of work, and the phone was ringing off the hook with more alteration jobs. Because Dotty was at home, her family never took her business seriously; they never offered any help with the regular chores. One hectic day her faithful sewing machine sewed its last stitch, and Dotty hadn't put any of her earnings aside to replace it. She had to rent a machine to finish the work she had already undertaken. Tired and disappointed, she gave up her business and got a job at Wendy's Old Fashioned Hamburgers.

Planning your business before you start taking orders can make all the difference. Being prepared means having a machine that allows you to do everything from monograms to bound buttonholes and that can accommodate metallic, velvet, satin, or lace fabrics. Being prepared also means deciding how much you can handle. And it means being confident of your ability (and the machine's) to make a doll's wardrobe or a poodle's coat, i.e., whatever your customer wants. Or you may decide to specialize in one or two areas (because of your expertise, the limitations of your machine, or heavy demand) and offer your services to a well-defined clientele.

If you have practical experience in designing clothes, you could stand apart from your competition in another way. If you can choose fabrics, styles, and colors to suit your customers' tastes and needs, you'll have them coming back for more.

Robin W. of South Dakota is a single woman confined to a wheelchair. She makes and sells camouflage clothing for hunters, including T-shirts, pants, jackets, and hats. She got the idea for her business when she saw her brother digging out his old army clothes to wear for hunting. She had been looking for something she could do to earn money at home—something interesting that would make her feel useful. Robin buys the camouflage-patterned fabric wholesale from a sporting goods company. She advertises in local gun shops and sporting goods stores and in some national hunting magazines. The orders come in from all over the United States and Canada. With her brother helping with packaging and mailing, Robin netted $4,600 last year.

Your business sense must include knowing what start-up funds you'll need. If you already own a reliable machine, your initial costs should be minimal. If not, remember that a good quality sewing machine can make your work easier and your product more professional. Prices range anywhere from under $100 to over $500, depending on the type of machine, its features, and the attachments that accompany it. You can buy a reputable machine for about $250. If you invest $500, you can get a machine that sews five styles of buttonholes and has an even-feeding foot that helps you work on knits, tricot, satin, and other slick or thick fabrics without bunching and an extra-wide zigzag stitch for heavy or easily frayed fabrics. Such a machine also offers several utility and stretch stitches and as many as thirty decorative stitches. After you have a machine you feel comfortable with, the rest of your supplies are fairly inexpensive: scissors, pins, needles, tape measures, hem markers, and thimbles are some items you may already have. If you decide to do dressmaking, an adjustable dress form, which can be purchased for under $50, is a must.

As a self-employed businesswoman, you must record your expenses (fabric, notions, machine use, electric bills) and the time you spend sewing, so you can determine what to charge your customers. Check with seamstresses in your area who do similar work. Your expert workmanship, combined with lower-than-department-store prices, should make your sewing skills a real find for people who think needles are only found on pine trees.

If you don't have a good sewing machine, you may still be able to earn extra cash with a needle. You might even use your skill in hand sewing or embroidery to earn money to pay for the machine you want.

Esther F. of Alabama loved to sew and used her mother's machine to clothe her family and decorate her home. When she moved to Missouri, she missed having a machine and couldn't afford to buy one. She began crocheting and knitting sweaters and hats and found an outlet for them at a local boutique. In three months Esther made $175, enough for a down payment on a new sewing machine. In a year's time, Esther paid off the machine and finished making draperies for her new home. Now she not only knits and crochets, but also sews knapsacks and sleeping bags to order, as well as purses to sell at the boutique. Esther's business earned her $1,200 last year.

If you sewed for your boyfriend in college or made a suit in home ec one year, you will probably have no trouble with straightforward sewing jobs. But how many people come to you with perfect figures or standard sofa measurements? If you've never sewn for others or if you'd like to polish skills you've been using all along, consider taking some of the many courses offered at stores that sell sewing machines or fabric. Qualified instructors teach you about new trends and techniques. Some classes start with the basics; others give advice on sewing with knits; advanced classes deal with tailoring, styling, and fashion. Such courses may also be offered by the YWCA or area colleges and fashion schools, or you can learn from someone you know who sews well. To gain hands-on experience and confidence, try working at a sewing center that gives lessons. Daily contact with instructors will help expand your knowledge and sharpen your sewing expertise.

You and Your Sewing Machine

Once you feel ready to take orders, the next question is how to go about finding a market for your talent. Make a list of the kinds of people who could benefit from your know-how. Then think about how you can reach them. People who wear large sizes and babies who wear in-between sizes are just two of the endless customer possibilities. Decide which of your sewing skills you want to capitalize on (your speed in turning out a blouse in a few hours, your patience in putting lace trim on curtains). Advertise accordingly: You might contact Weight Watchers and health spas about your wardrobe alteration service; maybe the hospital gift shop is just the place to sell your outfits for newborns. Market your sewing strengths carefully.

The following are but a few ways to earn money with your machine; you'll undoubtedly think of others. (We'll consider industrial sewing options later.)

Do you make draperies and slipcovers, napkins and placemats for your own home? Do you re-cover worn-out footstools? If so, why not do these jobs for others? Aside from skill with machine and scissors, sewing **home furnishings** demands expertise with a tape measure and a good eye for straight lines and square angles.

If you decide to do slipcovers, you'll need a cording foot for your sewing machine to make welting; you'll also need zippers and heavy-duty threads and pins. You may need transportation to customers' homes to measure their furniture. Of if you have room to store it, you may have the furniture brought to your home. Some seamstresses prefer the latter because they would rather fit the covers to the furniture as they go along.

If you plan to make draperies, your supplies will include lining, stiffening, rings, cords or shirring tape, and weights. Prices for custom-made drapes will depend on which fabric is chosen, whether they are to be lined, how much fabric is needed, and how long it takes to make them. A reasonable charge for lined patio-door draperies that are made of moderate-priced fabric and that take you about ten hours to make will be $170. Contact furniture and decorating stores that sell coordinating wallpaper and fabric. As a convenience to their customers, the store managers could have you available to cover a chair or to make drapery tiebacks to complement a sofa or match new wallpaper.

Uniforms are another good source of work for a seamstress. There are countless businesses that require their employees to wear special clothing. Restaurants, beauty salons, hospitals, theaters, and grocery stores are a few operations that use smocks or costumes. Many real estate companies have each of their salespeople wear a blazer with the company's emblem on the breast pocket. Contract with a local firm to outfit its entire sales staff. Local amateur entertainment groups (music clubs, for example) might be another outlet. Take advantage of your location. If you live near a military base, offer to do mending and sew chevrons and military patches for soldiers whose strengths lie in areas far from a needle and thread. If you have a boarding school in your area, consider offering to patch the clothing of children who live in the dormitories. Hospitals and prisons may need uniforms, scrub suits, and linens mended regularly.

Louise L. of Pennsylvania couldn't take a full-time job because she had three preschool children. When her husband's factory went on strike, she began looking around for a way to make some money to ease the financial pinch. Already a part-time seamstress at home, she went to several restaurants and catering businesses and talked about making tablecloths and napkins for them and uniforms for their employees. The restaurateurs were happy to give her the job when they saw her work samples and when they heard that she could buy the material in bulk from a textile mill. She could supply the goods at a fair price, selling uniform smocks for $25, tablecloths for $16, and napkins for $2. Louise kept sewing even after her husband's strike was settled, because she enjoyed the added income, which amounted to $6,000 the first year.

If you have ever bought **doll clothes,** you know how expensive they are. A collection of three outfits for a Barbie or Ken doll costs about $6. If you're a designer at heart, you could make your own patterns and feature everything from jogging outfits to evening gowns. The pattern pieces would be tiny and would demand good eyesight and nimble fingers, but your outfits would be unique. (And if you're good at fashioning doll clothes, the next step might be **baby clothes.**) A few carefully placed ads, especially about a month before Christmas, would generate plenty of response from parents. You might sell your miniature fashions on consignment, with shop owners keeping 10-25 percent of the selling price. Or you could sell your creations at church, school, and craft bazaars. A spin-off idea is to offer matching outfits for the dolls' owners.

A **wedding gown** is a special dress. Every bride is eager to find something perfect, something that blends with and reflects her personality. If you've made suits, dresses, and jackets, chances are you have the confidence and know-how to tackle the wedding-gown market. There are books available to tell you enough about bridal fabrics, lace, and trimmings, and about how to pick styles and design dresses, to allow you to make a $500 gown for $100. You'll design the dress and do all the adjustments and fittings on muslin, which is later taken apart and used as the pattern for the gown. As a wedding-dress maker, you must know about fabrics—their availability, practicality, and care. Handling satin as little as possible, making sure that the sole of your iron has no rough edges and keeping the sewing machine needle sharp to avoid puckers are tricks of the trade.

Custom-made gowns are sold at phenomenal prices. The manufacturer must usually figure labor and salaries, fringe benefits, taxes, utilities, insurance, rent, advertising, and profit into the cost of her finished product. She sells an $800 dress to the retailer for $400. The retailer's price, in turn, must cover the same kinds of expenses along with the cost of services like delivery, credit cards, and bridal consultants. Since labor and overhead are the biggest costs in the commercial wedding-dress business, you can make the gowns cheaper. You could even take on the task of sewing bridesmaids' dresses and special outfits for other prominent figures in a wedding, including parents and grandparents.

Choir robes for churches are another possible source of income for you and your sewing machine. And what about **high schools** in the area who need outfits for cheerleaders, flag corps, drill teams, and bands? Maybe you could be the costume designer for the next school play. Schools are beehives of activity, sponsoring parades, school parties (prom, homecoming), and week-long celebrations (student council "Western Days" or National Horticulture Week, for example). You could help outfit students for these special occasions.

Sporting goods stores could use your sewing expertise. Think of how many school jackets and sports uniforms from baseball to soccer need school names, letters, numbers, and emblems sewn on them. The sewing is done with a tiny zigzag stitch that most machines have built in. Bring samples of your work when applying for this job. You can use your skills creatively by designing alphabet pillows to sell in the sporting goods stores. Sell names of players, teams, coaches. Set a per-letter charge depending on how plain or frilly you make the letters. Fashion words or names from gingham and lace for a soft, delicate look a skater might enjoy, or use corduroy or canvas for a collegiate or hardy look appropriate for a wrestler. Monograms are in right now; offer them to customers who buy sweaters, scarves, and hats at the store.

Consider making **costumes.** Contact a costume agency serving theater groups in the area and offer your services. Call dance studios where children take ballet or tap dancing lessons. You could make the costumes for student recitals held throughout the year. Parents who work outside the home or who don't sew at all will be overjoyed to find someone to do the job. You may even get a contract to do all the sewing and costume alterations for a studio's recitals. Measuring squirming six-year-olds is a challenge; to be good at it, you'll have to get them involved in what you're doing by asking them how the outfits look and feel or get them to talk about the upcoming recital—anything to get their minds off having to stand still. You'll have to feel comfortable working on sheers, velvets, satin, taffeta, crepes, metallics, and nets to succeed in the costume business. The work will be time-consuming, but the rewards can be fantastic: Think of watching ten proud second-graders prancing on stage in costumes you created. You may also want to make outfits for ice skaters and roller skaters, riders in horse shows, costume-party guests, and hospital candy stripers.

You can make outfits for adults' social activities, too. **Square dancing and folk dancing** are popular with adults of all ages. Hundreds of square-dance clubs around the country meet regularly for hoedowns. The women wear full, swinging skirts, and the men usually wear shirts to match their partners' outfits. Check the newspapers for square-dance clubs to which you could supply dancing wear at reasonable prices. You'll charge according to the fabric used and the complexity of the pattern. You can offer suggestions on styles and colors and on coordinating the outfits, and always your bright-colored clothes must allow freedom of movement for the dancers. Prices vary, but dresses can run between $25 and $50; shirts, between $10 and $20. Your satisfied customers could be your greatest source of advertising.

Another costume-related moneymaking opportunity presents itself in **karate clubs** for adults and children. Advertised as a means of mastering self-protection, the clubs are popular as a way to meet people, get exercise, and work out aggression while learning. Special clothing is required for karate practitioners. You could make and sell karate garb that consists of a gi (a simple, loose white tunic that laps over and ties at the sides) and white kicking pants that are wide in the crotch to make kicking easier. These outfits normally sell for around $35. Price yours a notch lower, and affiliate yourself with a karate club; try to land a contract to sell them all their karate gear.

Consider offering **one-of-a-kind garments** that can't be bought in retail stores. Designing each outfit to suit the customers' needs (pockets along the bottom of a pants leg for a clown or lace around the collar for a princess in a fund-raising skit) and tailoring it to ensure a better fit (for long arms or a short-waisted torso) would be big drawing cards for this service. Also advertise to sew for the **hard to fit.** There are lots of people who don't have model shapes, and they have difficulty finding clothing that fits well. You could offer these men, women, and children more style and comfort than the standard sizes on display in stores.

Alice M. of Wisconsin has discovered a way to make money and perform a valuable service. When her son, Neil, was born, he weighed only three pounds, six ounces. Buying clothes and diapers for him was a nightmare, so Alice began making them. After reading in the newspaper about the number of **premature babies** born each year, she hit on the idea of making tiny clothes and selling them to hospitals. Several hospital gift shops now stock her "preemie" clothes, and some of the new mothers ask Alice to make wardrobes for their little ones after they come home. She now makes dresses, romper suits, and christening outfits for premature infants. Some department stores carry her line, and some of the clothes are sold by mail to people who have heard of her unusual business.

Sew for **displays.** Fabric stores are likely customers, as they frequently feature suits, dresses, and other clothing made from the fabrics they have for sale. You can offer to change displays seasonally or whenever new shipments of fabric arrive. Store displays may even lead to other kinds of work. Lila D. of Indiana landed such a job because the store where she bought fabrics and sewing supplies recognized her talents and asked her to display some of the suits she made for her husband. Customers admired the suits and the workmanship, and Lila now sells suits for $300 each to people who appreciate her expert labor. She makes about fifteen suits a year, and most of her advertising is by word of mouth.

One of the latest sewing fads is making your own **outerwear;** ski suits, vests, parkas, booties, mittens, caps, and knickers can be made from kits (available by mail from the Frostline Company and L. L. Bean). The kits contain material filled with down or polyester and sell for about half the price of the ready-made articles. Everything you need to complete the apparel is included in the kit. No special machine attachments are needed, but the smallest needle size (usually a 14 or 16) should be used. Making your own outerwear is a great inflation-fighting idea for do-it-yourselfers; you could offer your skills to people who don't sew but still want to save money. Stores that sell these kits are often looking for someone who can sew the items for their customers.

Alterations

In addition to sewing new creations (or instead of it), you may find a place for yourself in the world of alterations and mending. Replacing zippers in jeans and jackets, hemming coats and dresses, and letting out and taking in garments as needed are among the services you can offer. (See Chapter 16 for more on clothing repair businesses.) You'll need to know about sizes, fabrics, and styles to get the best fit for your customers. Department stores and dry cleaners would be good sources of work for you. Or line up a route that you serve regularly, picking up and dropping off clothing once or twice a week. When you apply for alteration jobs, show samples that demonstrate your abilities. Take courses in tailoring to brush up on techniques.

Oona P. of Iowa has an unusual alterations business that she got into by chance. Her husband, Tom, is a **plain-clothes detective** who wears a gun in a shoulder holster. The constant rubbing of his suit coat across the gun and holster was playing havoc with the suit. Oona inserted a heavy twill fabric into the lining of the coat, fastening it with Velcro so that it could be removed when the suit was dry-cleaned. Other detectives asked her to alter their suits the same way to prevent them from having to buy new ones so often. When the uniformed policemen heard of Oona's expertise, they began dropping off their uniforms to have her sew on buttons, fix ripped seams, and replace zippers.

In the alterations business, you never know where you'll find work. Donna Jean E. of Missouri rented a Cleopatra costume to wear to a Halloween party. Before wearing it, she had to replace missing snaps and put up the hem. On returning the costume to the rental agency, she commented on its poor condition and offered her services to keep the agency's other outfits in top shape. The manager agreed that his business was suffering because of the shape the costumes were in. So Donna Jean now checks all the outfits for rips, tears, missing buttons and snaps, cigarette burns, and stains. She makes repairs, removes stains, and sends each costume to be cleaned. She also suggests to the manager which costumes should be replaced. Donna does most of her work at home, charging $8 an hour. Last year she managed to make $3,200 in her part-time mending and alterations venture.

Industrial Sewing

If you produce high-quality work with your regular sewing machine, consider purchasing an industrial machine that has a stronger motor and can sew heavier fabrics. With it you'll be able to make that canvas butterfly-chair cover that your lightweight machine can't handle. You might rent a machine for several months, with your rental going toward the purchase price should you decide to invest in one. To rent or buy, check the Yellow Pages under "Sewing Machines—Industrial and Commercial." Machine rental may be impossible in small towns but should be available in larger cities. Some companies who want to hire you may have their own machines. New machines may run upwards of $1,000, but a good used one can be bought for several hundred dollars. With heavy-duty machinery at hand, you could make seat covers for recreational vehicles, slipcovers and cushions for furniture, and other bulky items. Contact businesses whose nonsewing customers might welcome your know-how.

The opportunities for an industrial seamstress are many, and sewing with an industrial machine is no more difficult than a regular one; it just makes sewing through heavy material like leather, suede, awning cloth, canvas, duck, sailcloth, ticking, and upholstery fabric much easier. Marina and boat shops might need you to make sails and boat covers; automobile dealers might want you to make new seat covers for vans, trucks, and cars; recreational vehicle stores might ask you to spruce up used pop-up trailers with new canvas tops. You could also do work for awning companies. Or advertise that you specialize in outdoor kits and make sleeping bags, covers for barbecue grills, and umbrellas for patio tables. You could consider sewing purses and even briefcases.

Lettie M. of Washington had worn out her living-room furniture and couldn't afford to replace it. For $30 she took a course in upholstering and learned how to retie the springs, replace the webbing, and restore the frames. She reupholstered her furniture with lightweight nylon material and was happy with the result. Neighbors commented on her skillful work, and she began getting requests for similar projects from them. Some of the jobs demanded the use of an industrial sewing machine, so she bought a good used one. She made a workshop in her basement, complete with fabric samples and style illustrations for customers to choose from. Her prices vary according to the size and difficulty of the project, but she charges around $125 for most chairs and $250 for standard sofas.

Hand Stitchery

A sewing machine is not a prerequisite to making money with needle and thread. You can make money by mending, decorating, and designing with your hands. It can be done at little expense to you, since the main tools are your experienced fingers. Some people believe that the various thread crafts are the "artsy" side of sewing. Hand-stitched creations passed down through generations along with the knowledge of how to make them are regarded as priceless by the families who share them.

Unlike sewing by machine, hand stitchery can be done almost anywhere—while watching TV, waiting in a doctor's office, or riding on a plane. The experts are comfortable anywhere and take pride in their detailed precision work. They have learned to cope with frustrations like having to tear out and redo tiny stitches.

Some women are professionals when it comes to hand sewing, embroidery, quilting, tatting, needlepoint, and other hand stitchery. They have perfected their skills and learned to do complicated, intricate work. **Hand sewing,** which can be functional or decorative, adds a look of elegance to linens or wall hangings in a way that a machine cannot. The detailed, sometimes tedious, work calls for patience and precision. **Embroidery** is decorative needlework done with a wide range of stitches. Experts know how and where to use a stitch that best interprets a particular design, and they recognize how the thickness and texture of the thread influence the effect of the finished work. **Quilting** means stitching together layers of fabric with padding in between. This is an old art that pleases the eye and warms the body. **Needlepoint** is embroidery done on canvas, usually in single, even stitches across counted threads. The result has the look of loom tapestry. These forms of stitchery, although all done with a needle (except tatting, which requires a shuttle), vary in technique and effect.

Aside from the decorative hand stitchery described above, there are other, highly practical money-making ideas that use needle and thread. Some people can't even sew on a button without piercing their index fingers, and others don't have the time or patience to do it. These are your customers—people who would be thrilled to have someone put a hook and eye on a skirt or fix a torn buttonhole for them. **Simple hand sewing** requires little apart from an ordinary needle and plain thread. A chalk pencil, a tracing wheel, a ruler, a tape measure, a pressing cloth, pins, a thimble, and traditional sewing-basket stock are probably all you'll need. Your earnings for sewing by hand will depend partly on how well you advertise your service and partly on how much of a demand there is in your area. But when you consider that a reasonable price for hemming one coat is about $10, chances are you could do well. If you are one of the nimble few who can wield those proverbial silver threads and golden needles with skill, don't keep your talent to yourself.

Embroidery on shirt yokes is fashionable these days; the Western look is especially in. Retail prices of clothing with embroidered patches and emblems are quite high. But your customers could buy plain shirts if they knew you would dress them up later. Simple stitches can add roses to a blouse collar or the image of a team mascot to a shirt pocket. Aim your advertising at the young at heart, and determine prices according to the amount of work, the complexity of the job, and the time it takes to do it.

Offer to **finish people's abandoned needle projects** stashed away in chests and closets. Advertise in newspapers, craft supply shops, and needlework magazines. Crewel designs with beautiful color combinations and interesting but difficult stitches could be brought to life with your help. To finish something started by another, you'll have to copy a particular style and try to match the original colors.

Enid L. of Oklahoma is a whiz at several forms of stitchery. She has completed crewel, macrame, crochet, and needlepoint projects left unfinished by her friends because of waning interest, lack of time, or insufficient skill. When she mentioned her "I'll finish it" hobby to the manager of the craft supply store she frequents, he offered to recommend her to his customers who complained about their undone projects. Since her conversation with him, she has finished several afghans and hooked rugs. The money she earns is spent for more needlework supplies.

Tatting is a nearly forgotten art. It is a delicate handmade lace formed by looping and knotting with a single thread and a small shuttle (a spindle-shaped device that holds the thread). The knots and loops are drawn into circles and semicircles, creating a fragile look. Its origin is in doubt, but examples of this kind of lacework have been found in the tombs of ancient Egypt. Tatting, as we know it, came from Italy in the sixteenth century, and people in America have been doing it since before the Civil War. Yet few people in the younger generation know of it. It's thought that tatting began as a way to decorate other fabrics, but today it is used in making doilies, jewelry, belts, ponchos, wraparound skirts, shirts, and dresses. It can make a fancy lace collar or be mounted and framed for its own beauty.

Jeanette R. of New Hampshire **recycles old needlework,** making it possible for her customers to display the treasures in their homes. For one job, she took a pair of rabbits done in bobbin lace (tatting), placed them facing each other on brown linen, and framed them. Jeanette has livened up quilts and pillows with pieces of old tatting and has even covered eggs with them. Old needlework is often soiled or dusty; she rinses it thoroughly in warm, sudsy water and irons it on a Turkish towel. Jeanette has even taken needlework with worn, stained, or damaged spots, finished the edges, and tacked it in place behind a piece of felt so that the undamaged part showed through a cutout in a familiar shape, such as a heart or a bird. She's always thinking of new ways to recycle the aged pieces. She does not work year round, but she makes $20-$130 on each project, depending on how much work is involved.

Repairing and restoring existing needlework is another service you can offer. People treasure the embroidered and crocheted handiwork of their great-grandmothers. Because of age and use, the delicate work often needs to be repaired. Sometimes just tying broken threads is enough to repair a piece. Other times you must try to match the thread used in the original, weaving in and out with your needle to duplicate the design. You must handle the needlework carefully as it may fall apart easily. Advertise in magazines such as *Yankee,* which attracts antique and history buffs.

Laura M. of Maine is an antique-lover who looks for pieces of old, stained needlework to restore in her spare time. She washes the pieces and bleaches them with lemon juice, diluted hydrogen peroxide, or non-chlorine household bleach. She keeps some of the needlework and sells the rest. Owners of antique shops and private collectors call on her for her expertise; though she restores many samples, she always warns that the pieces may be rotted beyond repair. She is paid well for her work and spends the money collecting more antiques.

Quilting is an honored tradition. If you do wadded, flat, corded or stuffed quilting, or have watched someone else labor over such a project, you realize the time, eyesight, steadiness, and perseverance required. Handmade quilts sell for $200-$500. Quilting frames (costing around $35) are used to hold material taut and on grain, enabling the quilt maker to sew tiny stitches easily. Even if you make only two quilts a year, that's a significant addition to your extra cash reserve. You might also consider **repairing quilts** for owners who value the sentiment that's sewn into many of them.

Iva C. of Kentucky learned quilting from her mother. When her husband, John, was laid off at the coal mine, she hung four of her quilts in the front yard with a "for sale" sign on them. Tourists in the area stopped to inspect them, and it wasn't long before they had all sold for $200 each. A neighbor later asked her if she would like to display her quilts at his gift shop in a nearby state park. Iva furnished him with six quilts; five of them sold in one summer. Four brought $350 each, and one—in the "cathedral window" design—brought $500. Besides supplying the gift shop, Iva now makes quilts to sell at flea markets in the winter.

Teaching

Sewing and needlework can be fun, lucrative ways to let your creative juices flow. Whether your expertise is in machine sewing or in some other kind of stitchery, you might want to consider sharing your enjoyment by teaching your skill to others. You could teach a woman who has always wanted an afghan to make one, or a bachelor who doesn't know a bobbin from a zipper foot to hem his slacks and mend his jeans.

If the sewing machine is your best tool, if you are knowledgeable about fabrics and styles, and if you know how to alter a pattern for the best fit, then your years of experience could make you the best teacher for others eager to make their own clothes. You'll probably want to keep your classes small, since you'll need space to set up machines and lay out fabric, patterns, and supplies. Have each person bring a portable machine and his or her own material. Offer one-hour lessons, and charge according to your expertise, the class size, and the competition's fees. You might consider offering separate beginner, intermediate, and advanced sessions if your students' abilities are wide-ranging.

If hand needlework is your area of expertise, you could offer your classes at local craft stores and advertise in community flyers. You can give individual or group lessons and recommend books to help answer student questions when you're not available. Lessons can be held in your basement or in a spare room, with students bringing their own equipment. The money you earn from your teaching venture will be equaled by the satisfaction of having shown someone "how to."

If you can whip up a fashionable skirt or crochet an afghan while watching TV, maybe needles and thread are your tickets to extra cash.

Suggested Reading

Basic Tailoring. New York: Time-Life Books, 1967.

Bergen, John. *All about Upholstering.* New York: Hawthorne Books, 1962.

Burns, Marjorie A. *Altering Ready-to-Wear. New York: Lippincott, 1976.*

Deutch, Yvonne, ed. *Sew-It-Yourself Decorating Book: Manual Making Home Furnishings*. New York: Thomas Y. Crowell, 1978.

Dillon, Karen, and Gail Brown. *Sew a Beautiful Wedding*. Portland, Oregon: Palmer-Pletsch, 1980.

Fraser, B. Kay. *Modern Stitchery: Stitches, Patterns, Free-Form Designing*. New York: Crown, 1976.

Mordle-Barnes, Mollie. *Making Children's Clothes*. New York: Good Housekeeping Books, 1977.

Mosesson, Gloria R. *New Clothes from Old*. Indianapolis, Indiana: Bobbs-Merrill Co., 1977.

The New Vogue Sewing Book. New York: Butterick Publishing, 1980.

Perkins, Margaret. *Teaching Needlecraft*. Exeter, New Hampshire: Heinemann Editions, 1972.

Scott, Toni. *The Complete Book of Stuffedwork*. Boston: Houghton Mifflin, 1978.

Snook, Barbara. *Costumes for Children*. Newton Center, Massachusetts: Charles T. Branford Co., 1969.

Thelen, Marilyn. *Sew Big: A Fashion Guide for the Fuller Figure*. Portland, Oregon: Palmer-Pletsch, 1980.

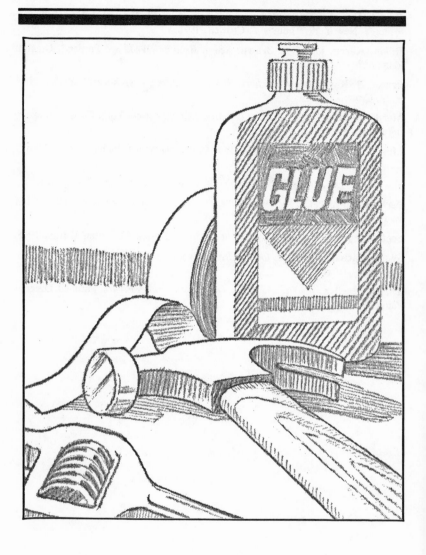

Fixin' to Make Money

16

(Jobs for the fix-its of the world)

Nothing lasts forever—not the purring sound of your new car's engine, the hair-splitting edge of your meat cleaver, or the unhindered flush of your toilet. Sooner or later the car will have to be tuned, the cleaver sharpened, the toilet repaired. Will you be forced to call a repair person at $5 to $25 an hour or can you rely on yourself?

With today's cost of living at an all-time high, it isn't feasible to replace every marred, scratched, or broken possession. Skilled repair people are the support system that keeps many households intact. If no one were capable of rewiring our dehumidifiers or regluing our porch swings, the city dumps would be running over with broken pieces of the American lifestyle. The touch of a master's hand—that's what many people think of when a meticulous repair person has restored the original gleam to their familiar Chippendale table, or the memorable chime to their hundred-year-old Seth Thomas. Those who don't know the difference between a nut and a bolt believe that the skilled hands of a repair person can perform miracles. Does the challenge of bringing *old* back to *new* excite you? Maybe you're destined to be the next Dr. Kildare of the repair world.

Nearly every woman has some sort of finesse in the fix-it field. Have you ever patched or replaced a frayed cord on the toaster or iron, or put a new washer in the bathroom faucet? Think of the money you saved by resealing your own driveway last fall. Sit down and make a list of the things you've repaired in your home in the last year. Surprised? Now think about getting paid to repair those same things for others. If you have always had the knack for doing these jobs in your own home, you may be well suited for running a repair service. If you don't do any repairs for yourself, don't plan on hiring yourself out to do them.

To do top-quality repair work, you should have certain personal traits to accompany your manual skills. You need a sensitivity to other people's feelings about their possessions. Your job could be to fix a broken leg on a bar stool that's been in the family for years or to cover a scratch on the paperweight someone won in a high school essay contest. You should give these objects the tender loving care you would give your own things. You should also be able to realistically evaluate a repair problem and decide if you can do the job and how much you should charge. Are you really up to repairing a stained-glass window if you've only worked previously with tiny stained-glass ornaments? Finally, you must be dependable—willing to work hard to get the job done on time. These characteristics will help you to build a good reputation in the business.

Training

Do you have the skills necessary to start a repair service? If you think you know what you're doing, but would like to know more, there are several routes to take. You can learn simple repairs and general fix-it tips from the countless how-to books and repair manuals in public libraries and bookstores. As models and styles of products change and some repair procedures vary, you can secure updated repair manuals from product manufacturers.

Other repair services require more preparation and training than you can get from a manual. High schools, vocational schools, the YWCA and YMCA, and college extension and continuing-education programs frequently sponsor refresher and advanced evening classes for adults. Repair courses are offered at reasonable fees and usually run for six to twelve weeks. If there are no classes available in your area, find a repair person in your field of interest and ask him or her to teach you what you need to know. Under the supervision of a more experienced person, you'll learn to interpret hints of trouble and to diagnose full-fledged problems. For example, what does it mean when a toaster makes a buzzing sound, works intermittently, gives an electric shock, or emits an odor?

For such repair jobs as snowblowers and lawn mowers, most of the work will be periodic maintenance, which many people prefer to have done for them. If you enjoy auto work, changing the oil and spark plugs and cleaning or replacing the air filter are routine. Most places that sell small engine parts also stock repair manuals. Look for these companies in the Yellow Pages under "Engines—Gasoline."

To do some kinds of work, such as electrical repair, you may have to take an accredited course and earn a license or certificate. Such work is specialized and technical—and often dangerous if you don't know what you're doing. The voltage inside some television sets ranges betwen 20,000-35,000; that's no place for an amateur to be messing around.

Setting Up Shop

When you've taken stock of your repair skills, you can begin thinking about how you will set up your business. Do you have adequate space to work in your home? Enough room to store your equipment and supplies? Most basements and garages can be fixed up as work areas. Be sure to call your local zoning board to find out if running a repair business is permitted in your neighborhood. If you plan to do the repairing at your customers' homes, is your car suitable?

Having the right equipment is essential. Depending on the kind of repairs you plan to do, you may already have many of the necessary tools. Equipment for a general repair business should cost you less than $100. A good hammer costs around $10, and pliers, saws, and wrenches are relatively inexpensive. Other common repair tools include a plunger, all-purpose lubricants, sandpaper, tape, a flashlight, screwdrivers, a combination wrench set, and all-purpose glues (epoxy and contact cement). Of course, more specialized tools will be needed for some repair work. For instance, you'll need a heavy staple gun for small upholstering jobs and a pipe wrench for plumbing repair. You may want to locate a wholesale hardware supplier to keep your costs down.

Be sure there's a market to support your repair service. You wouldn't think of repairing snow skis in Key West, but in upstate New York that could be a big hit. The demand for your service is probably not limited by geography, but you do need customers to stay afloat. If there's a clientele out there, serve it, but don't try to compete with the Roto-Rooters and Sears Roebucks. Large companies are usually happy to leave small jobs to small businesses, since they make their profit on commercial and heavy-duty jobs. If the things you repair are lightweight and easily packaged, consider having them sent by mail. This would work well with watches and small appliances.

Susan M. is an elderly widow living in Iowa. After her husband's death, she sold their jewelry store and their big house and bought a condominium. As the inflation rate rose, Susan's buying power shrank; she advertised in her church bulletin and around the neighborhood to **repair watches.** She had done this work for years in the jewelry store and had kept her repair equipment. Although she got some work, she couldn't bring herself to charge church members and friends as much as she would a stranger. So she contacted jewelry and department stores in her city, offering to do their watch repair. Several stores began mailing her the broken watches their customers brought in. Susan repairs them and mails them back to the stores, where the owners pick them up. Last year she cleared $3,200 in her repair business.

Money Matters

Setting competitive prices for your work is basic to survival in the repair business. Use the Yellow Pages to locate businesses who already offer the repair service you intend to start. Find out what they are charging their customers. In addition to checking the competition's rates, consider your time, the skills needed to complete the repair job, the complexity of the project, and the materials required. How will your repair business affect your gas, electric, and water bills? Can you make enough to cover expenses and still make a profit?

Are you adequately protected in your repair work? If fire or other damage results from your incorrectly rewiring lighting fixtures in someone's home, liability insurance may be your lifesaver. Check with your insurance agent for details.

To make your business more attractive, you might offer pickup and delivery on small items, plus a thirty-day guarantee on your work. (Check with a lawyer for more information on offering a guarantee.) You may also attract customers by advertising that you're on call for certain repairs twenty-four hours a day.

Cindy L. of Rhode Island started doing minor repairs in her home to fill up the times when her husband was out of town on business. She bought a set of repair manuals that explained how to **fix everything around the house.** She fixed the curtain rod and silenced the creaking bathroom door. She even changed the oil and spark plugs in her car. The high school in town offered a course on home repairs, and Cindy signed up. She passed easily because she had developed a real interest in how things were made and how to fix them when they didn't work. Since Cindy had spare time during each day, she ran an ad in the local paper for repair work. Now she changes her ad almost every week. One week she repairs toasters, coffee pots, and mixers; another week she removes scratches from furniture and rewires lamps. In the spring and fall she advertises to repair screens and to weather-strip homes.

Her customers wonder if there's anything Cindy can't fix. (She does turn down work for furnace and television repair because she isn't qualified.) Cindy charges by the hour for some jobs and offers a flat rate for others, depending on their complexity. She has a steady stream of customers, because her work is guaranteed for thirty days, and is done promptly and at a reasonable price.

Repair Specialties

We've listed some specialty repair businesses below. Your ingenuity will undoubtedly lead you to other moneymaking repair ventures.

Clothes Mending—Everyone agrees that clothing costs are high, and pocketbooks are already stretched before broken zippers in coats and jeans signal another trip to the store. Replacing zippers in pants or jackets can be one of the best services to offer. Hemming coats or dresses and doing other alterations can be another. (More on this in Chapter 15.)

Small Appliances—If you do it for yourself, you can do it for others. Fixing the cord, plug, socket, or switch on a small appliance is an easy repair job if you follow common sense safety rules—like unplugging the appliance and using appropriate tools. Be sure that any replacement part you use carries the Underwriters Laboratories emblem, which shows it's been tested and meets safety standards. Most major manufacturers sell parts for their appliances. You can usually charge less for repairs than a shop would, because they have to pay employees and meet other overhead expenses. Besides saving money, a customer who would normally mail a broken food warmer back to the manufacturer for repair can probably save at least two weeks by bringing it to you. Mixers, blenders, food processors, toasters, irons, and hair dryers are small appliances you can learn to repair. A vocational school course entitled "Industrial Electronics" may be just the place to gain some confidence and polish before you open your small appliance repair service.

Furniture Repair—You can rid wood furniture of scratches with supplies like colored putty and colored lacquer sticks. With a lot of patience and elbow grease, you can strip down and refinish old furniture, using paint remover and a putty knife. There are several methods of refinishing, each using different supplies, such as stains, varnishes, and sealers. Remember that a well-ventilated area is essential for this work.

Another common furniture repair job is tightening loose chair rungs. You'll need thread and glue and the know-how of an experienced fix-it person. With practice you'll learn some tricks of the trade, such as gluing toothpicks and tapping them around the rung after you've replaced it in its hole. When the glue is dry, you cut off the exposed part of each toothpick.

Furniture upholstery is another potential repair business for you. Evening classes or hands-on experience under the supervision of a professional will prepare you for this job. You'll need a hammer, upholstery tacks, and a staple gun, and you may want to buy a few other special tools. A sewing machine should be used to sew the welting.

Other furniture repair jobs include removing burns from wood furniture; repairing wicker, rattan, and antique furniture; and recovering outdoor furniture with new canvas.

Edith J. of Ohio adds to her husband's retirement income by upholstering furniture in a workshop in her garage. To prepare an old sofa or chair for its face-lift, Edith and her husband, Ernie, retie the springs and glue, brace and strengthen the entire structure. Edith sews the new fabric. These two home entrepreneurs also purchase used furniture at garage sales, flea markets, auctions, and junk stores. They renovate the items from top to bottom, inside and out. After the metamorphosis has taken place, the finished product is advertised for sale.

Knife and Scissors Sharpening—When a knife or a pair of scissors gets dull, many people don't know how or don't have the time or tools to restore its sharp cutting edge. And new knives and scissors cost anywhere from $15 to $50 or more. A sharpening service might be welcome in your area. You can learn to sharpen knives properly by getting a book on the subject and practicing with a box of dull blades. Collect the old scissors and knives you've been stashing away to get sharpened "one of these days." Ask your friends to donate worn ax and saw blades for you to practice on, too. Learn safety measures—like wearing goggles to protect your eyes from flying particles when you use the grindstone. Tools you'll probably need include a bench-mounted motor with a grindstone attachment, a honing stone, a whetstone, and several types of files.

Post notices in fabric stores for sharpening sewing scissors, in bait stores for hunting and fishing knives, in department stores for both knives and scissors. Place an ad in your neighborhood newspaper announcing your blade-sharpening service for lawn mowers and chain saws.

Home Repairs—How many home-owners haven't at one time or another had a broken garage door opener, a loose banister on the stairway, or a swollen front door? These problems are common, yet very frustrating and expensive to the less-than-handy person who doesn't know the difference between a wood chisel and a plane. You can help. Some of the basic tools and supplies you'll need are a hammer, a screwdriver, an electric drill, a brace and bit, pliers, vise grips, glues, drywall or plaster compound, and electric and plumbing supplies. Many vocational schools offer courses in home repair and home restoration, but quite often in-home repairs are learned best by *doing* them with the help of home repair manuals. Since these are repairs that can't be dropped off at your house, you'll need a reliable method of transportation to get to customers' homes.

Toy and Doll Repair—Is there a toy or doll made that is indestructible? If you have ever been around children, you've seen bald Barbie dolls, limping train cabooses, and wobbly-wheeled wagons. Start your own hospital for stuffed animals, trucks, wagons, dolls, and other toys. You will be one of Sally's and Billy's best friends because you'll have given new life to their favorite toys. Since toys are often less expensive to repair than to replace, their parents will love you, too. If you know children and understand their love for the stuffed animal they sleep with or the doll they have tea with every day, this may be the job for you.

Carolyn D. is a young mother in Illinois who quit her job to have a second child. Her four-year-old son, Billy, had been in a neighborhood day-care center for three years while Carolyn worked, and she was happy to be able to stay at home and spend more time with him. While awaiting the birth of her new baby, Carolyn started repairing her son's broken toys. Although it wasn't hard to do, she was proud when she fixed Billy's wind-up car that hadn't run for months. Remembering all the sick toys at the day-care center, Carolyn called the director and offered to fix the toys for much less than it would cost to replace them. Before long she had every toy in excellent shape. She has learned to keep toys that can't be salvaged and to use their good parts to fix other toys. Carolyn uses simple household tools, plus a few additional musts, such as a tiny screwdriver, and some Allen wrenches. After her daughter's birth, she hated the thought of going back to a nine-to-five job, so she set up a workshop in the basement where she could repair toys full time. She ran an ad in the newspaper and contracted with several other day-care centers in town. Carolyn is happy staying at home with her two children, and she loves her toy-repair business. Last year she cleared $2,100 by making sick toys well again.

Bicycle Repair and Maintenance—Bicycles are more popular than ever. Both the standard bike we've all ridden and the 10-speed bike we dream of racing require a certain amount of maintenance. Repairs can range from fixing flat tires and adjusting rear derailleurs to tightening spokes and replacing speed-selector cables. You can learn the world of bike repair by attending vocational school classes, by practicing, and by reading about bicycle anatomy. You'll need to be deft with a screwdriver, pliers, wrenches, bicycle grease and oil, punch, hammer, spoke tools, files, tire pumps, tire gauges, tube patches, tire cement, and other items needed for particular jobs. A bicycle-repair service could be very profitable in most cities, and near college and university campuses.

Picture Frame Repair—Many old family pictures lie in basements because the frames are in sad shape. They may be warped, mildewed, scratched, bent, or cracked. Frames exposed to excess moisture take on a chalky appearance. If this doesn't disappear after the frame is thoroughly dried out, you must sand away the dirt, polish, and varnish and apply a new finish. Some frames can be restored with simple plastic wood or glue. Many people are all thumbs when it comes to working with their hands; others don't have the time to get their picture frames in shape. They would gladly hire someone with the patience and time to restore old frames to their original beauty. Art galleries, antique shops, and the general public are your potential customers.

Machines and Instruments—There are various machines and instruments around the house or in offices that need occasional repair. Loose wires and broken belts can be fastened or replaced easily, but special training will usually be needed to work on other problems. Courses (Refrigeration, Heating and Air-conditioniong, for example) offered at vocational schools, and through community education programs and some commercial establishments, can teach you how to unravel the intricacies of these machines. With replacement costs so high, many people would rather repair than re-buy. Make *your* repair service quicker and better than the commercial establishments. With training and practice you could repair business machines, freezers, lawn mowers, radios, sewing machines, vacuum cleaners, etc.

Bonnie K. is the divorced mother of two teenage girls. Her ex-husband owned a business-machine repair and sales store, so typewriters, calculators, dictaphones, and adding machines were no strangers to her. After her divorce, she moved to New Jersey and started a repair service. She travels all over her city **fixing business machines.** She works on some machines in her basement workshop; others are repaired on the spot. Her small car is perfect for the job because it gets good gas mileage but has enough room to carry the parts and tools she needs and the business products she fixes. Her only large expense is the upkeep on her car. Last year she cleared over $12,000.

Nonmechanical Auto Repair—There's more to a car than

what's under the hood. If you're an all-purpose fix-it, consider repairing sprung glove compartment doors, broken speedometer cables, and ripped seat covers. To have these often simple jobs done in a repair garage that charges mechanics' prices of $25 to $30 an hour is extravagant. If you have a place to work (barn, shed, carport, or garage) and basic repair tools (pliers, screwdrivers, drills and bits, soldering iron, etc.), *your* price could be much lower. This kind of repair work is best learned by doing it. Some vocational schools offer it as part of a course in auto mechanics or body and fender repair.

Household and Decorator Items—Family living is hard on furniture, fixtures, and other household items. Many of these things are too good to throw out, and a competent repair person can make money for herself while saving her customer the dreariness and inconvenience of living in a run-down household. These repairs can be a steady and lucrative part-time business. Many families don't have "handy" members. If you don't mind doing work that is sometimes complex and detailed and sometimes physically demanding, you can come to their rescue by repairing some of the following:

barbecue grills	lamps
baskets and rattan pieces	marble
bird cages	mirrors
brass and copper items	rugs and carpets
china and ceramics	stained-glass objects
curtain rods	wood stoves

Hester W. of Maine was an English teacher who wanted to spend more time with her two-year-old son, Sean. She read in a magazine an article describing how professionals **restore old Oriental rugs** to their original beauty. Having huge rugs in her living and dining rooms, Hester went to work on them, using the method she had read about. When she saw how successful she was with her own rugs, she began doing the same work for her friends and neighbors. Using an artist's brush, Hester repaints the rugs with a thick homemade mixture of ordinary fabric dye, water, and salt. She has equipped her two-car garage with large sheets of plywood mounted on cement blocks. This is where she lays the rugs to work on them. Hester has built a good reputation in her city and has advertised her service in home decorating magazines. She now has rugs sent to her from all over the country. She has a large selection of vibrant colors for her customers to choose from if they would like a change. Otherwise she chooses the colors to match the original ones. She makes hundreds of dollars on each Oriental rug she rejuvenates.

Grace A. resides in Washington. She is a middle-aged wife and a mother of three sons. When her boys were growing up and roughhousing around, she was constantly finding things in need of repair—from broken bikes to pushed-out door screens. Grace was responsible for balancing the household budget, and the repair bills just made it harder. To lessen the blow of the repair bills, she decided to take a furniture repair course at the YWCA; next she took a small appliance course; then upholstery repair. After a few years of taking repair classes, she seldom needed to hire anyone to fix things around the house. She enjoyed the work and started doing it for others in her neighborhood. She replaced broken windows and caulked bathroom tiles—and got paid for it. She expanded her business by advertising in the newspaper. Today, with all the work she can manage, Grace also **teaches repair classes** at the local Y and in her basement workshop. She's especially good at teaching beginners because she was one herself not so long ago. (When she started, she didn't know the difference between a plain screwdriver and a Phillips screwdriver.) Her business has expanded so much that she has hired several of her students to work for her, and they are all benefiting from the added income.

Personal Possessions—No matter how torn or tattered some of our personal trappings become, they still hold a special attachment. Many items are passed down from one generation to the next, and repair of these sentimentally rich objects often requires careful handling by seasoned fingers using proper tools. Think of the deteriorating binding on your grandfather's second-grade reader. What about the chimeless anniversary clock from your parents? If you have an interest in and an understanding of how to repair some of the items below, you might consider starting a repair business that specializes in one or more of these categories:

art	jewelry
books	music boxes
cameras and projectors	shoes
clocks	silver
eyeglass frames	tape recorders
handmade doilies, table- cloths	watches

Photographs—Pictures can be damaged by sun, tarnish, and stains; they can crack and fade with age. Repairing these priceless memories is reserved for the skilled and steady hand of an expert. The start-up cost and equipment needed depend on the type of repairs involved. The price for doing this work is high, because of the skill and amount of time involved. Your subjects are often interesting, as you will be working on old family photographs, celebrities' pictures, and historical documents. Since these are irreplaceable, their owners are willing to pay well for restoration. A word of caution for those contemplating this kind of work: Training is difficult to find. Some universities offer a noncredit course, and a few books are published on the subject. Check with local photographers who might be able to suggest training sources.

Sports Equipment—Darlene C. of California is a college student studying to be a physical education teacher. She has been involved in sports all her life and has played everything from softball in grade school to tennis as the star player on her college team. Since tennis is her favorite sport, she owns several rackets and has learned to restring them like a professional. When her teammates complained that the sporting goods store was charging them $30 to restring their rackets, Darlene offered to do the job for $20. When word of Darlene's affordable rates got around campus, her business blossomed. She enjoyed the sudden burst of extra money and wanted to keep it coming. She put notices on bulletin boards in all the dormitories and at the student recreational center on campus. She called on the managers of sporting goods stores near campus, who hired her to restring the rackets brought into their shops. Darlene's lucrative part-time business earns her enough to pay for extras like concert tickets and weekend ski trips.

If you do a lot of repairs for yourself, you probably enjoy fixing things—and you're probably good at it. Why not earn some money doing it? Many not-so-handy people will gladly pay for your skills.

Suggested Reading

Basic Bicycle Repair. Emmaus, Pennsylvania: Rodale Press, 1980.

Boye, David. *Step-by-Step Knifemaking*. Emmaus, Pennsylvania: Rodale Press, 1977.

Carbo, Dorothy. *Fix-It Guide for Women*. New York: Arco Publishing, 1976.

Caring for Photographs. New York: Time-Life Books, 1975.

Carrell, Al. *Do-It-Quick-But-Do-It-Right: Home Repair Hints*. Englewood Cliffs, New Jersey: Prentice-Hall, 1981.

Consumers Guide editors. *Electrical Repairs Made Easy*. New York: Beekman Press, 1980.

Consumers Guide editors. *How It Works and How to Fix It*. Skokie, Illinois: Consumers Guide, 1974.

Darr, Jack. *Fix Your Small Appliances*. 2 vols. Indianapolis, Indiana: Howard W. Sams & Co., 1974.

Fawcett, Clara Hallard. *On Making, Mending and Dressing Dolls*. Riverdale, Maryland: Hobby House Press, 1949.

Grotz, George. *The Furniture Doctor*. Garden City, New Jersey: Doubleday, 1962.

Grotz, George. *Instant Furniture Refinishing and Other Crafty Practices*. Garden City, New York: Doubleday, 1966.

Peterson, Franklynn. *How to Fix Damn Near Everything*. Englewood Cliffs, New Jersey: Prentice-Hall, 1977.

Powell, Evan. *Complete Guide to Home Appliance Repair*. New York: Popular Science Publishers, 1974.

Reader's Digest editors. *Fix-it-Yourself Manual*.New York: Norton, 1977.

Saunders, Richard. *Collecting and Restoring Wicker Furniture*. New York: Crown, 1976.

Savage, Jessie D. *Professional Furniture Refinishing for the Amateur*. New York: Arco Publishing, 1980.

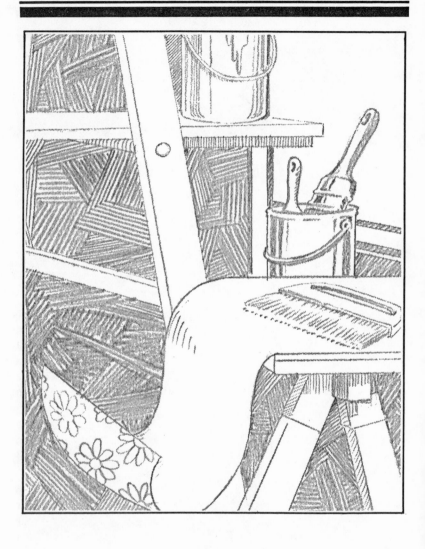

Paint, Paper, Decorate

17

(From wallpapering to rug painting in homes and offices)

A house might be a dwelling, but until you laugh, cry, argue, romp, and entertain there, it isn't a home. And not until you give it those special touches that make it a reflection of you (the hall lamp you found at the flea market, the burlap wall in your den, the zigzag paint job in the bathroom) does it qualify as a castle. But castles get worn, and newness fades. If you're like the average homemaker, you know the budget can't handle the velour couch in the store display window and that white shag carpeting isn't practical with five children and a dog. So if you're bent on a new look, you bravely wield a paint roller or wallpaper brush with one hand and whip up a new pair of drapes on your trusty sewing machine with the other—all in the name of beauty and comfort.

Sprucing up a home has many rewards. Not only is it an outlet for creativity, its a genuine spirit booster. Putting a parquet floor in the foyer or giving the bedroom a textured ceiling can change your attitude toward your 15-year-old bungalow. A house has a higher market value if it is well maintained and just as taking care of it now may eliminate costly repairs later on, careful decorating and design today will mean you'll still enjoy the mural in the hall ten years hence.

Though few people are born with paint roller in hand, many try their luck at using one as a defense against the cost of hiring a professional. But not everyone feels comfortable with ladders and paint odors. Some people don't have the confidence, talent, skill, or physical ability to fill their own decorating needs. Painting and wallpapering jobs require bending, lifting, carrying, climbing, and stretching. A steady hand, patience, and attention to detail are essential in attacking a busy-looking room or a bland hallway. Design and decorating call for keen perceptions of spatial relationships and the ability to coordinate structures and colors to achieve the effect intended.

If you're a do-it-yourselfer who doesn't mind paint flecks in her hair and enjoys the challenge of fitting a purple tweed chair into a mint-green room, you may want to learn the fundamentals of home decorating and eventually make money from your skills. Even if you papered your son's bedroom and put up a bamboo room divider, you'll probably benefit from more practice. You may need some formal study, too. After all, you may be competing with college-trained designers who work for large firms and run their own ventures on the side.

Commercial classes may be the place to start. Paint and wallpaper stores, department stores, hardware stores, and home improvement stores often give lessons (free or for a nominal fee) in everything from laying floor tile to paneling a basement. Practice in your home; then offer to paint your neighbor's kitchen or paper her dining room. You'll gain experience in friendly surroundings, and if you do good work, you'll have the recommendation of a satisfied customer to pass along to potential clients. Be sure of your capabilities before accepting a job. Your family may not be particular about how well the brown wallpaper matches the design in the couch, but if people are paying money for you to give their den a dignified look, you'd better be able to match the browns perfectly.

Learn by observation. There are tricks of the trade that only someone in the field can teach you. The pros can show you shortcuts and easier methods. They can teach you how to repair your mistakes and how to avoid making the same ones again. Practical experience under an expert's watchful eye is probably the most valuable training for a beginner.

Lila P. of Oklahoma did her own indoor painting for years, but she recognized that her paint jobs were less than perfect. Enjoying the work and wanting to improve her finished product, she attended classes offered by a local paint store. After a few lessons she answered an ad in the newspaper and got a job as a painter. She was supervised by the foreman of her work crew, and she absorbed all the information he shared with her (e.g., how to prepare the surface, mix the paint, and choose the equipment for each job). After two years she was confident enough to go into the painting business on her own.

When you've honed your skills and bolstered your confidence, advertise your services, offering free estimates on the decorating jobs for which you're qualified. Contact paint and wallpaper stores that might refer customers to you. Be prepared to take on assignments from unexpected places. One woman we talked with was given her first decorating job by the contractor who built her new home. When he came back to do some repair work on the month-old home and saw the way she had decorated it, he asked her to do the condominium units he had under construction. Have pictures of your past work available to show customers. They'll be more apt to hire you if they can evaluate your expertise by seeing what you've done.

Find out what other people are charging for similar work, and set competitive rates. You may be surprised at how much is being paid for the jobs in the following lists. Some of these will be discussed in this chapter; check the suggested readings for further references.

Painting Jobs

ceilings, walls	floors
doors, windows, trim	furniture
brick and other masonry	stairs
metal shower stalls	appliances

Papering Jobs

ceilings, walls	bed headboards
dividing screens	doors, windows, accents
portable wardrobes	room borders

Decorating Jobs

arranging rooms	decorating with plants
creating atmosphere	changing the focal points
revitalizing rooms	of foyers
recommending furnishings	designing playrooms
(drapes, carpet, furniture)	decorating for parties

Plan your business carefully; know what you're getting into. Start small, and build your reputation by doing your best on each job.

Phyllis P. of California started a painting and decorating business with her two best friends, Sally and Ann. In the beginning they all worked hard to get their business off the ground. When Sally became pregnant and was forced to drop out, the work load became exhausting for only two partners. After several weeks Ann's husband said he could tolerate TV dinners no longer. That left Phyllis on her own, desperately trying to hire some dependable help. Business started going downhill; Phyllis was cranky and couldn't get the jobs completed on time. Finally, in disgust and weariness, she dissolved her venture and vowed never to start another home business.

Before plunging headlong into a partnership that sounds good, recognize the pitfalls of the arrangement, too. Have contingency plans ready for emergencies. Have an alternative source for supplies. And don't accept a job unless you can guarantee you'll have it done on time—with the quality of workmanship that has been agreed upon. Insist on a deposit before you begin, and charge more for rush jobs that may cause you to postpone other work. Investigate special liability insurance. Accidents happen; spills and stains are not unheard of. Check with your insurance agent to find out what kind of insurance and how much you should have.

Offering only one service—painting, for example—has its advantages. Besides allowing you to do what you know the best and enjoy the most, you can advertise yourself as a specialist. (That's how Colonel Sanders made his reputation.) You can usually charge a higher price for a specialty service than for general home decorating. The start-up cost for a one-service busines is lower, too, since you need fewer tools and supplies and less space to store them.

But there are pluses to being adept at more than one decorating skill. For instance, if someone is redecorating an entire house, it's easier for him or her to deal with *one* person or company than to hire a separate one for each decorating phase.

Painting

Maybe you first learned to paint when you bought that older home that screamed for a new coat or when one of the kids scribbled with crayon along the baseboard in the living room. If you've taken care of those paint jobs and if people compliment your work or ask who did your family room, you may want to consider painting for others.

The cost of going into the painting business is relatively small. You'll need high-quality equipment. For indoor painting, good brushes and rollers, two or more stepladders, a couple of planks, and some buckets, rags, and drop cloths are basic; for exterior painting, you'll have to add extension ladders to your inventory. Working in painters' whites will make you look more professional; add this to your equipment list as well. You'll usually furnish the paint for your customers, so a reliable supplier is important. Look for a supply outlet or a paint and hardware store that caters to professionals. You may be able to buy tools wholesale or at a discount there if you have a bona fide business, and the clerks can give you invaluable advice. It will probably cost you around $100 (not counting paint) to get your business rolling.

In addition to traditional painting methods, spray painting is another service you might want to consider. Skilled hands are necessary, and it takes a lot of practice to be able to get the paint thickness just right. Almost any paint that can be brushed on or rolled on can be sprayed, but the technique is used mostly for fences and large wall areas or furniture that can be placed in an open space. Masking windows and doors is necessary when spray painting, so you must decide if the time gained will make up for that extra work. Spray equipment ranges from attachments to use with vacuum cleaners to large air compressor sprayers (these can usually be rented). Certain precautions must be taken when spray painting: Keep the room well ventilated; wear a mask to avoid breathing paint vapors; have a fire extinguisher handy; store flammable liquids in safety cans. Read the directions before using any spray equipment, and clean it thoroughly after each use with a solvent such as lacquer thinner.

To succeed in a painting business you must be able to give potential customers fair and accurate estimates of the price and duration of each job. Prices are determined by whether the house is occupied, how much furniture it has, how many different colors are requested, and how much surface preparation is needed. Add one-third of the usual charge to the price if you're painting an occupied house; it takes longer to paint because you must take care not to damage carpeting and light fixtures, and because you have to move furniture. Charge more for several color changes because of the time involved in cleaning brushes between colors. Remember also to figure the cost of the paint into the total bill.

Though painting prices vary throughout the country, the current going rate near us is about $.50 a square foot for interior painting. Painting the interior of a sixteen-hundred-square-foot house costs about $850. Exterior painting of a three-bedroom ranch house costs about $1,800. Exterior house and barn painting demands special consideration. You may decide that working with a partner is best for big jobs. Be sure you feel comfortable working at various heights and in hot (depending on where you live), muggy summer weather.

Ruth C. and Marylou M. are next-door neighbors in Alabama. Once when Ruth's husband was out of town on business, the two friends decided to paint the outside of Ruth's ranch-style house. The job took two weeks, but they enjoyed the work because they could chat while they painted. Marylou jokingly suggested that they should go into business painting houses. After taking stock of their time, tools, and skills, they decided it really was a good idea. After checking with other painters in town, they set their rates. They decided to paint only one-story houses, since neither of them wanted to climb very high. They got several jobs the first summer, and word spread of their efficient partnership. They've been painting houses for four years now. Last year, working from spring through fall, they made $7,500 apiece.

Advertise to **paint or seal basement floors and walls**. People often want the concrete floor painted because otherwise it produces a chalky dust that clings to shoes and gets tracked into the main part of the house. Applying a rubber-based paint with rollers usually solves the problem, and also gives the basement a cleaner look. Many basement walls are damp and leaky; painting with waterproof paint eliminates the dampness and the musty odors. Besides home owners, businesses that store items in their basements might welcome your specialized painting service.

Painted house floors are also popular, especially for vacation homes and recreation rooms. Most are done in bright, shiny enamel. First the floors are washed with a heavy-duty commercial cleaner such as trisodium phosphate to remove wax and glossiness from the surface. Floor enamel undercoat is applied with a brush or a short-napped roller; then the floor is sanded lightly, vacuumed, and dusted. A good floor-and-deck enamel is applied thinly and evenly in many coats (letting each coat dry before sanding it and applying the next one). Some floors have painted designs that make them look carpeted. Patience is a must in doing this kind of painting. No shortcuts are allowed. Never paint a dirty, greasy, or waxy surface. Avoid enameling floors when it's raining outside or when the humidity level is high. Get experience by working with professionals skilled in painting floors.

Sandy K. and her husband have a summer cottage in Maine that they bought at a good price because of its run-down condition. One of the last things Sandy did in remodeling the cottage was to put twelve coats of bright lemon-yellow enamel on the floors, to protect them from the gritty sand tracked in all summer long. When her neighbors saw her work, they asked her to do their floors. Now she works most of the summer. Sometimes she paints just one room, other times the whole cottage. Last year she netted about $2,000 painting floors.

Paint concrete porches, patios, and driveways that have become stained with oil, grease, and rust. You'll remove oil and grease by applying hydrochloric acid to stains, taking care not to leave it on so long that you remove part of the surface itself. Avoid touching the acid or breathing its fumes. Use rubber or plastic gloves and chemical safety goggles. When the surface is ready, apply an alkali-resistant latex masonry paint that's made to cover tough, unsightly stains on concrete. Expect to be especially busy with this service in the spring, when everyone wants to freshen up the outside of the house.

Private **swimming pools,** which were once luxuries, are becoming more common in neighborhood backyards. Since they require painting about every three years, this could be a source of income for you. Pools are painted with rubber-based paint that resists wear and abrasion. The job is done with a paint roller and takes only a few hours. The average cost to the owner for a pool sixteen by thirty-two feet is around $300.

Unfinished furniture is a big seller these days. Advertise that you will paint, stain, or antique it for the buyers. Paint is applied to decorate or protect the furniture, while antiquing gives the appearance of age. Stain contains a dye that sinks into the wood, giving it the desired color. If you're skilled in tole painting, you can also offer to trim the furniture in painted flowers or other designs. Redwood furniture, sun decks, and fences also need periodic staining. Many people can't be bothered with doing these big paint jobs themselves in the hectic spring and fall.

Appliance painting has become popular in the last several years. Some people want to paint their old stoves or refrigerators to cover scratches; others want to change the colors to match new decors. This type of painting demands some know-how. Appliances are cleaned with trisodium phosphate and water or sanded once lightly to roughen the surface before painting with epoxy enamel. You can practice on discarded refrigerator doors retrieved from the local dump. Once you are proficient, ally yourself with appliance stores, real estate offices, and builders—for their own business or referrals.

There are **other small items** around the house that need an occasional paint job. This could be your best bet for getting a foot in the door. If you advertise that no job is too small, you can start out painting picture frames, lamps, hanging light fixtures, toilet seats, and ceilings. Many professional painters won't bother with small jobs like these because their profit is made on large volumes of work and they can't always justify the costs of time and transportation for fifteen-minute paint jobs scattered around town. But *you* don't have the overhead of heavy advertising costs and large paint inventories. And if you have your own transportation you can carve out your own territory. You can work on a more personal level with your customer and get more business by word-of-mouth advertising. Get to know a big painting outfit; the people there might be willing to refer small jobs to you.

Wallpapering

There's more to wallpapering than matching patterns and fitting corners. Wallpaper stores often give instructions on papering and its special tools, such as seam rollers and wheel-type paper cutters. But the best way to learn the business is to work with a pro. There are countless tricks that only a veteran can teach you.

Before you decide to do wallpapering for others, make sure you know how to hang all types of paper. You'll need special knowledge to hang vinyls, flocks, foils, textures, scenics, and grasscloths. Flocked paper resembles damask or velvet brocade. Foil wallpaper is a thin, flexible sheet of aluminum or simulated metal with a paper or fabric backing. (It comes in many colors and is quite expensive.) True grasscloth is made from the herb, arrowroot. There's a shortage of this plant, though, so nowadays most grasscloths are made from synthetic materials laminated to paper backing. You'll also have to know how to work with prepasted paper, which needs only moistening before application. Another type of wallpaper comes in peel-off squares that are easy to put up and remove.

The cost of starting a wallpapering business is minimal. Most of the tools are inexpensive and easy to use. A plumb bob is necessary to mark a true vertical line for hanging your first strip. Other than that, stepladders, planks, pails, paste brush, smoothing brush, cutter, and seam roller are the basic tools. It's also helpful to have straightedges and a decent three-foot level. A worktable for cutting, trimming, and pasting is essential. Supplies you'll need to buy from time to time include paper remover, sizing (to condition walls for best adhesion), wallpaper paste (in powder or liquid form), paper conditioners (which reduce the susceptibility of paper to stain or soil), and paper cleaners (which come in doughs, sprays, liquids, and powders). Basic tools and supplies can be purchased in local paint and wallpaper stores for around $100.

To be good at wallpapering, you must be able to figure out how much paper is needed for each room (e.g., an eight-by-ten-foot room will need nine single rolls; a twelve-by-twenty-foot room will take sixteen). Of course, you'll need more if you're doing a room with high ceilings or using a paper with a large design. To do a professional job, you must have the patience to prepare the surface properly by cleaning and patching before you begin. You should be able to tell your customer about the wear and washability of each paper. Hanging the paper without marring ceilings and woodwork is also part of your expertise.

After learning all you need to know about hanging paper, determine what you will charge for your services. Most paperhangers charge by the roll, taking into account the type of paper used and the difficulty of matching the pattern. For example, foil paper is difficult to hang, as even a slight crease or scratch can impair its appearance. Paperhangers often charge around $25 per roll for foil and $12-$15 per roll for ordinary paper.

Decide whether you prefer working alone or with a partner. On your own you'll make more money because you won't have to share the profits. And you'll save by not paying for social security, liability insurance, and unemployment insurance for another worker. Working with someone means that you have help in carrying tools and supplies and in setting up for work. The job goes faster because while one hangs the paper, the other can cut and paste. And having company while you work may appeal to you.

Call on contractors and home builders to get jobs wallpapering their newly built homes and the old homes they've bought to remodel and re-sell. Leave your business card with apartment managers and office building managers, who often use washable wallpaper, grasscloth, or landscapes on the office and rest room walls in their buildings.

Most people will have a definite idea of the type of wallpaper they want to coordinate with their appliances, draperies, or carpeting. But your decorating eye will often be called upon for suggestions. If you're wallpapering in an office building where slick modern furniture is to be used, appropriate wallpaper would be tweedy textures, abstract designs, grass-cloths, stripes, geometric patterns, or Oriental motifs. Being able to help your customer choose just the right wallpaper could set you apart from others who just hang the paper.

Liza R. of Indiana wallpapers offices for dentists and doctors. She started when her brother Mike, a pediatrician, commissioned her to choose the paper, furniture, plants, and other decorations for his new office. She created a circuslike waiting room, hanging clown-and-animal wallpaper and brightly striped curtains. She put up shelves and stocked them with fluffy stuffed animals. The result was a friendly atmosphere for young patients. Mike's letter of recommendation has brought her other customers. She charges $12 a roll to hang wallpaper and $10 an hour to plan and shop for draperies, carpeting, furniture, and other room accessories.

Once you know the ins and outs of the wallpapering business, you might consider teaching others. Offer your services through stores that sell wallpaper. Give lessons at the store, or if you have adequate space and supplies, you could hold the classes in your own home.

Sarah Jane B.'s husband, an electrical engineer, was transferred by his company from Nebraska to Ohio. Sarah Jane had to give up a good job, and she began to look for a new way to earn extra cash. She had always done her own paperhanging, and after redecorating her new home, she decided to go into business for herself. She and a neighbor took classes from a local wallpaper store, then had a garage sale to help fund the business. They bought supplies and ran an ad in the local newspaper, calling themselves The Papermates. They got an enthusiastic response and after two years had more work than the two of them could handle. So that they could hire "experienced help" for their own business, they decided to give lessons in paperhanging, offering their students jobs upon completion of the course. Now they supervise several crews of paperhangers.

When Carla M. of Rhode Island was on vacation in Arizona, she stayed in a motel that had a wallpaper mural showing a mountaintop view. She wanted the same view on her family room wall at home, so she asked the hotel manager where it came from. She found the wallpaper by contacting the hotel's decorator and succeeded in hanging it on her wall. When her friends raved about it, she decided to try hanging scenic wallpaper on a part-time basis. Over the years she has hung seascapes, farmland scenes, and historical settings, as well as special murals on stairway walls in elegant homes in her town. Last year she decided to do office buildings as well as private homes. She began advertising her business as The Scene Setter. Since then she has hung a world map mural in the public library and a forest scene at the Sierra Club building nearby. Recently she began covering folding screens with scenic paper and selling them as room accents. Carla clears $6,000 a year in her more-than-part-time business.

Decorating

Some women have a talent for decorating and know how to give the dreariest room a lift. They've redecorated Grandma's kitchen and the lounge at the bowling alley hundreds of times in their minds. How do you know if you have the decorating bug? If you can walk into a room, identify what's wrong or missing, and suggest what the room needs to give it a total effect or a particular atmosphere, you're probably a decorator at heart.

But having the urge isn't enough. You probably need some training in design, and you'll have to keep up with changing fashions. You need a thick skin and a tactful manner—especially with the hard-to-please woman who insists on a black leather couch in an early American decor. You have to know what people want, show them what will work, and plan with them to achieve a pleasing compromise.

Professional decorators can be quite expensive, and many homemakers are hesitant to hire them because of the small budgets they have to work with. As a decorator, you can advise a client on what should be done in a room, or you can do the work yourself. Show customers how you can spruce up their drab kitchens inexpensively. Since you'll be working from your home, your overhead will be lower than a professional decorator's. You can charge lower prices and still make money.

The tools and supplies you need will vary, depending on what area of decorating you decide to work in. If you plan to make custom draperies, you'll need a sewing machine; if you intend to make, build, or reconstruct furniture or accessories, you'll need a workroom; if you plan to offer purchasing services (picking out the drapes, plants, paper, and everything else), you'll need a car.

If you're interested in decorating, but would like more training (in design, color schemes, furniture styles, fabrics, etc.), you could improve your chances of making money by taking classes at area department stores, colleges, or vocational schools or even through correspondence schools. Then practice in your own home or your husband's office. Work on whole rooms, or specialize in accessories and room accents. Take photos of all your finished projects, to use as samples of your work in recruiting customers. Since rooms are often difficult to photograph, you might consider hiring a photographer if you can afford the expense (which would be deductible).

As a decorator, you'll have to take into account the customer's wants, the family's living habits, the various functions rooms have, the traffic flow through a house, and the customer's budget. You must be able to create practical room arrangements, minimize house defects, and carry out color schemes. When Kathy R. of Illinois found out how heavily traveled one customer's living room was, she advised against the particular shade of pile carpeting the customer wanted. A home decorator must be understanding of a customer's wishes and yet tactfully honest about what will work in a particular situation.

Julia B. of California was overjoyed when her boyfriend asked her to redecorate his apartment, which was done in "early junk" donated by relatives. Julia started out by hanging natural-colored, wood-slatted blinds at the windows; since her boyfriend was a nature lover, she decorated the apartment in earth tones. He was so pleased with the transformation that he asked her to do his law office. Her success has lead to jobs decorating other bachelor apartments and offices in the city.

Decorators can dream up ways of giving new looks to room dividers, bookshelves, windows, and other often-neglected household items. Make plain **window shades** into decorator blinds, either by covering them with fabric to match the room decor or by putting original handcrafted stencils on them. Along the same lines, make decorator **valances** to match draperies. Buy wood at a lumberyard, and cut it into the design your customer wants. After clothing the wood with padding material, cover it with cloth that matches or complements the drapes, and make a welting to go along the edges. **Lamp shades** are frequently overlooked decorator items. They're often very expensive to clean or replace. Consider re-covering lampshades in silk, taffeta, burlap, or other material that coordinates with a room's furnishings. The only supplies you'll need are fabric, scissors, glue, needle and thread, and maybe piping for trims.

Advertise your skills to **redecorate boats and camping trailers**. Years of wear and tear make some recreational vehicles less than homey. You can re-cover seat cushions, make new drapes, and paint cupboards, or you can tell customers what they could do themselves to make their RVs inviting again. How can they liven up drapes that hang limp and faded from the sun of several camping seasons? What can they do with the tattered seats worn from children's shoes and tracked with sand and dirt? Reach potential customers by advertising in camping magazines and newsletters. Have "before and after" pictures ready when customers want to see your work.

What about **store windows**? Who dreams up the clever displays that lure shoppers in for a sample of the vanilla fudge or a closer look at the stitching on a quilt? If you have a good sense of what will catch a customer's eye, contact small businesses in your town (craft shops, drugstores, boutiques, florists, bakeries, etc.) and ask to "trim" their windows. Offer to do a couple of freebies to show them the quality of your work.

If you think you have **an original decorating idea**, you may be able to sell it to a decorating magazine or interior design publication that features readers' contributions. You'll be required to send your idea or design, with instructions and a clear photo, to the managing editor of a publication that solicits reader ideas. Be sure to check *Writer's Market,* however, for the specific submission requirements of design and home magazines. Your decorating design can also be copyrighted. For information on copyrighting a work of art, see Chapter 14.

Katie S. of Virginia is a young mother who likes to be a trend setter. A few years ago when her ten-year-old son wanted his room redecorated. Katie decided to give it a touch of nostalgia by making his bed resemble an antique car. She drew an automobile shape on a large piece of plywood and had the shape cut out. She padded it and covered it with bright red Naugahyde before bolting it onto the existing bed frame. Finally, she hand-painted the details of a classic sports car. Her son enjoyed sleeping in his auto-bed. After many of her friends and their children showed enthusiasm for the novel idea. Katie got another one: making and selling unusual headboards and sideboards. Now she earns a nice spare-time income by turning ordinary beds into everything from cars and flowers to people and animals.

Start your own **decorating service**. As a consultant, you'll be dedicated to creating livable, pleasing work and home environments and to helping your clients develop an atmosphere in which they can function optimally. Offer your services to professional offices, beauty shops, real estate companies, and private individuals for home or party decorating. Your fees will be lower than decorators who work through department stores. You will charge an hourly rate, plus a percentage of the purchased items if you help your customer select furniture, drapes, carpeting, and room accessories like plants and light fixtures.

Sally M. worked in an office in Washington, D.C., typing insurance policies. After several years of this, she found her life rather boring. Her only interests were holding office in several organizations, her bowling league and church group, etc. As an officer, she was often involved in planning and decorating for many of the organizations' social activities. She decided to try her hand at professional **party decorating** as a sideline. She made up business cards and sent them to party houses, churches, country clubs, restaurants, and hotels. At first she was called for small jobs—adult birthday parties or business luncheons. But as people heard of her decorating expertise, she began getting requests to spruce up restaurants for various holidays. She also does decorations for wedding receptions and private parties. Sally is still typing insurance policies, but now she has an exciting part-time business, too.

Specialize in decorating **one kind of room.** Foyers, bathrooms, and hallways can usually use some character building. They can be decorated formally or informally, in any style or period. Foyers take on distinctive atmospheres with the addition of mirrors, coatracks, accent lighting, and umbrella stands. Hallways are often narrow and poorly lighted. They can come alive with bright colors, mirrors, attractive wall hangings, and bouquets of flowers. Wicker, houseplants, new wallpaper, and special window treatments can make bathrooms more attractive. Help customers change their "ho-hum" rooms into nice places to be with finishing touches such as wind chimes, mobiles, baskets, pictures, and table accents.

Edie T. of Nevada took an evening class in home decorating at a local high school. After completing the course, she put her knowledge to work by putting mirrored tiles on one wall of her tiny bathroom to make it look larger. She then changed her living room by grouping the chairs to make conversation easier. She wallpapered her kitchen and made matching curtains. The manager of the store where she bought fabric asked if she'd be interested in making draperies for his customers and advising them on how to solve their decorating problems. Edie's **drapery and decorating service** has grown because customers appreciate her advice; her bank account has grown, too.

Painting, papering, or decorating could be the way to beef up *your* bank account. If your house is considered the most beautiful one on the block and you'd like to do something to make other homes just as pleasant, maybe it's time you put your designer's eye to work.

Suggested Reading

Geary, Don. *The How-to Book of Interior Walls*. Blue Ridge Summit, Pennsylvania: TAB Books, 1978.

Gilliatt, Mary. *The Decorating Book*. New York: Pantheon Books, 1981.

Home Care Guide. New York: Wallaby Books, 1981.

How To Paint. New York: Wallaby Books, 1981.

How to Wallpaper. New York: Wallaby Books, 1981.

Libien, Lois, and Margaret Strong. *Paint It Yourself*. New York: William Morrow & Co., 1978.

Reader's Digest editors. *Complete Do-It-Yourself Manual*. New York: Norton, 1973.

Tattersall, Bob. *Decorating*. (Tricks of the Trade Series). Central Islip, New York: Transatlantic, 1978.

Van Lear, Denise, ed. *Decorating with Indoor Plants*. Menlo Park, California: Lane Publishing Co., 1980.

You Ought to Be in Pictures

18

(Making money with your 35 mm)

When's the last time you heard someone say, "Wish I had a picture of that!" Maybe he or she wanted to capture the moment when Big Sis got stuck in the bathroom window or wanted a portrait of the gang from high school at their twentieth class reunion. With the right equipment and some know-how and ingenuity, you could get paid to take that save-it-forever photograph. It seems we're always looking for something tangible to help us remember those occasions that flee quickly or that hold special meaning for us. And a picture's value was recognized long before Kodak started making commercials.

In the 1840s photographers out West preserved history by taking daguerreotypes of the American Indians. Those pictures were recorded on chemically treated metal plates instead of on film. The metal plate itself was the photograph; there was no negative. So to get more than one copy of a picture, you had to rephotograph the subject.

Photography buffs today have a much easier time of it. Since the advent of the 35mm camera in 1924, technology has refined the single-lens reflex (SLR), added wide angle, telephoto, and zoom lenses, developed electronic cameras that even focus for you, and introduced time-lapse systems that capture flowers blooming. And taking good pictures is no longer exclusively the work of professional photographers. Affordable equipment and training are available to anyone dedicated to excellent photographs. If your escapades as a shutterbug have had good results you might have the right ingredients for an exciting part-time business.

The Market

Your clientele is the world, because photographs are a part of everyone's life. As personal keepsakes, they help us remember and make us laugh or cry. As learning tools, they teach us about faraway people or unfamiliar places and things. In both cases, they make us wonder. Pictures answer questions: "Did Sharon wear her green or her pink dress to our wedding?" They motivate us: "If I was that thin then, I can do it again." And pictures can be a part of other generations' lives because, with proper care, they can last for many years. You can show your grandchildren the uniform their grandpa wore in his first Little League game, or the '76 Mustang you polished every week.

Though some people seem content with a snapshot from their Instamatics, they often qualify their enthusiasm with comment, like, "I guess I was standing too far away to get the Yankees' emblem on the uniform," or "That's not a bad picture for a $20 camera." In short, they're often disappointed with second-rate pictures. There are others who feel that a first-class photograph underlines the importance of an event, and if they're all thumbs when put behind a shutter, they'll be willing to pay you for a clear, accurate representation of their real popcorn-decorated Christmas tree or of mom receiving a community service award.

There are many other reasons why reputable photography businesses are flourishing around the country. Many people would rather hire a photographer than risk messing up the job by doing it themselves. (Remember: Your son only graduates from high school once.) Others don't have the time, patience, or desire to learn the techniques involved in taking meaningful pictures. Still others don't want to interrupt their party fun to shoot pictures of the festive occasion. Finally, there are those who are intimidated by any camera they have to do more with than point; they gladly leave the picture-taking process to someone else.

The Photographer and Her Equipment

A photographer does more than take pictures for extra cash. She sees life with an aesthetic eye and uses the tools and understanding of her trade to capture it on film. She is able to frame a thoughtful, pleasing composition whether she's focusing on a birthday cake with candles or on an award-winning quilt. She is observant, attentive to detail (she notices a turned-up collar before shooting a family portrait), and patient enough to wait for a two-year-old to "look this way." She's able to make people relax and be natural, and she herself is cool under pressure—ready to click the shutter the instant the diver hits the water—because she's confident of her expertise and command of her equipment.

If you're still with us and already dreaming about making money with your camera, consider a few more things, such as how well your budget and your schedule can support your venture. The amount of time you can spend and the equipment you have will determine the scope of your operation. The rock-bottom basic equipment for a home-based photographer consists of a 35mm single-lens reflex camera with a 50mm normal lens, a flash unit, wide-angle and telephoto lenses, a collapsible tripod, a gadget bag, and, of course, film. Any one-time needs (a medium-format camera, photofloods, an extra-long lens) can usually be rented. "Hidden" expenses of the business include photo processing, transportation costs, and photo display supplies (frames and proof holders). Start-up equipment costs vary depending on your needs and tastes (and on the current exchange rate, since many SLRs are imported), but a basic system could range anywhere from $300 to $700.

If you plan to do black-and-white photography, having your own darkroom is the cheapest way to go, since black-and-white processing is expensive when done commercially. A bathroom darkroom can be set up for little money. The biggest expense is an enlarger; you can get a decent one for $100-$150. Resin-coated paper doesn't absorb water. Although it's available in fewer textures and grades than uncoated, fiber-based paper, you won't have to buy a dryer if you use it. To complete your darkroom you'll need a timer, opaque bottles, a developing tank and reels, tongs, trays, and an easel. The total cost will probably be under $200, not counting chemicals and paper. If you don't have a darkroom and aren't interested in printing your own pictures, color photography is your best bet.

Before You Start

If you're still sold on the idea of a home-based photography business, chances are you've been a camera enthusiast for a while. But to refine some of your techniques and refresh your memory about the tips you once gleaned from a how-to book, you may want to take an intermediate or advanced photography class at a nearby university, technical school, or adult education program. Or you might want to tag along with a professional photographer-friend for some on-the-job training. This would be a great way to learn the hidden risks and unanticipated snags involved in taking pictures for others. For example: How do you deal with parents who want to pose all the shots themselves? How do you write up a fair contract that protects you from customers who decide not to pay because they don't think you took enough pictures of the party decorations they made? The answers are best supplied by those who've handled similar situations. Classes can teach you technique; other photographers can teach you the practical side of the business.

Once you know what you're getting into, you can think about advertising and pricing your work. If you keep in mind your costs, the demand for your work, the complexity of your operation, and what "the other guys" are charging, you should be able to charge lower prices than some other photographers because, working from your home, you have lower overhead than commercial studios. You can attract customers by offering a little extra, e.g., speedy service and options like enlargements, frames and albums, in-the-home services, and one-free-print bonuses for large orders. Special photographic techniques, such as double exposure and the use of multiple-image lenses, vignetting attachments, and soft-focus filters, would also be attractive extras for customers looking for more than a traditional album or picture. List your special services in your Yellow Pages ad. Finally, your personal attention and interest in serving your clients are what can set you apart from the competition. Word-of-mouth publicity is invaluable in this business.

Despite the raves of your family and friends about your candids of the Fourth of July barbecue, start small. Accept only jobs you know you can handle. Have an album of your best shots (showing available sizes, special effects, poses, and backgrounds) to show customers. Work with them to outline exactly what they want. Based on your experience, make suggestions about what works and what doesn't. Let them know you care about the finished product.

Moneymaking Ideas

The following is a list of moneymaking picture-taking ideas that you could turn into reality with the right mix of planning, skill, and your own special brand of genius.

Portraits. Taking informal portraits of children, families, and pets is an especially good way for beginning photographers to break into the business. If something goes wrong, you can always restage the shots. Begin with friends and relatives to get used to arranging people and composing pictures. You can also practice taking candids and learn the art of putting your subjects at ease. At the same time, you'll be building a good portfolio to show customers. Aside from shooting candids, you might consider doing more formal portrait photography in the customer's home. You can put your subjects in a familiar background or carry portable backdrops with you. These are available in camera supply stores and come in paper or canvas, selling for $25-$100.

If you've ever taken a child to a photo studio, you understand the hassles. By the time you get there, your nerves are frayed; the baby's outfit is decorated with slobber, and your son's shirt looks ready for tie-dying because he's been rolling around in the back of the station wagon. Making **portraits of families in their own homes** is often more convenient than trying to get everyone to your home studio for a sitting, especially when basketball practice, business meetings, and play rehearsals tie up three nights a week. Photographing the clan at home in the family room or backyard is also less threatening for them.

Pet photography is another good way to break in. People who own show dogs and other purebred animals have them photographed regularly. And the owner who proudly walks his "Heinz 57" mutt around the neighborhood would be thrilled to have a framed 8x10 of him on the desk in the den. Advertise in-the-home pet portraits if you feel comfortable with animals and have the patience it takes to get them to react the way you want.

Rhonda R. of Ohio is a young woman who has been earning extra cash for years as an animal photographer. She takes pictures of horses, goats, cattle, dogs, and cats at shows and fairs. She takes some photos for pet owners' enjoyment and others for advertising purposes for breeders. (If an animal owner wants to sell his stock or offer them for breeding, the only thing better than a good photo is a string of blue ribbons and trophies.) Rhonda charges $35-$100 (depending on the number of poses taken and the difficulty of the shots) for an 8x10 color photo and, for an extra charge, frames the pet portraits. She enjoys the excitement of capturing an Irish setter's majesty or a Siamese cat's sveleteness.

Special Kinds of Portraits. Local **sports teams** are a good source of work for a photographer. Contact league leaders or coaches and offer to shoot their teams. You can also shoot company golf leagues, bowling tournaments, and city tennis matches. Your work could appear in company publications, school yearbooks, and community newsletters. Color portraits of the sports teams could be awarded to members at the end of a season or could be bought by the individual members. Bring a sample of your work and a price list so team managers will know what you have to offer. Be sure your portfolio is filled with the kinds (size, style, sport, pose, and setting) of pictures you'll be taking for a particular group.

High school activities are another potential outlet for your services. You can work with the school's photography club in getting shots of the band, cheerleaders, the intramural volleyball squad, and the choir. Plan to shoot **school festivities,** too, like the prom and the homecoming dance. Set up an attractive display as a background for couples' pictures, which they can buy directly from you. You might design a backdrop appropriate to the theme of the dance.

Sadie W. of West Virginia is a retired history teacher who has turned to photography as a source of extra income and fun. She has always loved learning about **famous couples in history and fiction,** and she dreamed up the idea of photographing couples in the style of dress of various celebrities. Her portable studio consists of an 8x10 view camera, wardrobes of the past, and beautiful canvas backgrounds with collapsible aluminum frames to hold them up. She carries her gear to shopping malls and community and school celebrations. People attending last year's homecoming dance enjoyed dressing up in period clothes for keepsake pictures with their dates. Sadie's customers dress up as characters like Bonnie and Clyde, Scarlett O'Hara and Rhett Butler, Abe and Mary Lincoln, Mark Antony and Cleopatra, Napoleon and Josephine, and John Smith and Pocahontas.

Special Occasions. Photograph adult parties and contests, local appearances by clowns, St. Patrick's Day dances, children's birthday celebrations, and doings sponsored by community and church groups. These are the things that studio photographers don't usually get involved with. You'll have to be observant enough to spot a good shot on a crowded dance floor, quick enough to snap the expression on a seven-year-old's face when he sees his two-wheeler, and composed enough to put up with all the smoke, noise, and congestion of being in a crowd.

Once you've gotten plenty of practice and established a good reputation, you may be ready for **weddings and bar mitzvahs.** Photographing these memorable occasions demands the expertise that comes with experience. It's pretty hard to restage a church ceremony after a quick check of the camera reveals you lost a half-dozen shots because the film wasn't wound properly. If you're going to do weddings, you must have a backup camera and flash unit in case your main equipment fails.

Gayle M. and Linda A. of South Carolina specialize in bridal photography. Gayle is the photographer and Linda, an interior design major, is the album coordinator. Gayle uses a 35mm camera with a good flash unit for taking church, home, and reception pictures. Linda plans the "must" shots and works with the couple in deciding the kinds of extra features and special poses the album will contain. She then designs each album to personally suit the couple in style, color, and arrangement, using 30-40 photographs of varied sizes. The women usually do only two weddings a month; so they have a few free weekends to share with their families.

Greeting Cards. You can make lovely Christmas, birthday, anniversary, and other greeting cards from at-home family portraits. These greetings let faraway friends see how the family has grown and changed. Pose the group in various settings around their home and yard, and let them choose the pose they want for the card. One method of making the cards is to mount the picture on a medium-weight textured paper and, using a stylus, apply press type for the caption. The supplies can be purchased at an office supply store. Xerox the captioned card on a color copier. Printers often have several types (glossy, matte) and colors of paper to choose from for quality reproductions. Be sure to check into the cost of supplies and photocopying before setting a price for this service. Another method is to have a photo lab make the cards for you. Add the cost of producing the cards to your fee for taking the pictures.

Arts, Crafts, and Hobbies. Photograph the work of artists, craft workers, and hobbyists. These people frequently submit pictures or slides of their creations to galleries and art and craft fairs where they hope to exhibit or sell their work. Offer your photography service to builders of dollhouses, model trains, boats, cars, and planes. They might enjoy photographic portfolios of their projects. A taxidermist might also use your services. You'll have to be especially attuned to selecting appropriate lighting for these still-life photos, taking shots at various angles, and choosing backgrounds that complement and highlight your subjects, which could include sculptures, wall hangings, and miniature Model Ts.

Toy W. of Florida was an amateur photographer for many years, snapping photos of children, pets, and wildlife. Her husband, Mike, who is president of a local **model airplane** club, once asked her to photograph the club's annual flying show. She took her SLR, standard lens, wide-angle lens, flash unit, and tripod to the exhibit. Some of her photos were published in the club's newsletter, some were used for advertising, and some were framed to hang in the club's meeting room. She also photographed some of the member's planes for their own homes. Toy charges $20 an hour and $25 for each 11x14 color print; framing and album prices depend on customers' tastes. She does all the work herself, except for the developing. After a year of photographing planes and amassing a thick portfolio, she advertised her services to **model boat, train, and car** enthusiasts. With this additional business, she earns about $6,000 annually.

Things. Photograph antiques, jewelry, and other valuables for homeowners' **insurance records.** This is something many people might never think of having done, until they see your ad in the paper and recall the bike that was stolen from the garage and never found because there was no picture record or serial number on file. In performing this service, you would date the photos and photograph separately any identifying marks on the items (e.g., initials, serial numbers, and scratches). Advertise in insurance agents' offices and through the newspaper.

You could also take **pride-of-ownership photos.** People love to have pictures of their cars, motorcycles, train sets, and homes to share with friends. Telling someone about the features of your new Kawasaki is not quite as satisfying as showing a picture of it. These photos can be displayed on the rec room wall or in an album to pass around at a family reunion.

Take photos for ads in catalogs and trade magazines. Many businesses want pictures of their **products** for display at trade shows and conventions. Since professional photographers often handle these jobs, part-timers should concentrate on serving small, family-run businesses, unless they have the equipment and setup to compete with the product-photography pros. You might offer your services to individuals who are trying to sell handmade objects or original designs. You could end up helping another home-based entrepreneur get her business off the ground.

Other things to photograph for sales or advertising purposes are houses, apartments, and condominiums. **Real estate** offices may also need your help in taking pictures of vacant buildings and land for development. Send your business card to a local broker's office, and check with the multiple-listings agency in your area.

Illustration. A lot of nonfiction writers need photos to accompany their **book and article manuscripts.** Cookbooks, exercise books, and how-to and craft books are more appealing when they use good photographs to illustrate their copy. If you're able to travel to take pictures for an author who needs a photo of something on the opposite coast, put an ad in a magazine for writers, such as *Writer's Digest*. If transportation limitations and home responsibilities cut your travel radius to fifty miles, spread the word around your own community. Plan to collaborate with local authors by supplying photographs that will add to the salability of their works. Chances are the pay won't be great, because writers can't afford $40 a picture, but you can usually negotiate a fair price, and perhaps more importantly, you'll earn credit and public exposure when the book or article is published. The experience and the additional photos in your portfolio will help you land jobs with other writers.

Joy M. is a Kansas woman who takes pictures for local groups that self-publish their books. She got started in the business when her brother was in an auto accident and couldn't fulfill a contract with a local church group to take pictures for their fund-raising cookbook. Joy was an amateur photographer; she had never taken pictures for anyone else. With her brother's coaching, however, she managed to finish the project and ensure its success. Joy took some noncredit photography courses at the university and subsequently took on other book projects. The photos in her portfolio reflect assignments on such diverse topics as woven baskets and yoga. The pay is low, but the experience is valuable because Joy hopes one day to be a professional photo illustrator for a major publication.

Leave your name, your phone number, and a list of your credits with the **small newspapers** in your area. When staff photographers are busy, editors may ask you to fill in on unexpected assignments or on big stories that require several photographers. Gamble a little and shoot some pictures on speculation, without any payment guarantee. (Submit the parade picture that no one else got because a blaring ambulance siren drew attention away from the marching juggler.) You may not need a model release (signed permission to use the photo), but whenever you can, get the names of people in the photos you take on spec; the newspaper editor may fall in love with them and want captions. The pay is not phenomenal, as some pictures sell for as little as $2, but you can make a lot of contacts and get some public exposure this way. Be sure you get a credit line for every photo the paper uses.

Shoot tourist sites and other points of interest for **travel brochures.** We know of a woman who really capitalizes on this idea.

Daisy P. of California is a photographer whose in-laws own a campground in the northern part of the state. They asked Daisy to photograph the entire complex for some promotional brochures they were planning to pass out at an upcoming travel and vacation show. With her 35mm Minolta in hand, Daisy took shots of the tennis courts, pool, campsites, office, restaurant, recreation rooms, and laundry facilities. The brochures turned out so well that she decided to offer her services to other resort businesses through ads in camping journals and by writing directly to motels, restaurants, and tourist attractions nearby. Now she has her own promotional booth at travel and vacation shows in California, and her part-time work earns her around $3,500 a year.

Where there is technical writing, there is often a need for photographs. **Operating manuals and instruction pamphlets** need the benefit of clear, detailed photographs to clarify the text (some people know a monkey wrench only when they see one). With either formal training or practical experience in photographing everything from milling machines to toy assembly, you can offer your technical photography service directly to manufacturers and trade show representatives and advertise in business and industry publications.

Jill V. of New Jersey is a technical photographer who works with her friend Carole, a technical writer. Their partnership began when Carole was writing an operator's manual for a new machine designed and built by a local manufacturer. Carole suggested to the manufacturer that pictures of the machine parts would make the complex processes the machine performed much clearer for its potential buyers and users. Jill's photos won high praise, and the brochure was acclaimed for its impact and clarity. Since then Jill has photographed everything from exercise machines to corn pickers and manure spreaders to accompany Carole's freelance technical writing jobs.

There are dozens of ways to make money with your camera. The initial investment is higher than for many kinds of home enterprises, but a photography business could be your opportunity to turn a favorite hobby into an exciting and profitable adventure.

Suggested Reading

Ahlers, Arvel W. *Where and How to Sell Your Photography*. New York: American Photographic Book Publishing Co., 1979.

Baker, Frank J. *One Hundred One Ways to Make Money in Photography*. Chicago: Contemporary Books, 1980.

Berner, Jeff. *The Foolproof Guide to Taking Pictures*. New York: Bantam Books, 1981.

Calder, Julian, and John Garrett. *The 35mm Photographer's Handbook*. New York: Crown, 1979.

Cavallo, Robert M., and Stuart Kahan. *The Business of Photography*. New York: Crown, 1981.

Cribb, Larry. *How You Can Make $25,000 a Year with Your Camera (No Matter Where You Live)*. Cincinnati: Writer's Digest Books, 1981.

Hedgecoe, John. *John Hedgecoe's Complete Course in Photographing Children.* New York: Simon & Schuster, 1980.

Kelley, Victor. *How to Get into the Business of Photography.* Sedona, Arizona: ETC Publications, 1981.

Langford, Michael. *The Darkroom Handbook.* New York: Random House, 1981.

Linsley, Leslie, and John Aron. *PhotoCraft.* New York: Dell, 1980.

Lutz, Robert, ed. *1982 Photographer's Market.* Cincinnati: Writer's Digest Books, 1981.

Scanlon, Henry. *You Can Sell Your Photos.* New York: Lippincott, 1980.

The $ound of Music

19

(Jobs for musicians and vocalists)

A melody that hums in your mind all day long, background music in a mall or a dentist's chair. Upfront music at a concert or piano recital. A harmonica's moan, a banjo's twang. A choir's voice or a mother's lullaby. Harmony, dissonance, in tune or out of tune, the silence of a rest. Music is everywhere. It fills a need. It guides us around a crowded dance floor; it fills our minds with recollections of a fifties sock hop or a Virginia reel. Be it the highly charged *Star Wars* sound track or the soothing strain of a Chopin waltz, music is a uniquely human experience. It's universal. Whether or not you're gifted with perfect pitch or a flair for rhythm and blues, music means something to you; if you're a music maker of sorts—or maybe just a music lover— it could also mean extra cash in your pocket.

Maybe you used to play the organ at church; or you set your high school class motto to music for graduation; or you practice your flute every Saturday morning. If you're one of those talented people who can read music, compose it, sing it, or play it, you're not lucky; you're gifted. And your musical gift is one you can give to others. Musically inclined people recognize and appreciate any number of musical sounds, from the tumult of the Rolling Stones to the serenity of a chamber ensemble. If you get excited about the sounds of electronic music and the occasional harmony of a third-grade choir, you have a respect for music that's begging to be shared. The rewards and satisfactions of making your own kind of music or encouraging others to make theirs can be far greater than season tickets to the Met or the chance to sing backup for Barry Manilow.

We learned of two enterprising women who decided to share their enthusiasm for music.

Dreama W. of New York is a former choir director who teaches young children to appreciate music. She wanted to teach such a class because when she was a youngster, her aunt spent many hours showing her the variety, value and need for all kinds of music. Dreama realized that without an appreciation of melody and sound, she would be missing out on a great deal. She wanted to enrich others' lives, so she advertised her class in a local magazine. Her ten-week course consists of thirty classes. The classes are small (usually no more than five children), and the students range in age from three to ten. She teaches nursery rhymes and choral singing to begin with. "Mary Had a Little Lamb" and songs from *Mary Poppins* come alive in her classroom. Her students learn folk music, too, singing ballads like "John Brown's Body" and "Barbara Allen." They go on to learn about classical music such as Tchaikovsky's *Nutcracker Suite* and Mussorgsky's *Pictures at an Exhibition*. They listen to *The Nutcracker* and talk about the feelings the different dances stir up in them. If the class is in session at Christmastime, Dreama takes them to see the city ballet company perform the classic fantasy. She charges $300 a child for thirty classes.

Stella A. is a North Dakota homemaker who earns extra cash as a square dance caller. Her husband, Al, has had a square dance band for many years. Stella always cheered from the audience, but she wanted to be involved in the activity on stage. Square dance calling always appealed to her, so she learned the lingo and tried out for Al's band. The band members were pleased. Now she's a regular, earning $50 every Saturday night; her strong, articulate voice is a big hit with the dancers. Stella's favorite dances are Alabama Jubilee and Little Liza Jane.

Whatever your musical preferences, think about ways to share your talents at weddings, parties, and special occasion festivities, either by playing, composing, singing, or dancing. Advertise wherever people gather—community centers, party houses, schools, churches, and clubs. Build a reputation for skill, talent, dependability, and enthusiasm.

Making Money with Your Voice

How many times have people said to you, "You have such a lovely singing voice. Have you ever thought about using it professionally?"

Maybe it's time you did. You've probably been in choirs and amateur musicals all your life, and you've tried to emulate musical idols—performers who've made it big. You hum with the radio, sing along at a concert, and make up songs in the shower. Singing is natural for you. Are you ready to sing for others?

If you think your self-confidence would benefit from a few voice lessons, take some. At least ask an expert to evaluate your talent and its potential for making money, especially if you're not convinced that Aunt Mildred and your dad aren't just a little biased about the merits of your high C. Though many vocalists have made it big without any training, taking lessons can't hurt your chances for success. You'll learn how to take care of your voice, and how to breathe and stand for optimal voice projection. And taking lessons will put you in touch with people in the business who may be valuable contacts when you begin looking for work.

College voice instructors often give private voice lessons on the side, and one may be willing to add you to the schedule. Or check with a music store that might be able to recommend a voice teacher. Voice lessons generally range between $25 and $40 a month for a thirty-minute weekly lesson. Group lessons (five or six students) will cost less than private lessons; training given by a prestigious music institute or a well-known instructor is likely to be much higher than average.

Using your voice to make money is especially attractive because the initial start-up costs for your business are usually minimal. You already have the equipment; all you need to do is practice and prepare various musical programs to offer your potential clients. To learn a stage presence that's right for you, sing in front of a mirror, in front of your family—or in front of the pet canary if you're trying something new and can't bear the thought of boos and criticism just yet. But *practice*. Have a demo tape made or perform on the spot for prospective customers. Your best publicity is your own performance and the praise you get from satisfied listeners.

Offer your services as a **wedding soloist**. Many couples want vocalists to contribute a lyrical touch to their wedding ceremonies. Have a repertoire of songs available, and be flexible enough to learn new songs or hymns at the bride's and groom's request. "Oh, Promise Me" is a little old-fashioned, so if it's still your number-one offering, think about updating your program. Pay attention to what's being sung at weddings you attend. Discuss popular wedding songs with your church organist. Then you can also act as a consultant to couples who need help in choosing appropriate, meaningful wedding music. How many selections you sing for a wedding may depend on the couple's preference, the church they're married in, or the kind of ceremony they plan. Charging between $25 and $35 for four songs is a reasonable rate.

Ally W. of Wisconsin is a college senior, majoring in music. She's been getting solo singing parts in choirs and play productions for as long as she can remember. To earn some extra cash and to help herself feel like a part of the music industry, she began singing for weddings during high school. While at college, she's been singing in **nightclubs** around town. She takes private voice lessons, and she pactices in the school auditorium every day. Ally hopes to have a singing career someday, but for now she's content to earn enough to pay for her tuition and some of the expenses of living in a campus dorm.

Small **dance bands** often use vocalists. Some bands appear nightly in restaurants and supper clubs; others perform for special functions such as festivals, parades, and weddings. You'll have to audition to join such a band, so be sure you know the tricks of singing into a microphone and of projecting to the back of a smoke-filled room. You might get a foot in the door by offering to act as a standby in case a band's regular singer is ill or unavailable. If you do join a band, you may need to purchase clothes that go along with the group's image. Keep that in mind as you estimate your start-up costs in this business. Bands and their vocalists practice a lot, to maintain the quality and the sync of their music and to stay professionally in tune. A minimum of fourteen hours a week is common, on top of the actual performances. Your earnings in this job will depend on many things, including how much experience you have, who hires you, and how much they're earning. A fairly established vocalist may earn $50 a night.

Could you sing a message? Call companies listed in the Yellow Pages under "Singing Telegrams," and ask if they need anyone to help deliver their messages around town. If not, or if there are no such companies in your area, consider starting your own **singing message service**. You'll be hired by parents, friends, lovers, husbands, and wives who want messages delivered to their favorite people. You'll need a strong voice, a means of transportation, and a good-size ad in the Yellow Pages. Singing telegrams is a great part-time idea if your town is large enough to support the venture. To be a hit, you can't be at all bashful or timid.

Jackie T. of Illinois is a homemaker who started a singing message service five years ago. She dresses in colorful costumes, which she designs and makes, and delivers singing messages for Christmas, Easter, Valentine's Day, and other holidays. For Valentine's Day she sings dressed as a satin heart with an arrow through it; for Halloween she's a wicked witch. She also delivers birthday and get-well messages. Her spare-time work brings her about $200 extra cash each month.

Making Money with Your Instrument

Where there's music, there's probably some kind of musical instrument and an artist who brings it to life. There are thousands of unknown musicians whose talents are shared around campfires, during church services, and in classrooms. Some of these closet musicians could undoubtedly be getting paid for their years of practice and effort. Are you one of those who survived finger exercises, scales, and breathing techniques? Are you glad your parents forced you to practice the oboe when you could easily have given in to TV or the movies? Or maybe you're a born musician who never had a formal lesson but can play the piano by ear. Maybe you eyed the old guitar in the corner of grandma's dining room for years, but were unable, until you were grown and on your own, to muster up enough nerve to take lessons. Whatever your introduction to musical instruments, if you've been entertaining your in-laws at family reunions or getting your teenagers to listen while you pick a difficult chord pattern on the bass guitar—if people ask you, "Where'd you learn to play like that?"—maybe you should think about earning extra cash with your musical instrument.

Before you hire yourself out, though, consider all the pros and cons of the job. Are you ready to play for others? Are you good enough to call yourself a professional? Get an outside opinion; it might convince you that your friends haven't just been polite over the years when they've asked you to play for them. Are you prepared to handle criticism, rejections, and maybe a scarcity of work, especially if you play an unusual instrument (bells, zither, or harp, for example) not much in demand?

Do you have a list of good references to show potential customers that you play a mean fiddle? Other people's recommendations are valuable publicity tools for you. A good show is also a valuable calling card. In place of a portfolio, you'll have to make demonstration tapes of your work or play in person for potential customers. Is your musical instrument in good working order? A Stradivarius won't get you the job, but a poorly tuned instrument or one in dire need of repair will make your audition less than professional. Will you need any special clothing, maybe a costume, for the job you want? And what about transportation and working hours?

If you can handle all those preliminaries, you're ready to begin reaping the joys of your moneymaking venture. You'll be making people happy with your music and expressing yourself creatively; you'll be earning money doing what you enjoy.

Play the organ or piano in church on Sunday mornings. This isn't a high-paying job, but you can expand its moneymaking potential by playing for weddings as well. Many churches have weddings every Saturday, especially during the summer. Leave your card with all the churches in town. Point out that with your knowledge of church and wedding music besides your playing expertise, you can help couples plan special wedding programs. It's common for an organist to earn $25-$50 for providing the music during a marriage ceremony.

Many churches now hire part-time or full-time **music directors**. This job requires that you plan and conduct musical selections and programs for regular and special church services. As music director, you teach hymns to the congregation, direct the choir, and play the organ for weddings, funerals, rehearsals, and other services. Formal training for the job is not always necessary, but much experience and a background of working with people who have little or no musical training are important prerequisites. Music directors are usually hired after a successful audition. Could your church benefit from an organized music program? Why not talk to your minister or church council about the idea? You could even offer to do the job without pay for a trial period, during which the response of the congregation to your efforts could be monitored.

If you enjoy making music with others, start your own **musical group**. What kind of music will you play? What sound will you strive for? When you know the answers to these questions, you're ready to advertise for the players who can help you create the sound—maybe a woman who plays rock piano or a tenor sax player who can also handle a trumpet. Choose carefully the instruments and the people in your group. Seek out skilled musicians who share your dedication to the group's success, with whom you can work well, and with whom you can spend long hours. You'll be sharing plenty of time with them, developing programs, practicing new music, and rehearsing to achieve a pleasing sound. You'll work together closely planning your various shows. For wedding receptions, for example, you'll need a variety of dance numbers; if you work as a backup group, you should have an ample selection of current hit tunes in your repertoire.

Start-up costs may include matching costumes (with each member generally paying for her own) and advertising expenses. If you only want part-time work, advertise your group to organizations (churches, schools, and clubs) that occasionally use outside groups for their social activities. For more steady work it's best to find a reputable booking agent.

Donna R. is the owner of a music store in Arkansas. She sells instruments, music, and supplies to musicians of all ages.

She herself is a veteran clarinet player who, with three other women, formed a combo (clarinet, bass fiddle, piano, and drums) to play for church dances, wedding receptions, and other local doings. They perform three or four times a month and are building quite a reputation. The group practices three times a week for about two hours, and the members share equally the $125 they earn for two hours of playing at a wedding reception. They play a variety of dance music, from old rock 'n' roll to current hits. Donna's job as a part-time entertainer allows her to keep up her clarinet playing.

Hire yourself out as an **accompanist** for other musicians and vocalists. Piano accompanists may play for both organized choirs and informal singing groups. They accompany soloists who compete in contests and auditions. They play practice music in dance studios and they play for dance recitals. They play background music at parties, roasts, and other gala events. Accompanists have a flexibility that enables them to work with other performers to give each audience the best possible show. They have the knack of picking up a soloist's strengths and capitalizing on them; a skilled accompanist works with a performer to minimize weaknesses in a song or program. Though they don't get much public acclaim for their efforts, skilled accompanists are renowned among performers, who appreciate their special expertise.

Earn cash as a **folk musician**. If you play the guitar, banjo, or fiddle, and can sing too, share your brand of folk songs—perhaps those that tell a tale of history or a story of the imagination—with others. A creative folk singer can make up songs about politics, environmental concerns, fantasy, and history. Old favorites, like "Puff, the Magic Dragon," will warm hearts and bring back memories to listeners nostalgic for a gentle sound. Offer your services to coffee houses, restaurants, and seminars and conferences in search of "half-time" or luncheon entertainment.

Greta M. is a New York woman who earns extra cash by **singing and playing the organ** in a neighborhood shopping mall. She's a natural who's been playing and singing since childhood. Greta always wanted a musical job that wouldn't drain all her spare time and energy. One day she was browsing through the mall and saw the organs on display. Greta sat down and played a short song, softly singing along with the music. The store owner was impressed with her impromptu performance and asked her to do a few other songs. She did, and he offered her a job demonstrating his organs. Greta now plays for three hours on Thursday and Friday evenings and for five hours each Saturday, with a fifteen-minute break each hour. She earns $5 an hour, playing and singing current hits and popular oldies. Greta is pleased with the arrangement, which gives her extra cash and doesn't interfere with her other profession, wife and mother. The store owner is also pleased; his sales have nearly doubled since Greta began singing. He has recently asked her to appear on local television advertising his music store.

Other Music Money-makers

Are you an amateur songwriter? The one who composed a family chant or wrote a parody of a classic Christmas song? Whether you write music or lyrics—or both—there may be opportunities for you in the **songwriting** world. You can try selling your music to an artist directly (John Denver, Anne Murray, or more realistically, your town's prize tenor), or to an artist's manager, a music publisher, an independent record producer, or a record company. This is a tough market to crack. Rejection is the name of the game, and there's no guarantee of success. But perseverance may one day bring you a hit, and unless you share your songs with people in the business, you'll never know whether your tunes have that potential.

Check the current edition of *Songwriter's Market* for markets that seek songs and services of songwriters and for information on how to make your mark in this competitive, rewarding field (including how to prepare a demonstration tape, how to protect your songs, and how to submit them for consideration).

You'll probably do best to start small. Get practice and notoriety by sharing your talents with anyone who needs a song. How about offering to write a sentimental piece for a fiftieth wedding anniversary or a tune to celebrate the birth of a baby? A new lawyer might get a kick out of hearing a jingle called "You Done Good" after passing the bar exam. You might offer your songs, musical plays, and advertising shorts to local performers, ad agencies, schools, churches, and little theater groups. You could negotiate work-for-hire arrangements with your clients. Or you could decide to copyright your songs (see Chapter 15) before you make them public.

If you enjoy working with musicians, start a music group **talent agency** by advertising to find jobs for bands, small combos, singers, dancers, and entertainers. You'll need a strong musical background—study, practice, and experience as a performer—to do well in this business. You'll book jobs for performers at dances, weddings, bar mitzvahs, holiday parties, conventions, and country clubs. You must be able to distinguish between good talent and the not-ready-for-a-booking performers. Rather than representing any one performer, you'd be dedicated to giving your customers superior entertainment. Your job could include placing talented musicians in supper clubs and restaurants that could never afford a Frank Sinatra or a Kenny Rogers. You must be able to match the right person with the right job. Advertise your musician placement service in newspapers and through musicians' guilds and unions. Be on the lookout for promising entertainers to add to your roster.

Start-up costs for this business would be minimal, the biggest expenses being advertising, telephone, and transportation. A reasonable commission for your services would be 15 percent of the performer's take. A contract with each performer would establish specifically when and how much you'd be paid. Performers who fail to comply with the conditions of a contract or to fulfill their responsibilities to one of your clients would be removed from your files and would no longer be represented by your agency.

Jean K. of Texas is a former professional performer who started her own entertainment agency. She played the saxophone in an all-woman trio until she was seriously injured in an auto accident four years ago. Jean had been the spokeswoman for the group, and during her long recuperation she got many calls for their services. She knew that her partners needed the money, and she felt obligated to help them get work. She advertised in the newspaper for a female saxophone player to replace her and found an experienced performer in a nearby town. She began accepting jobs for the trio again and, with their approval, kept 15 percent of their earnings as her commission for scheduling their bookings. It wasn't long before she advertised for and auditioned other talent, taking on those performers she judged to be salable. She has musicians, singers, dancers, magicians, actors, and poets listed in her "active" file. She mails letters locally advertising her service to her many professional contacts in the entertainment field. When she gets a call for a specific talent, she can usually find a ready person. Though Jean still plays the saxophone, she does it only for her own enjoyment now; she finds much joy in locating jobs for other performers.

What about **dancing**? It's an artistic interpretation of music and, as entertainment, comes in many varieties: folk, modern, jazz, disco, ballroom, and more. Dancing is both a musical and a physical art form that can be offered to night clubs, supper clubs, dinner theaters, party houses, and private parties. People enjoy sitting back and relaxing after dinner to watch the fancy footwork of good dancers. If you're light on your feet or belong to a group that enjoys dancing for others, offer your talents to those who enjoy watching. Since dancing lessons are popular as a social activity, you might consider teaching dancing as a way to extra cash, if you're patient and skilled at showing other people how to do what you do.

Joyita and Carlos are a New Mexico couple who earn extra cash by dancing at private parties. Joyita is a professional flamenco dancer, and her husband plays Spanish guitar for her. They became intrigued with flamenco dancing many years ago when they were vacationing in Mexico. Joyita took lessons and at first performed only for friends. Word of Joyita's dancing prowess spread, and she began charging a fee for her performances. Now nearly every weekend Carlos, dressed in Spanish garb and armed with a finely tuned guitar, and Joyita, in a full, lace-tiered dress, with a rose in her hair and castanets in her hand, perform the emotional music and dance. They earn nearly $200 a night delighting enthusiastic audiences.

If you play a musical instrument well, maybe you could **teach others to play**. Giving music lessons doesn't require any license or certificate, but it does require that you have a complete understanding of your instrument and music and that you can share that knowledge with others. You'll have to communicate your enthusiasm for the piccolo or accordion and be very patient with students who may be learning not just a new instrument but a new language—music.

If you give music lessons in your home, be sure to have a room where students won't be disturbed by telephones or slammed doors and where they won't be subjected to criticism from outsiders. If students come to your home for lessons in playing a large instrument, such as a piano or organ, you'll have to provide a good instrument that can withstand all the blunders of beginners. Smaller instruments, such as guitars, flutes, and violins, are generally brought to your home by the students.

If you plan to teach children, remember to keep lessons short (usually thirty minutes), and don't try to cover too many new things in one lesson. If you hope to teach adults, you may have to learn how to put them at ease in their new learning venture. They may feel self-conscious about starting at the beginning; how far they go with their lessons may well depend on your encouragement and support.

Advertise lessons in your home, offer to go to students' homes if you have transportation, or contact a music store or school to give lessons to their students. Securing a music teaching job may be difficult without some verification of your training and letters of recommendation from those who have benefited from your teaching. Pricing for various music lessons depends on the instrument, where the lesson is given (in a store where rates are set by the owner; in your home; in students' homes; at school), the region of the country, and your reputation. In our part of the country, a thirty-minute piano lesson at a music store ranges between $5 and $10.

Maybe you enjoy tinkering with musical instruments, as well as playing them. Do you have experience repairing some of them? If you've cleaned instruments, and put new strings on guitars, and new pads on clarinets, maybe you could team up with a music store in town and do their customers' repairs. An **instrument repair service** could also be offered to churches, schools, and bands in your area. The costs of starting a musical instrument repair business will vary, but basic equipment includes wire cutters, round-nose pliers, screwdrivers, pad slicks, mallets, a hammer, a punch, an anvil, a ruler, razor blades, a mouthpiece puller, a spring hook scraper, an alcohol lamp, piano tools, a tuning crank, a decentering tool, and a key brushing tool.

If you've tuned pianos, you might be welcomed by the musical community in your town. A good piano tuner is sometimes hard to find. To learn the trade, you should apprentice yourself to a professional. Check with the Piano Technician's Guild, 113 Dexter Avenue N., Seattle, WA 91809, for complete details about becoming a registered piano tuner and repair person. The going rate for tuning a piano is $40-$60.

Abra P. of North Carolina is a homemaker who repairs musical instruments for extra cash. Her husband, Mac, is a part-time instructor who has a large clientele of would-be musicians. Mac used to teach students to play woodwind and stringed instruments in the back room of the local music store, but he and Abra have converted their basement into a studio, both for giving lessons and for repairing instruments. Abra plays several instruments and is especially intrigued by antique guitars, violins, and pianos. Over the years she has earned a nice profit by buying old instruments from flea markets, garage sales, and private individuals, repairing and cleaning them, and reselling them. She also cleans and repairs Mac's students' instruments. Abra tunes and repairs both upright and grand pianos for individuals, businesses, and schools in the area. She carries her tuning crank, pitch meter, and repair tools in her Datsun. Her skills as a musical fix-it earn her about $4,000 annually.

If you've been nurturing your musical skills for a while, it may be time to put them to work. Talent, dedication, and perseverance can mean success and extra cash. You don't have to be a recording star to make money with your music.

Suggested Reading

Banek, Reinhold, and Jon Scoville. *Sound Designs: A Handbook of Musical Instrument Building.* Berkeley, California: Ten Speed Press, 1980.

Bastien, James W. *How to Teach Piano Successfully*. 2nd ed. San Diego: Kjos Music Co., 1977.

Boye, Henry. *How to Make Money Selling the Songs You Write*. Rev. ed. New York: Frederick Fell Publications, 1975.

Enoch, Yvonne, and James Lyke. *Creative Piano Teaching*. Champaign, Illinois: Stipes Publishing Co., 1977.

Glaser, Hy. *How to Write Lyrics That Make Sense and Dollars*. Smithtown, New York: Exposition, 1977.

Kuroff, Barbara Norton, ed. *1982 Songwriter's Market*. Cincinnati: Writer's Digest Books, 1981.

Livingston, Peter. *Country Swing and Western Dance*. New York: Doubleday, 1981.

Reblitz, Arthur A. *Piano Servicing, Tuning and Rebuilding*. Vestal, New York: Vestal Press, 1976.

Shinn, Duane. *How to Sell Music by Mail*. Central Point, Oregon: Duane Shinn Publishing, 1975.

Silverman, Jerry. *How to Play Better Guitar*. New York: Doubleday, 1972.

Stanley, Burton. *Instrument Repair for the Music Teacher*. Sherman Oaks, California: Alfred Publishing Co., 1978.

Whitley, Roger D. *How to Get Started Singing*. Kannapolis, North Carolina: Reveal Publications, 1979.

Wilbur, L. Perry. *How to Write Songs That Sell*. Chicago: Contemporary Books, 1977.

Zalkind, Ronald. *Getting Ahead in the Music Business*. New York: Macmillan, Schirmer Books, 1979.

Real People

20

(Mini stories of women who've made money with truly unusual job ideas)

During our research for this book, we uncovered some truly ingenious women actively involved in unusual moneymaking projects and in new twists on old ones. This chapter is a smorgasbord of their job ideas, ranging from welding to underwater modeling. It's exciting and satisfying to hear about women who capitalize on a practical idea when they see it or invent a workable one when they don't. They refuse to let financial hurdles or scheduling obstacles stand in the way of making some extra cash. These women are intelligent and ambitious and have creative ability to match their drive. We're betting that you'll be as pleased as we were to discover them.

Desiree T. of Louisiana is a young welder who loves to fashion objects from **wrought iron.** She creates some very ornate, very intricate wrought iron designs. Desiree started welding when she was a teenager on a farm in northern Louisiana. She was an only child and always helped her father with the repairs; welding broken farm equipment was part of the work. Welding became more fun than work to her, and she started welding projects of her own. For example. one summer she built a pontoon boat from pipes. She used every piece of pipe available, even her old swing set. Today, Desiree's iron work is noted for its elegant designs. Some of her pieces carry astrological themes such as crescent moons, shooting stars, and signs of the zodiac. Others have earthly motifs: a staunch row of cornstalks or graceful deer and other wildlife. She paints her ornamental works and sells them all over the country for use as hand railings, gates, doors, and window guards.

Diana P. and Amber K. are physical education teachers from Wisconsin who've been friends since college. They accepted teaching positions in the same school district, but after a few years they realized that a teacher's salary just didn't keep pace with inflation. Five years ago they decided to capitalize on what they knew best: **gymnastics.** They made arrangements to rent the school gymnasium two nights a week during the winter and four nights a week in the summer to teach youngsters the how-to's of balance beams, trampolines, and floor exercises. They secured the gym equipment on a lease-purchase plan and later bought it with their earnings. The response to their gymnastic program was tremendous. Parents were happy to find an additional outlet for their children's energy. Now Diana and Amber work full-time in their own gymnastics club.

Jenny D. of Florida is an attractive young woman who's an expert skin diver. She was working as an instructor for a diving club when she was approached by an ad agency to do **underwater modeling** for some vacation brochures and magazine ads. She jumped at the offer and now gets to dive in some of the most beautiful waters in the world. An underwater photographer goes along to capture her on film. Jenny loves the work, and the income goes a long way toward financing her education to become a marine biologist.

Kathy F. of Maryland lives near one of the state's busiest fishing spots, Chesapeake Bay. She knows that sport fishermen love the glory of angling—getting their pictures taken with gorgeous largemouth bass and feasting on their catches—but that few of them get excited about cleaning and scaling their fish. She decided to take advantage of their lack of enthusiasm for the job. Kathy had learned to clean, scale, and fillet striped bass, shad, and other fish by helping her husband with his own catches. She enjoyed taking part in getting their dinners from the bay to the frying pan. During the fishing season she now uses her garage as headquarters for her **fish-cleaning business.** The fishermen bring their daily catches to her and pick them up the next morning. She has all the necessary tools (including pliers, fish scalers, and fillet knives) and stocks ample packaging supplies. She cleans the fish for $1.75 a pound, bags them in plastic, and refrigerates them until they're claimed by the proud owners.

Sally H. of Michigan got so tired of looking at snow between October and May that she decided to start pushing it around. Sally's husband,

Jack, is the owner and operator of a service station in the upper peninsula. He had to keep the snow cleared off the station lot, and that meant buying an expensive, heavy-duty truck with a snowplow mounted on the front. To help pay for it, Sally decided to use it herself to **clear snow** off driveways, church parking lots, mobile home parks, and shopping center lots. Every time there's a heavy snow, Sally's ready to go to work before daylight. She's always adding new customers to her list of "steadies," whose snow she plows whenever they give her a call. Her plowing schedule is jam-packed; sometimes even Jack has to wait his turn for the plow. When Sally isn't moving snow, she uses the truck to tow Jack's customers. Summer or winter, she's one woman who knows how to profit from the weather.

Norma G. is a homemaker from a small town in Kansas. She'd had a weight problem since childhood but had never been able to stay on an exercise program. There were no health spas nearby, and Norma knew she would never stick to an exercise routine unless she had company. She decided to get other women to join her in a **health spa** venture. The first thing she did was to have all of her accumulated exercise equipment checked for safety. She consulted her insurance agent and added appropriate liability coverage to her existing insurance policies. A local retired physician agreed to be on call when her spa was in use. She advertised in beauty salons and grocery stores. She decided to charge members monthly fees, depending on the individual schedules they set up. The groups meet in the huge basement of Norma's house on Tuesday and Thursday mornings and Wednesday evenings. They do toning exercises and aerobic dancing, use barbells, and work out on Norma's exercise bikes. After vigorous workouts the spa members relax with diet drinks and discuss eating habits and the preparation of nutritious low-calorie meals. Norma is slimmer than she's ever been before, and she continues to maintain her weight, while encouraging others in their reducing programs.

Helen Q. of Illinois is a retired foreign language teacher. After leaving the classroom, she needed some extra income to help her keep pace with the cost of living. Since she speaks six different languages fluently, she decided to take advantage of her knowledge by teaching her skills to others. She had some business cards printed and mailed them to all the travel agents in town, offering them her language expertise. A few days later she followed up with a visit to each agency. Now when someone buys a travel package to Russia, Egypt, Denmark, Spain, Italy, or France, he or she is directed to Helen for a **beginning language course**, which consists of ten one-hour lessons in two weeks' time. Half of the course fee is paid by the travel agent. The travelers learn language fundamentals for their trips, such as how to introduce themselves, ask directions, and read menus, plus special instructions they might need to ensure a good visit. Many of the students continue with the lessons after their trip is over.

Bobbie Jo D. of New York **roller-skates** for money. She started skating when she was only six years old, and she skated nearly everywhere. She ran errands on skates, skated to her piano lessons, and she even wanted to skate in school, but the principal refused to let her through the door with wheels on her feet. When she was twelve, she entered and won the first of many skating contests. Now married and the mother of a seven-year-old son, Bobbie thought she could supplement her husband's income with a skill she'd practiced for years. She offered to skate in public at the local roller rink where she practices twice a week. The manager recognized that she would be a great promoter for his business. Since the rink is located in a busy part of town, he decided to ask Bobbie to skate in the huge glassed-in area facing the street. Bobbie Jo skates in this improvised showcase in full view of passersby, who are fascinated by how easy she makes spins and splits look. Many casual watchers have been excited enough to give roller skating a try. Some sign up for lessons given by qualified instructors at the rink. The rink's manager considers hiring Bobbie Jo the smartest promotional move he ever made. Bobbie Jo skates on Fridays, Saturdays, and Sundays from four to seven, with a ten-minute break each hour, and she earns $12 a day. She gets plenty of exercise, and she's glad the work helps her to stay physically fit; but mostly she just loves to skate.

Denise L. is an Ohio native who comes from a long line of wine makers. Her great-grandfather had a vineyard in southern Ohio before the Civil War, and her parents started a winery near Lake Erie when she was a child. Several years ago Denise decided to operate a **winery** of her own. She wanted to break away from the traditional wines and offer some unusual flavors. Though she knew a lot about making wine, she had to give her money-making idea much thought. What state laws and health codes had to be met? Would the market support the exotic flavors she hoped to offer? How much revenue would she need to make a profit? After months of careful planning, she was ready for business. In her gracious one-hundred-year-old home, she makes and sells her specialty wines, which include rhubarb, red beet, dandelion, red clover and honeysuckle. She also holds wine-tasting parties at Denise's Wine Cellar for groups of up to one hundred.

Pat M. of New Mexico has an unusual way of **wrapping gifts:** She cans them. She came up with this idea after she received a canned gift from her sister as a joke. She found a company that produced corrugated cans with snap-on tops. She has them in all sizes, one tiny enough for a diamond engagement ring, another large enough for a huge stuffed animal. Several department stores have hired her to can their merchandise as gifts, by first wrapping them in colorful tissue paper, then stuffing them into the right-size cans. Since the plastic lids snap on, sealing is very easy. Pat's cans come in a plain brown color, so she decorates them with a variety of wrapping papers and ribbons. Her prices range from $2 to $10 depending on the size and the amount of decoration. Her gift-wrapping idea has caught on like wildfire.

Carol M. of Alabama had plenty of open space on her farm, so after checking with firearms officials, she opened a **rifle and pistol range** for the gun enthusiasts in her area. Her husband, Alan, a firearms expert, is always available to instruct those who want to improve their aim or learn more about their guns. Every week Carol's rifle and pistol range is booked up with gun-toting hobbyists—men, women, and teens.

Marty J. of Iowa is a beautician who didn't like the nine-to-five routine of working in a hairdresser's shop. She wanted a new challenge, something she could take pride in doing. She tried to think of people who could benefit from her cosmetology skills. After a co-worker at the shop mentioned the possibility, Marty applied at some of the funeral homes in her area for the job of **doing the hair of the corpses.** She admits, "It doesn't sound very pleasant or exciting, but it's an important job. Seeing loved ones as they remember them is comforting to the families of the deceased. I'm doing my part to ease the pain of their loss." Marty also does hair for people in hospitals and rest homes and for those shut in at home. She currently has more customers than she can handle.

Jackie S. of Texas **massages feet.** Those who've benefited from her strong, skilled hands include her husband, her children, and friends in the hospital. She's built up such a reputation that when anyone's feet hurt, someone in town naturally recommends Jackie's foot massage. From some formal study of human anatomy and by working under the guidance of her uncle, a podiatrist, she learned the intricate workings of the twenty-six small bones in the foot. She learned that each foot must have toned muscles, strong ligaments and a good arch to function well. Unfortunately, many people's feet are in poor shape because of ill-fitting shoes, lack of exercise, too much walking on concrete sidewalks, and other abuses. She massages their feet by rubbing them with a special peach oil; she uses mustard leaves or hot pepper plants for skin stimulation. She has massaged pregnant women's feet, which were sore from the excess weight they were carrying; she has soothed the soles and arches of people who stand up for a living—e.g., salespeople. nurses, and teachers. She also recommends herbal foot baths, a combination of dried lavender flowers, rosemary leaves, dried mint, comfrey roots, and thyme—herbs that she grows, dries, packages, and sells to her customers. Jackie does foot massaging in her home, her customers' homes, nursing homes, and hospitals. She charges $7.50 if the customer comes to her, $10.00 if she travels to the customer. Jackie earned $520 last year soothing feet and their owners.

Randi R. of California is a young woman who earns part-time money by sitting in a hot tub. She's a physical education teacher who wanted to bolster her income; she answered a newspaper ad and was hired as a **demonstrator for a local hot tub company.** She welcomed the chance to work by relaxing; she's always on her feet in the school gym. She was given a crash course in hot tubs: the various types, their construction, normal maintenance (including proper water temperature and pH), and the working of the filter and heating systems. On Friday and Saturday evenings at five, she puts on a bikini and climbs into a hot tub in the company's showroom. She stays there till nine (with regularly scheduled breaks) and earns $5 an hour. As the customers browse through the store, Randi answers their questions about hot tubs. She saves the salespeople from having to spend a lot of time with people who are "just looking." She also helps educate the serious customers, who can then approach a salesperson with specific questions on financing and purchase. Word of Randi's pleasant personality and professional sales manner has spread, and the store's owners feel her presence in the showroom and her ready answers have increased sales significantly.

Garnet W. is an Idaho homemaker who **makes compost for sale.** She and her husband, Josh, own a farm; Josh operates a large horse-boarding stable there, earning the family's main income from home. Garnet always kept her eyes peeled for a home-based job for herself. Where there's a horse, there's manure; manure can be turned into compost and compost into profit. Instead of spreading the manure on her neighbors' fields for free (something she'd been doing for years), Garnet decided to use it to make some money. First she did a lot of reading about compost making, then she cooked up her own recipe. Her ingredients include manure, rotted hay, wood shavings, earthworm castings, and the leaves that fall in the woods on their farm. She mixes them and piles them in a way that creates optimal conditions for decomposition. Once a week she even collects bags full of hair clippings from a few beauty and barber shops in her area. (Hair is very high in nitrogen and a great additive to any compost bin.) The first year she made only $80 supplying gardeners in town. But as more weekend gardeners learned about Garnet's compost, her business grew. Josh has built several large bins, and Garnet keeps the compost "cooking" year round. She sells her "black gold" in four-cubic-yard bags. It's also sold loose by the pickup load to small nurseries nearby. Garnet earns $3,500 annually with her spare-time business.

Della M. of Colorado performs an unusual service from her home. **Hand analysis** (palm reading) is something she grew up with. People came from up to fifty miles away to have her grandmother read the lines and markings etched on their hands. As a child, Della had her grandmother teach her what the lines and markings meant. Though she'd been away from palmistry for several years, her interest was resurrected when she picked up a book on hand analysis at a local bookstore. After buying the book and taking it home, she refreshed her memory on the science of reading palms and learned more than she had known before. She started reading palms for friends as a hobby and really enjoyed it. People wanting advice or peace of mind, and others out of curiosity, asked her to read their palms and tell them about marriage, money, and health. She began to charge for her readings. Most of her customers want to know about their love life—whether they'll marry, whether there will be a divorce, whether a potential marriage is wise, whether they'll marry into wealthy families. She took her readings seriously and finally placed an ad in the newspaper, advertising her palm-reading service both to individuals and to party hostesses, who could hire her to entertain their guests. Della charges $25 for each individual reading, and a group rate for parties, where the price depends on how many people attend. Although she doesn't make a lot of money, she has steady customers who keep returning for her assessments of what has happened or will happen in their lives.

Delsey B. of Pennsylvania is a retired science teacher who **rents out her land for weekend outings.** She never married, and when her parents died, the family farm was left to Delsey. After many years of teaching fifth graders, Delsey was content to stay at home, manage the farm, and enjoy the breathtaking surroundings. She rents most of the tillable land to a local farmer. She keeps a few chickens and a cow for eggs and milk and also has a team of draft horses, four barn cats, and one old English sheepdog. She hires Rollie, a young man who lives nearby, to help with some chores like splitting wood for winter and putting up hay for the horses. Eight years ago a local church group asked if she would rent them her land for a one-day church picnic. When they told her how much they enjoyed the picnic, and made the same arrangement for the following year, she got the idea of offering her property to others. She advertised to school and community groups and to individuals. Now Delsey's farm is used by hundreds of people enjoying daytime hayrides, walks in the woods, wiener roasts, picnics, and reunions. Rollie does much of the preparation and drives the hay wagon. Delsey conducts nature tours and uses her training in biology to give informal talks on conservation of the environment. Many of her customers are city dwellers who've never had the opportunity to see what farm life is all about. On Delsey's farm they enjoy all the seasons—spring buds, summer growth, fall harvest, and winter peace. A covered pavilion accommodates people on rainy days and helps to keep the weather from dampening spirits. Except for Rollie's wages, Delsey's monetary output is minimal; she already owned many of the needed items (wagons, old hunting trails, a cleared area for bonfires, a tool barn converted into a cabin). She carries plenty of liability insurance and meets state and local regulations regarding the health and safety of her customers. She charges $100 a day for the use of her farm; the money goes into farm improvements (new siding on the barn last spring, for example). But Delsey's greatest reward seems to be the look on people's faces when they begin to understand rural beauty.

Susan G. of Ohio is a young wife and mother of four. Trying to clothe and feed a family of six on her husband's income made bargain hunting an important part of her life. She felt as though she knew every place in her city where a bargain could be found. She and a friend decided to compile a list of those places and find someone to print it. A local company printed the *Bargain Hunter's Directory* for $.17 a copy. With directory in hand, they contacted grocery stores, drugstores, and book stores in their city and placed the guide (priced at $1.50) for sale in these stores. It wasn't long before Susan and her friend sold out their first printing and had to have more printed.

They were contacted by a local distributor of magazines, who wanted to take over their distribution. They were tired of running all over town to restock, so they gave him the job. His commission was set at $.50 for each guide, but the women still came out ahead, because the distributor sold many more copies each month. Their gasoline bill was cut considerably, and they weren't burdened with trying to collect every month from several stores. Now they receive a check each month and a new order for directories. They update their guides once a year, and the distributor does the rest.

Jann B., Maribel Q., Rona G., and Cassie V. are Florida neighbors who wanted to do something to bring in extra cash. One morning while they were having coffee together, they hatched the idea of renting the vacant space at the local shopping mall. The rent was too high for one person, but they thought that four people could afford it. After paying the first month's rent, they **divided the store into four sections,** allowing each of them to operate her own "shop" and sell her own merchandise. They named their store Different Strokes. Each woman installed tables and shelves to suit her product lines. Jann's section sells wine and cheese, while Maribel sells houseplants and fresh-cut flowers. Baked goods and candy are Rona's specialty, with Cassie's corner featuring fresh fruit. Shoppers at the mall love the store and keep the owners quite busy. The foursome finds that when people come in for a particular item, they almost always browse around the other three quadrants. Customers say it's convenient to walk twenty feet from where they just bought Muenster cheese and be able to select delectable citrus fruits for the brunch they're planning. And the women find they enjoy coordinating their inventories to fit the needs of their regular customers. When the women advertised in the local paper, they offered to make up gift baskets with their combined merchandise. They hired another neighbor to deliver the gift baskets. Jann, Maribel, Rona, and Cassie are very happy with the business arrangement and can't wait to get to work each day. Their novel idea has paid off.

There are hundreds of other women who've made their money making ideas work. If your goals are realistic and you're willing to work hard, you can be one of those women. We hope the stories in this chapter have given you new ideas or inspired you to put your own pet notion into action.

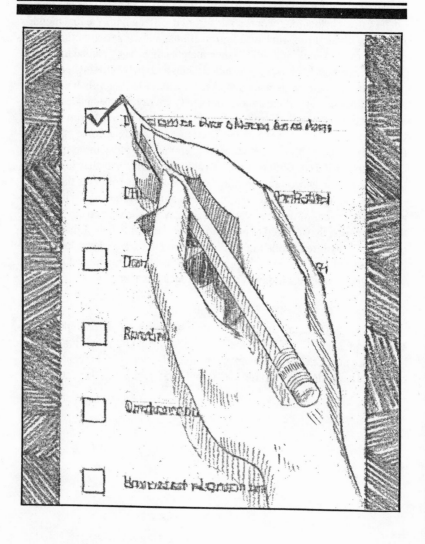

Before You Try Your Wings 21

(A final look at what to consider before you start your home business)

Any way you look at it, starting a home business is hard, time-consuming, and frustrating as well as rewarding. It may look glamorous on the surface, but if you plan to succeed, have plenty of elbow grease and midnight oil on hand. In many ways starting a home business is like stepping into the "twilight zone." You have fears and expectations—and not much assurance of what you'll find. You may be surprised or disappointed, encouraged or disheartened by your moneymaking venture. The extra cash and warm feelings of accomplishment will be easy to handle. But the financial booby traps and legal snarls you might find could throw you if you're not prepared.

Every business has its own set of pitfalls, and we've alluded to many of these in previous chapters. But there are also common snags and general considerations facing any new home-based entrepreneur. And this is our last chance to bring them home before you forge ahead in your own business. An awareness of what to expect is the best defense against failure.

1. The key to business success is planning. If you don't have a strategy, don't expect to be a big hit. The business life is filled with rewards of all kinds—extra money, self-esteem, confidence, achievement—but without a clear and thorough plan of attack and an eye to watch out for the legal and personal hurdles in your path, you may never realize those benefits.

Your head is probably spinning faster than a whirligig. Am I smart enough? Can I do it? Should I do it? Will my family suffer? My marriage? What if I fail? What if I don't? Will success change me or my life? These are questions you can't afford to ignore; the answers don't take care of themselves.

2. Get the cooperation of your husband, family, and friends. The people close to you should be aware of your new commitment and how it will affect them. Keeping the telephone tied up from seven to seven or using the free parking space in the garage for storing a ton of basket-weaving material may upset your spouse, for instance. A new home business will take up much of the time you used to spend making life comfortable for the members of your family. Your children might start complaining about not having clean Levi's for two weeks or never getting to use the family car because it's always filled with artificial flower arrangements. What about all those years you were there with a smile on your face, brimming with enthusiasm for your family's projects—the tree house in the cherry orchard, the expensive shelves in the garage that warped after one winter? Now it's their turn to rally round, so don't feel guilty about expecting cooperation.

But you may not always get it from the people you love and nurture, especially when your business gets into full swing and your days (and nights) are packed with chores other than homemaking. And you may not get much sympathy when the local newspaper leaves the word *rug* out of your rug-hooking ad. Your best bet is to try to get them involved in what you're doing. Get their reactions to untested notions. Explain what you're doing and how and why. Ask for their advice on how to solve these new family problems. A family powwow never hurts. In the end, however, you may discover that your family and your home business just can't coexist.

3. Have a specific place from which to run your operation. That means you should have room to work, store supplies, make calls, meet people, or do whatever your business demands. Where would you put a ton of potting soil, fifty lamp kits, or enough refrigerated food supplies for five wedding receptions? Plan ahead. Arrange to use one part of your home exclusively for business purposes. A spare room, garage, basement, loft, barn, or laundry room, a corner of the bedroom, or maybe even a large walk-in closet will do; but be sure to keep the area "strictly business." And be sure everyone in the family knows it. It could save you some money.

A work area is considered a legitimate business expense if it's designated as the headquarters for your full-time or sideline business operation. If a room or area does qualify, a percentage of the depreciation and operating expenses (insurance, utilities, repairs), based on the portion of the whole house occupied by the office, may be deducted. Recent changes in the tax rules are more lenient toward home-based entrepreneurs, but be sure to check with your accountant or the IRS if you need clarification or have questions. (See Chapter 2 for more tax information.)

4. *If your new home business requires heavy use of the family telephone, plan accordingly.* If conflicts develop between you and your family over phone use, have a second phone line installed and ask clients to call you at the new phone number instead of your home number. The additional phone could cost anywhere from $10 to $50 a month, depending on the type of service you select. (You may be required to pay for business service.) A telephone message recorder (around $250) may alleviate your having to be tied to the phone when you'd rather be with your family or relaxing with a novel in the backyard. Your phone messages will be recorded and you can return the calls when the family is gone or busy and you have time set aside for telephone duties. It will also record messages when you're out or when you're too busy to be bothered with calls. Or consider an answering service to take your calls when you aren't available or don't want to be interrupted. Your messages can be relayed to you at a convenient time. Look in the Yellow Pages under "Telephone Answering Service." The service will probably cost you about $60 a month.

5. *Investigate all the legal requirements for running a home business in your area.* Check with your local zoning board about the various codes (safety, zoning, fire, health, etc.) in your neighborhood. Seldom will zoning restrictions prevent you from conducting business from your home, so long as you don't harm the neighborhood. Don't let your customers block streets and driveways or park in "no parking" areas. And while you're in city hall, check on the permissibility of signs, and how to get a vendor's license if you'll be selling anything. (Are you permitted to erect *any* type of advertising sign in your yard? Get this answer before paying a sign painter for something you can't use.) If you're starting a food-related business such as catering, cooking, or baking, be sure to check with the boards of health concerning mandatory permits and licenses. (Refer to Chapters 2 and 3 for further discussion of these regulatory considerations.)

6. *Handle money matters (your own and your customers')* *with care.* Doing it carefully can mean the difference between success and failure. For any small business, cash is always the best method of exchange. Large companies operating on big budgets can afford to wait for payment from credit customers or take a risk on check-paying clientele. But you probably can't. A transaction by check is technically a cash deal, but it may only take a few bad checks to put your business under water. Credit dealing can al-

ways be done through companies like Visa or MasterCard, but the service is expensive. Credit card companies will charge you monthly rates. Thus if you offer this convenience to your customers, the amount you're being charged must be reflected back to them in the way of higher prices for your product or service. Offering credit card privileges can also be quite cumbersome because of the added paperwork. We discourage this type of service for any small business. If you want to extend personal credit, try to minimize the risk as much as possible. Give credit only to someone you know—a friend, neighbor, or relative. The same rule applies to accepting checks, but as an added safety measure, you should ask for two pieces of identification. If you feel that extending credit and accepting checks just don't fit into your business plans, simply post a very visible sign: "CASH ONLY."

7. *Keep accurate records.* A thorough account of your expenses, deductions, and income tells everything about your business. Without this information it's nearly impossible to make intelligent business decisions. Incomplete records won't make filing your income tax return any easier, either, and that could result in a lot of red tape and extra paperwork on and after April 15. Set up an office area where you can keep your books. Your office can be only a few drawers, an adding machine, and some ledgers with columns for listing your business dealings. Your professional responsibility for maintaining good records can't be overstated. (This subject is discussed in more detail in Chapter 2.)

8. *Start on a small scale and suit your business to your needs.* This may be the best advice you'll ever get. How much money do you need to earn? (You'll find tips on determining your financial needs in Chapter 2.) How much time and money can you afford to invest? Will your idea support a full-time venture or only a part-time or weekend commitment? It's difficult to stay employed full-time as a clown for birthday parties, but there's always plenty of work for a typist. Be realistic about even your most cherished business scheme. Remember that every business has to start somewhere. In 1886 a railroad agent, Richard W. Sears of Minnesota, started one of the world's largest department-store chains by selling mail-order watches in his spare time. Starting small—with a small initial outlay and only the most realistic expectations—lets you test your market without monumental risk. Maybe you're certain your home-baked brownies will be a success, but for some unanticipated reason (people's tastes, the cost of chocolate, dentists' campaigns against sugary treats), they might not sell. If you haven't invested your entire savings in the venture, you won't starve if the business fails. And by starting small you'll learn the business inside out because you'll have your hand in every phase of the operation. You may even do your own monthly bookkeep-

ing, using the services of an accountant only on a quarterly basis. If you start small, you'll have less time, money, and energy invested. And if things don't work out, you'll have enough momentum (and money) left to plan your next move.

9. *Know yourself.* Is the life of a businesswoman really for you? After reading about some of the problems that might arise, do you still want to do it? Are you a person with a head for business? Do you really have a salable service, product, or talent to offer? Do you have the determination and drive to make it work? Can you set long-term goals for yourself? Do you have the patience to wait and work for them? Weigh and balance all the pros and cons before deciding. It may be the most important decision you'll ever make. If the answer keeps on coming up "yes," then go to it.

You probably have the desire to be a home businesswoman, or you wouldn't have bought this book. We've supplied you with workable ideas, guidelines for running a business, and a hearty dose of motivation. The rest is up to you.

Index